MARQUESAS OR WASHINGTON ISLANDS

Faitohu
Hiau I.d
Small I.
Reef
Var. 4° 24' E.
Mottuaity I.s
Nookaheeva
Hooahooga
Fetugu
Hooapooah
Ohevahoa
Ohitahoo
Onateava
Ottaheoah
Rock resembling a ship

Tiburones

I S L A N D S

King Georges I.s
Oitscha
Rocks
Spiridoff
Romanzoffs I.
Disappointment I.s
Var. 5° 8' E.
Doubtful I.
Palliser I.s
Ulitegan
Karsheff I.
Wolchonsky
Chriheff I.
Merrils I. 1832
S. Pablo doubtful
Raraka I.
Tolly I.
Arackscheef
Predpriatige
Sacken I.
New I. 1832
Camboy I. 1832
Shoal
Margaret I.
Shoal
Nigeri
Furneaux I.
Resolution I.
S. Narcisso
Adventure I.
Doubtful I.
Chain I.
Birnies I.
Tuscan I.
Bird I.
David Clarks I.
Bunyers Group
Two Groups
South I.
Bow I.s
Serles I.
Averell or Tenniere I.
DANGEROUS ARCHIPELAGO
Thumb Cap
Lagoon I.
Henrys I.
Gloucester I.
Queen Charlottes I.
Cumberland I.
Egmonts I.s
Whitsunday I.
Surrey I. 1821
Turnbull
Litho I.
S.t Miguel
Margarets I.s
Coronados
High I.
Gravsfort I.
S.t Elmo
Blighs Lagoon
Hoods I.
Osnaburg I.s
Matildas I.
Gambiers I.s
Crescent I.
Bonds I.
Martha's I. 1822
Oeno I.
Var. 6. E.
Elizabeth I.
S. Juan Baptista
Pitcairns Island
Osbornes Reef
Oparo I.s
Four Crowns (doubtful)
S.t Elmo (doubtful)

Islands from the Spanish Ch
I. seen by Capt.n Mitchel 1825

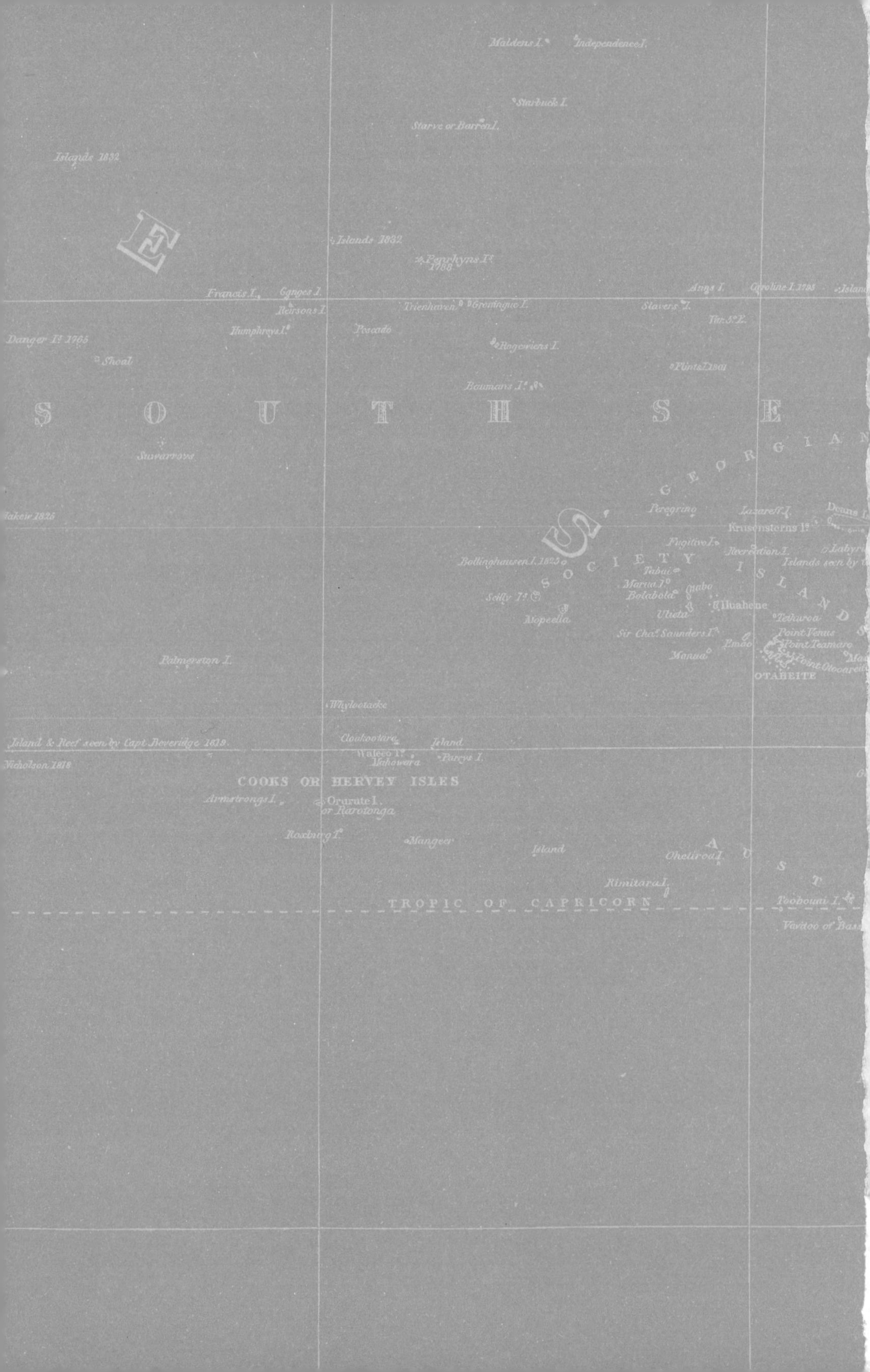

Maldens I. Independence I.

Starbuck I.

Starve or Barren I.

Islands 1832

E

Islands 1832

Penrhyns I.s 1788

Francis I. Ganges I.

Anna I. Caroline I. 1795 Island

Peirsons I.

Trienhaven Groningue I.

Slavers I.

Vin: S.t I.

Humphreys I.s

Posado

Danger I.s 1765

Rogewiens I.

Shoal

Flints I. 1801

Baumans I.s

S O U T H S E

Staarrows

GEORGIAN

Baker 1825

Peregrino

Lazareff I.

Deans I.

Krusensterns I.s

S

Fugitive I.

SOCIETY ISLANDS

Recreation I.

Lahyr

Bellinghausen I. 1825

Tabai

Islands seen by

Marua I.

Scilly I.s

Otabo

Bolabola

Huahene

Ulieta

Tetuaroa

Mopeeha

Sir Chas. Saunders I.

Point Venus

Emao

Point Teamaro

Manua

Point Otooareit

Palmerston I.

OTAHEITE

Whylootacke

Island & Reef seen by Capt. Beveridge 1819

Cloukootaro

Island

Nicholson 1818

Wateeo I.s

Mahowara

Parrys I.

COOKS OR HERVEY ISLES

Armstrongs I.

Ururute I. or Rarotonga

Roxing I.s

Mangeer

Island

Oheteroa I.

AUSTR

Rimitara I.

TROPIC OF CAPRICORN

Toobouai I.

Vavitoo or Bass

A Thousand Leagues of Blue

A Thousand Leagues of Blue

The Pacific Whaling Voyages of Charles and Susan Veeder of Nantucket

Betsy Tyler

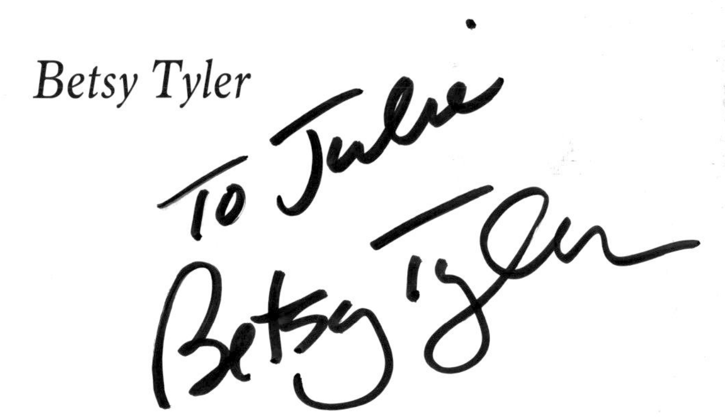

Nantucket Historical Association research fellow Betsy Tyler was the inaugural Obed Macy Research Chair of the NHA from 2012 to 2016 and is the former editor of *Historic Nantucket.* She is the author of *Sometimes Think of Me: Notable Nantucket Women through the Centuries* (NHA, 2010); *'Sconset Actors Colony: Broadway Offshore* (NHA, 2011), and the *NHA Historic Properties Guide* (2015). Tyler has written extensively about Nantucket houses and neighborhoods for the Nantucket Preservation Trust and is the author of more than forty individual house histories and histories of public buildings.

Published by the Nantucket Historical Association
15 Broad Street
P.O. Box 1016
Nantucket, Massachusetts 02554
(508) 228-1894
www.nha.org

First edition

Printed and bound in South Korea by Four Colour Print Group, Louisville, Kentucky
ISBN: 978-1-882201-07-5

All images from the collection of the Nantucket Historical Association,
except where noted.

The quotation on page 119 is from Homer, *The Odyssey,*
translated by Robert Fagles (New York: Viking, 1996).

Edited by Michael R. Harrison

Designed by Eileen Powers, Javatime Design
Set in Linotype Marion and PT Serif

Frontispiece:
Portrait of Susan Veeder by a Chinese artist, circa 1858.
Gift of Barbara Johnson, 1994.28.1

. . . now the long supplication of my youth was answered;
that serene ocean rolled eastwards from me
a thousand leagues of blue.

—Herman Melville, *Moby-Dick,* chapter 111: "The Pacific"

The Nantucket Historical Association gratefully acknowledges the generous support of the following donors to this publication.

Patrons

Melinda and Paul Sullivan

Subscribers

Susan and Bill Boardman

Ellen and David Ross

Merrielou and Ned Symes

Supporters

Patricia and Thomas Anathan

Mary Randolph Ballinger

Janet and Sam Bailey

Pam and Max Berry

Lisa and Porter Dawson

Kelly and Scott Ferguson

Diane and Art Kelly

Helen Lynch

Carolyn and Ian MacKenzie

Ronay and Richard Menschel

Ann and Craig Muhlhauser

Franci Neely

Bonnie Sacerdote

Scheerer-Schwanbeck Charitable Fund

Janet and Rick Sherlund

Jason Tilroe

Susan Zises Green

Contents

Prologue

Researching the life stories of ordinary people from the past is no small challenge, even if the subjects of inquiry were caught up in extraordinary circumstances, or hailed from a storied place. It's like finding that old jigsaw puzzle with the water-stained image on the cover. Inside are pieces left too long in the sun, or chewed by the dog, or just plain missing, but still there are tantalizing nuggets that can be put together—a palm tree, a ship, a woman—that are beautiful and intriguing and lead you to imagine the missing connections. My quest for details of the lives of Susan and Charles Veeder began with two nuggets, or two whaling voyages, one in 1848, the other in 1868. Susan accompanied Captain Veeder on the first voyage; he never returned from the latter one.

Traces of the old whaling captain must exist somewhere in French Polynesia, but they are unrecorded, deeply buried, sunk, or blown away. He was last seen in Papeete, Tahiti, in 1872, after his crew mutinied and left him there. The final year of his life for which there is any record was spent sailing among the atolls of the Tuamotu Archipelago and the Marquesas Islands, ostensibly in search of sperm whales, but in reality floundering with something scarcer and less tangible: an escape from his family, his responsibilities, and his home island in the Atlantic Ocean—Nantucket. With the help of large quantities of alcohol, a Polynesian mistress, and a frightened and desperate crew, he successfully fell off the map.

I had no real hopes of finding him, but a voyage on the *Aranui* transported me through his last known stomping ground and gave me an appreciation of the part of the Pacific that captivated him. The only ship that now sails regularly in the same part of the world the old whaling captain from Nantucket once favored, the *Aranui* is a freight and passenger transport that travels from Tahiti to the Marquesas delivering cement, gasoline, beer, an occasional car or outrigger canoe, and the varied stock of small general stores—from ketchup to popsicles to pencils—to the six inhabited islands in the group, their names suggestive of drum beats and falling coconuts: Nuku Hiva, Hiva Oa, Ua Pou, Ua Huka, Fatu Hiva, and Tahuata. At each bay, the ship purchases the cash crop of the islands, copra—the dried flesh of coconuts—which is shipped to refineries and made into coconut oil through a process reminiscent of trying-out whale blubber. With only a few small airplane landing strips in the islands and a limited schedule of flights, everything the villagers need, or want, arrives on the *Aranui*, and the only strangers on shore besides the occasional yachtsman are the passengers from the ship.

During a decade at sea, the engineer of the *Aranui* has seen only eight other ships on the eight-hundred-mile-long passage from Papeete, Tahiti, to Taiohae, Nuku Hiva. In a vast expanse of blue there is nothing in sight but clouds and the swell of immeasurable gallons of seawater rocking the ship. No sails, and no whales either; he has spotted only three whales in his dozens of two-week-long trips to the Marquesas Islands. The mysterious life beneath the surface of the ocean is hinted at early one morning by flying fish zipping above the waves as if shot out of slingshots, their silvery fins vibrating like hummingbird wings. They are leaping for their lives, but the source of their terror is hidden from view. All we see from the deck of the ship is sky and sea and lots of it. One day, a frigate bird hangs above us for a few minutes like a piñata, his bright red neck shocking against the blue. His kind are reputed to travel only thirty miles from land, so there must be an atoll nearby, but our map doesn't show it.

Between Tahiti and the Marquesas lies the Tuamotu Archipelago, a string of atolls mapped by Captain Charles Wilkes of the U.S. Exploring Expedition in 1839. Two of his boundary lines are particularly intriguing. The first extends roughly along meridian 145 west and is labeled: "To the

East of this line the Missionaries have not extended." The next dividing line snakes through the eastern Tuamotus carrying the cautionary statement: "The Natives east of this line were supposed to be cannibals." The Marquesas lie east of the line. Nantucket whalemen on the ship *Essex*, sunk by a large sperm whale in 1820, so feared the cannibals of the area they decided to sail their small whaleboats to the coast of South America some three thousand miles away rather than attempt to seek help at one of the Polynesian islands. A fatal irony ensued.

The man I'm following, Charles A. Veeder (1809–1878?), knew the missionary-tamed Marquesas well enough fifty years after the *Essex* tragedy to arrive at Nuku Hiva in search of provisions, with rum at the top of his list. Veeder was one of a pantheon of respected and successful Nantucket whaling captains in an era when Nantucket Island was at the height of its prosperity in that global industry. Oil from sperm whales lubricated the industrial revolution and lit the streets of Boston and New York, London and Paris. While other seaports might send whalers after right whales, or humpbacks, or into the Arctic after bowheads, Nantucketers were primarily sperm-whale fishermen, chasers of the largest toothed whales in the ocean, and Charles Veeder was one of the more successful whalemen: in four voyages as captain of Nantucket vessels—*Christopher Mitchell*, *Empire*, *Nauticon*, *Ocean Rover*—he brought home more than 7,500 barrels of sperm oil, turning 125 or more of the leviathans into illumination, lubrication, and cash.

The complicated endeavor, with its heavy toll on mariners and whales, was about light, the simple idea of extending the day and moving beyond the rhythm of the natural world into that of the man-made as the industrial age kicked into gear. And, of course, it was about money: ship owners and whale-oil merchants could become very wealthy, and although Nantucket Quaker whalemen might not approve of singing and dancing and wearing colorful clothing, they had no problem counting their profits. Nantucket boys had family connections in the oil industry, they grew up listening to tales of the sea, studied mathematics and navigation, learned to swim and row when they were young, and aspired to become whaling captains. Inexperienced boys and men without that background, or crew signed on in the Azores or Pacific Islands, generally had no idea what they were in for and how little they would get out of it if they survived. At the entry level, it was an occupation of last resort for the ignorant and desperate and the occasional educated adventurer down on his luck, like twenty-two-year-old Herman Melville, who signed on as a seaman on the whaleship *Acushnet* out of Fairhaven, Massachusetts, in 1841. That year, Captain Veeder was sailing home in the whaleship *Christopher Mitchell*, his first command, with more than 2,700 barrels of sperm oil in the hold, an excellent haul. And waiting for Veeder in Nantucket was his wife, Susan, and their young sons George and Charles Edward.

Susan Austin Veeder (1816–1897) became the first Nantucket woman to accompany her husband on a whaling voyage from the home port seven years later, after the captain had completed another lucrative voyage. She packed her trunks and, with two of her three boys, boarded the *Nauticon* in September 1848 for a voyage that lasted four and a half years. She kept a journal, a terse record that on rare occasion overflowed with emotion, and she illustrated it with watercolor paintings of islands and harbors in the Pacific world.

Twenty years later, in 1868, her husband sailed off in the New Bedford whaleship *William Gifford*, happy to leave the island that was in the throes of a shocking decline—half the population dispersed, the major industry sunk, and town fathers pondering a new livelihood: tourism. Elected one of the town's selectmen in 1865, Veeder was on the first Committee for Tourism, exploring a way to make a living that many viewed as the only hope for the economic survival of the island. But to an old sperm-whale fisherman who had ridden the waves of maritime prosperity and international respect that Nantucket garnered in the 1830s and '40s, the proposed reinvention of the island might have seemed an embarrassment.

The family voyage on the *Nauticon* and Captain Veeder's final voyage on the *William Gifford* are widely disparate tales, and each is an atypical episode in an industry that was full of drama: there was no such thing as an uneventful whaling voyage. Men fell from aloft and were drowned or broken, they deserted, they were injured during the hunt, and they suffered from malnutrition, exposure, and despair. Ships wrecked on uncharted reefs, were damaged in storms, lost their way. Mutinies, clashes with foreign cultures, pirates—travel on the ocean could be treacherous. For those reasons, and other, more personal ones, few women chose to accompany their whaling husbands at sea. Even fewer kept journals of their voyages, and only a handful attempted to illustrate their travelogues, but Susan Veeder went armed with watercolors and pens and paintbrushes, eager to record a world she had heard so much about but could not imagine. And although sailors desperate to escape the confines of stinking factory ships deserted with regularity—especially in the tropics—whaling captains rarely abandoned their ships and families and disappeared on remote Pacific islands. That both these events occurred in a single family is unusual; that two journals survive recording these voyages is extraordinary. Most surprising is that the close-knit community of Nantucket, one that relished its tales of mutiny and other catastrophes at sea, kept silent about the captain's betrayal and scarcely remembered Susan's remarkable journey.

The rise and fall of Charles A. Veeder and the rise and fall of Nantucket whaling follow the same timeline. The depression that hit the island in the 1860s overwhelmed the captain, too. Lack of resources and a viable plan for the future were temporary setbacks as the local populace figured out how to make a living on their remote sand pile, eventually transitioning from a whaling center to a tourist mecca. Veeder took a different course, his personal resources exhausted and his plan for the future vague. But stalwart Susan, left on Nantucket with a niece and daughter to care for, opened the doors of the family home on Orange Street to summer boarders, just as many of her neighbors did, offering genteel accommodation with a splash of historical romance. This woman walked the Broom Road in Tahiti, visited the descendants of mutineers on Pitcairn, watched a volcano erupt in the Galápagos, and saw a polar bear stroll across the frozen Arctic close to her ship. The shells on her mantle were from Lazareef and Peacock Island. Her journal, with watercolors of her laundry drying on Cocos Island, was on the parlor table; her husband's portrait hung above the fireplace mantle. Their story is replete with adventure, danger, exotic locales, and interaction with a culture so different from their own it was as if they had entered an alternate reality, a land of opposites, one to be witnessed, recorded, and left behind by Susan, but one that drew Captain Veeder through the looking glass never to return.

Note to Readers: Sources and Suppositions

THIS BOOK RECONSTRUCTS the lives of Susan and Charles Veeder of Nantucket and tells the story of two voyages to the Pacific that changed their lives a hundred and fifty years ago. The work is based on extensive research I conducted in libraries and online, in journals, documents, genealogies, newspaper accounts, and numerous other sources. You may refer to the Notes at the end of the book for references and additional information about people and events.

The book is also informed by my own personal experience. My deep interest in the Veeders' story took me to the other side of the world, for a brief taste of life at sea on the *Aranui*, a very comfortable passenger freighter cruising from Tahiti to the Marquesas through the Tuamotu Archipelago. I saw the same blue waters, green islands, and coral atolls that Susan and Charles Veeder sailed through a century and a half before on wooden ships stinking of whale blubber.

In her *Nauticon* journal, Susan Veeder records what she considered noteworthy events, but her entries rarely describe her relationships with her husband and the crew, how she cared for her children, the details of life on board the ship, or her impressions of Polynesian life—topics we'd certainly wish to know more about. I have filled in some of this void with brief imagined scenes based on an informed and sympathetic reading of her journal. These scenes are prefaced by qualifiers like "must have" or "would have" or "perhaps." The journal that informs us about the last year of Captain Veeder's last voyage is much more detailed and explicit than Susan's journal and requires less supposition. Although at times that account seems fanciful, it isn't, as evidenced by a report of the U.S. Consul in Tahiti in 1872.

Nantucket's first historian, Obed Macy, author of *The History of Nantucket* (1835), kept personal journals throughout his life, recording his thoughts and observations about local, national, and international incidents and occurrences. Although he did not know Susan and Charles Veeder and made no reference to them, he made the following comment, which aptly applies to this account of their lives:

> *. . . although in many instances it may not be literally correct, yet the author believes the whole is substantially true.*
> (Journal 6, 1844)

A Thousand Leagues of Blue

Title page of Susan Veeder's *Nauticon* journal.

Gift of the Friends of the Nantucket Historical Association, Ms. 220, Log 347

CHAPTER ONE

Islands Seen by the Ship Nauticon

Discharged our pilot and steered our course for the Cape de Verd Islands, nothing of any note occurred until the 15th, then we had a strong gale for three days and myself and boys very sick.
(September 15, 1848)

RETCHING IN HER CHAMBER POT while steadying her feet on the rolling deck, Susan was bombarded with the awful music of the ship—the creak and groan of the wood, the slap of the sails, the jarring slam of the hull in the trough of the waves. She made a feeble attempt to comfort frightened six-year-old David, who would soon enough be more at home on the ship than his mother. George, at fourteen, suffered his own awkward initiation into the life of a mariner, but he, too, would soon prove that he was cut of the same cloth as his father. Captain Veeder came below to tease his sons while he smoothed Susan's hair and helped her sip some tea, assuring them all that such weather would soon be recognized as a minor impediment; the Pacific was just around the corner.

Thirty-two-year-old Susan Austin Veeder, five months pregnant with her fourth child, sailed on the Nantucket whaleship *Nauticon* in 1848 with her husband, Captain Charles A. Veeder, and two of their sons on a journey hunting sperm whales that would last four and a half years. Her account of the voyage from the home port is the earliest one by a Nantucket woman that is currently known. A contemporary of Herman Melville, Susan was not a literary woman, but her journal gives us a glimpse of her passage through the world that was the setting for much of Melville's work.

Her reasons for uprooting her family—leaving ten-year-old Charles Edward, her middle son, at home with her parents—were complex. Like so many other Nantucket women, she felt like a widow when her husband was at sea, and feared that she would become one. Sparse information about the progress of his voyages—an occasional letter, a brief notice in a newspaper, or personal news delivered by another Nantucket captain who had met him at sea—provided ample opportunity for anxiety as the statistics of disaster and tragedy in her maritime community were well known; local genealogies of Nantucket families are heavily peppered with the comment "lost at sea." Susan understood the necessity of quelling a morbid imagination with hard work and frequent socializing with her extended family and her women friends, and her children kept her busy enough, even if she was lonely. During the fourteen and a half years of their marriage before her maritime adventure, while she ran her household and cared for their boys, Charles was at sea more often than he was ashore. His documented voyages as captain of a whaleship total six and a half years before he sailed the *Nauticon*, plus another three years as first mate, and he was certainly at sea for at least two voyages before that, working his way up to positions of more and more responsibility. Since she pledged her seventeen-year-old heart to him on November 28, 1833, he had been at sea nine and a half years, sailing first as mate on the *Christopher Mitchell* in July 1834, when Susan was seven months pregnant with their first child. Charles met his son, George, a month before the boy's third birthday, when he returned in the late summer of 1837. The voyage was successful—the couple bought a new house on Orange Street in the busy heart of downtown Nantucket—and Veeder was chosen as captain for the next voyage of the ship, sailing away in the spring of 1838 and returning in 1841 to meet his second son, Charles Edward, born in November 1838. Following that voyage, he took some time off, bought a farm

Built at Mattapoisett in 1834 for Charles Mitchell & Co., the *Christopher Mitchell* made eight whaling voyages in twenty-six years. Charles Veeder was first mate 1834–37 and captain 1838–41. Ship portrait is by an unknown artist, circa 1835.

Gift of Robert M. Waggaman, 1979.8.1

in Shimmo, on the south side of Nantucket's Great Harbor, and was home to witness the birth of third son, David, in 1842. The opportunity to command another whaleship came his way in 1843, and Charles began his career with ship owners George and Matthew Starbuck, sailing their new ship *Empire* off on a four-and-a-half-year voyage. He returned home in November 1847 to a family he hardly knew, and, when it was time to go to sea again ten months later, he and Susan broke the traditional maritime-family mold. She was pregnant and not keen on waving goodbye, and he was torn between a flourishing career and a growing family. Strong, capable, curious, and determined not to be without her husband when her next child was born, Susan agreed to sail off to the other side of the globe on a voyage that held no guarantees for her safety, health, or sanity. Few women of her milieu took such a leap of faith into the Pacific Ocean.

* * *

THAT THE OWNERS OF THE *Nauticon*, brothers George and Matthew Starbuck, were married to educated, cultured women active in progressive social causes probably worked in Susan's favor; they were open to new ideas. Prior to their decision to send Captain Veeder and family off on their new ship, the Starbucks and their wives would have met Susan to assess her suitability as a companion to her husband on a lengthy and arduous voyage that had one purpose only, to kill enough whales to make enough oil to realize a profit on their investment and maintain their elegant lifestyle as denizens of Main Street, Nantucket. In no way did they want her to interfere with that objective. Invited to one of the brothers' identical stately brick mansions for tea and conversation, Susan would not disappoint. Although not of the same social circle, she could hold her own with George's wife, Elizabeth, who was described as having a "commanding personality." The women had much in common; they were lively, multitalented young mothers. Elizabeth's oldest son, George, was fourteen, as was George Veeder, and both women were, coincidentally, five months pregnant, although that fact may not have been mutually recognized or discussed. Elizabeth had five more children than Susan, however, because her wealthy ship-owner and whale-oil merchant husband stayed home while Charles's long absences provided the only guaranteed method of birth control at the time, if a wife was faithful. Catherine, Matthew's wife, was two years younger than Susan, with three small children. She and Elizabeth were literary women; they wrote poetry and later belonged to Sorosis, a local women's literary club, so they may have encouraged Susan to keep a journal, something they would surely have done if they were in her place. Although familiar with the official logbooks of their husbands' ships, we can imagine the women would have been eager to read an account of whaling from a woman's point of view; it would give them a glimpse of a world they would never see but could then better imagine from the comfort of their identical parlors, in front of their identical black marble fireplaces. George and Matthew listened to their wives, trusted Charles Veeder, and sized up Susan: she had gumption, she had spirit. She was more than acceptable. And if there were any suspicions about the captain's propensities toward alcohol and native women that would surface two decades later, Susan and the children would remind him of his responsibilities.

Known as the Three Bricks, these identical houses on Main Street were built in the late 1830s by whaling magnate Joseph Starbuck for his three sons. Stereograph by Charles N. Shute & Son, 1870s.

GPN-Shute-46

With the seal of approval bestowed upon her, Susan began to pack her trunks and arrange for middle son, Charles Edward, to stay on Nantucket with her parents. At ten years old he was a schoolboy who would miss four crucial years of education if he joined his family at sea; older brother George had already completed his formal education, and David was young enough to catch up when he returned. If Charles Edward was to be a successful mariner like his father, he could not afford to neglect a study of mathematics and navigation that would be the foundation to set him apart from other greenhands on a whaling voyage. Another consideration that might have weighed on Susan and the captain was the possibility that if something tragic happened to them, at least there would be an heir on Nantucket to carry on the family name and inherit their property. And who knows, maybe Charles Edward was rambunctious, a bit of a problem, too much for a pregnant mother to handle on a ship at sea. The 1850 U.S. Federal Census for Nantucket places eleven-year-old Charles E. Veeder in a household with Susan's parents: George Austin, sixty-one; Susan Austin, fifty-seven; their daughter Eliza Foster, twenty-four; her husband, Clement; and their one-year-old daughter named Susan Veeder Foster. Surrounded by close family, Charles Edward was safe and well cared for, although excluded from the family adventure.

In the corner of one of her trunks, Susan tucked in a blank journal, pens, ink, watercolors, brushes, and blotters, ready to record the noteworthy events of her life at sea. Her journal is not the typical sturdy account book favored by many log keepers, the ones sold by stationers in New Bedford and Boston, fourteen inches or so tall by ten inches wide, with more than two hundred tightly bound pages. It's surprising hers survived at all, as it is more delicate, a simple, slim eight-by-ten-inch notebook with a skinny leather spine, the cover a thin board made lively with marbled paper. One hundred and seventy-two lightly lined pages, all she anticipated filling in more than four years at sea.

The typical trunk of the time had a shallow tray that fit in the top, where her hairbrush and mirror, combs and pins, jewelry, and small items for her toilette were carefully placed. Knitting needles, a thimble, scissors, thread and etui of needles made up her sewing kit. Beneath were dresses, nightgowns, shawls, stacks of diapers, and the layette she would soon need. A bolt of calico, slippers, books, her favorite teacup from home, a small box for letters. There was no suggested packing list for a woman off on a four-year voyage with a ship full of whalemen and a baby on the way. Susan had to anticipate her needs, do without, or find a substitute for any items of importance she forgot to include. While the ship was being outfitted at Nantucket she could arrange the tiny stateroom, supply it with pillows and linens, and have Charles deliver a small carpet and rocking chair to the after cabin. Would she need a rocking chair? The ship would rock enough perhaps; an upholstered armchair might be more suitable.

* * *

THE FIRST MATE OF A WHALESHIP kept a logbook for the vessel's owners, often a rather dull record of weather; longitude and latitude; where whales were seen and killed and the number of barrels of oil rendered from each; ships spoken (other ships seen at sea and communicated with by signal or conversation); and sites where wood, water, pigs, fruit, and other provisions were collected in the Pacific. Some logbooks were later used by granddaughters of mariners as scrapbooks, with illustrations from *Godey's Lady's Book* pasted over accounts of mutiny and other disasters. Others were tossed when attics were cleared, and some are still treasured by descendants. Despite the vagaries of preservation, thousands of accounts of whaling voyages are in libraries and archives around the word, not all of them "official" logbooks: other crewmembers besides the first mate often kept private journals, and those can be most illuminating. The log kept by the first mate of the *Nauticon* has not surfaced, but third mate James F. Roberts kept a very dry journal of the voyage, obviously practicing for his future role as keeper of the ship's log. He included no more than half a dozen brief personal comments among the litany of wind and weather before his account ended in October 1851. Susan is mentioned only once. A disgruntled young journal-keeper on Captain Veeder's last ship, twenty years after the *Nauticon,* painted a vivid picture of a voyage gone awry, and in observations not commonly recorded in logbooks helps us understand why the captain never came home.

Journals kept by whaling wives, the rarest of all, present an entirely different perspective of life at sea, one that often involved childbirth, laundry, and loneliness. Among women's journals, Susan's is one of the most valuable, not only for its unique account of her life on a whaleship—a notoriously odiferous, cramped environment populated by a multinational crew—but because of her artistic renderings of exotic locales. Although some women's whaling journals include sketches of ships and animals and islands, no other woman's journal yet discovered includes full-page color paintings.

Susan overcame whatever anxiety she may have had, and, holding David firmly by the hand, boarded the 106-foot-long wooden ship to sail off chasing whales in the Pacific, even though there was no doctor on board, no female companionship in the foreseeable future, and no set course across the watery portions of the globe—wherever sperm whales gathered, there they would go. Examine her painted portrait and you will see a woman who appears solidly self-possessed. She is serious and elegant in her black velvet dress, exotic gold earrings, and pearl studded pin, staring calmly and a little sadly at the viewer. There is an uncanny resemblance to the *Mona Lisa*: both paintings depict women with limpid eyes, black hair parted in the middle, carefully placed hands, the suggestion of a smile, the aura of contentment mixed with something else—in Susan's case, resolution. Attributed to a Chinese artist, her portrait was based on a miniature painting or daguerreotype taken before 1855, when Captain Veeder left on the *Ocean Rover* on a three-year whaling voyage that found him at anchor in the harbor at Hong Kong for six weeks in early 1858, making repairs to his ship. Plenty of time for him to commission the painting and have it framed to hang in his cabin for the return voyage, a

Portrait of Susan Veeder by a Chinese artist, circa 1858.

Gift of Barbara Johnson, 1994.28.1

substitute for his now land-bound wife. The portrait shows us Susan more than half a dozen years after her voyage on the *Nauticon*, after a heavy dose of loss. In 1848, she may have had more sparkle in her eyes, the healthy glow of pregnancy, a lighter step, a genuine smile.

Whether from encouragement by Elizabeth and Catherine Starbuck or by her own design, Susan planned to keep a journal and illustrate it, and she set to work immediately, even though she felt wretched. She was a proficient painter, carefully delineating isolated islands—some uninhabited, others featuring harbors crowded with ships—seen during the course of the voyage. In fact, the striking title page of her journal, depicting their ship tossing on waves near a point of land where a lighthouse and keeper's house stand, is framed by the painted words "Islands Seen by Ship Nauticon." One of her incentives for joining her husband was a desire to see exotic places and to paint landscapes entirely foreign to her, and *everything* was foreign to her. Married at seventeen and a mother at eighteen, she had been bound closely to Nantucket while Charles was roaming the Pacific; there is no reason to assume she had been farther afield than New Bedford, or, maybe at the farthest reach, Boston.

Susan's ability to paint ship portraits was learned on Nantucket, where William Wilkes Morris advertised a mariner's school in the 1820s and '30s, offering instruction in mathematics, navigation, and "ship-drafting—to cut rigging and sails with accuracy." Morris scribbled the names of some of his students and the fees due him for their instruction in his own journal, and among the names were those of several girls, evidence that boys and girls were taught some of the same subjects; Susan may have been his student. The Quaker belief in equal education for boys and girls was a long-held tradition on Nantucket, dating back to the eighteenth century when that faith became predominant on the island, and even after most of the believers had given up the increasingly restrictive Quaker doctrine, the emphasis on education still held. Private schools and tutors were available to those who could afford them and public schools were in place on Nantucket by 1827. Susan, although slightly orthographically challenged, had been schooled, as had her brother, Edward Austin, who became a ship captain. It is obvious that she studied painting, in particular ship's rigging, the delicate spider's web of lines that run from mast to deck in all manner of vessels in the harbor scenes she depicted in her journal. If she didn't study with Morris, perhaps Edward did, and she sat with him in the evenings drawing ships on rag paper by the light of an oil lamp while he filled her head with nautical details, instilling an eagerness in her for firsthand knowledge of the world he would soon inhabit.

* * *

ALTHOUGH HER HUSBAND thought she got along fine at sea, Susan had her moments of doubt.

> *24th we had another strong gale we took in our boats and sent down some of our masts. I think that if I could of got on shore I should of given up the voyage for I was very sick.*
> (September 24, 1848)

The *Nauticon* followed the usual route of whaleships traveling from Nantucket to Cape Horn, sailing the Gulf Stream toward Newfoundland and then taking the southern curve of that warm-water conduit down toward the coast of Africa, briefly stopping at the Cape Verde Islands for provisions—pigs, chickens, oranges, and plantains—but no excursions on shore for Susan. In the vicinity of the islands, the *Nauticon* met a brig bound for Lisbon and first mate James Archer went aboard her for a gam, or conversation and visit with the captain, who sent Susan some birds, along with a pet monkey for little David. The birds may have been a nice addition to the family quarters, their cage swinging while they sang, but it's doubtful they lasted long in rough seas, or had much to sing about then. As for the monkey, a six-year-old on a whaleship with a monkey is either the stuff of a children's book or a mother's nightmare.

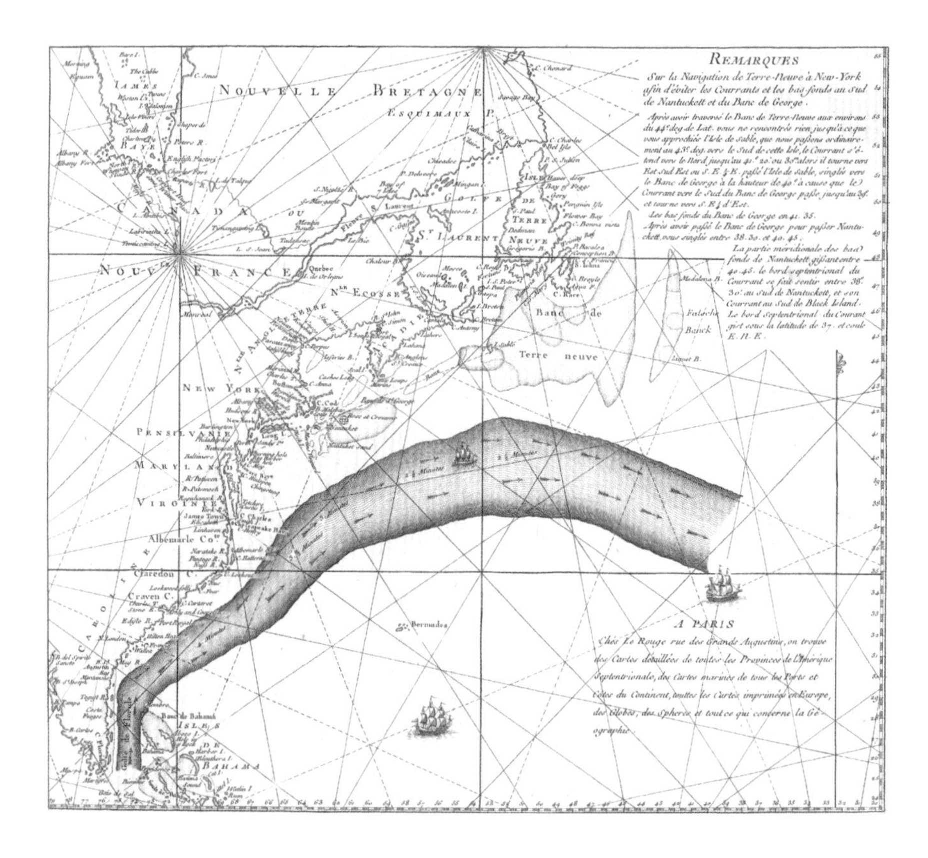

The parameters of the Gulf Stream and its effect on sailing vessels were well known to Nantucket ship captains in the eighteenth century. Timothy Folger, whaleman and merchant captain, plotted the Gulf Stream in 1769 at his cousin Benjamin Franklin's request. Franklin, then residing in London, arranged for the earliest chart of the Gulf Stream to be printed in London that year. The second version, printed in Paris by Le Rouge circa 1783, is pictured here.

Gift of the Friends of the Nantucket Historical Association, Ms. 1000.2.2.10

Gams would become a highlight of Susan's long voyage, and every little gift, whether monkey or jam, broke the monotony of shipboard life. The first watercolor illustration she painted in her journal is a one-page panel with three horizontal scenes: *St. Nicholas Island Dist. 2 Miles*; *St. Jago Island Dist. 3 Miles*—both in the Cape Verde group—and *Staten Island, Dist. 10 Miles*. The *Nauticon* sighted Staten Island, east of the tip of South America, on December 11, three months into the voyage that took them away from an approaching North Atlantic winter across the equator to summer and then farther south to some of the roughest seas on the planet.

Susan writes very little about the voyage to Cape Horn, noting a few ship sightings, and remarking that her sickness had begun to wear off on November 8, after eight weeks at sea. By December 13, she was feeling spritely, noting, "the Captn is all attention and says he is very happy to think I am hear and incourages me by saying that he thinks I get along first rate."

The family's first Christmas on board the ship was a non-event: Susan merely wrote "squally and some rain." They were rounding Cape Horn, and on December 26 met with the strongest gales yet; it was not a convenient time for festivities, if they had been desired. Unlike many whaling wives who kept journals, Susan does not mention religious holidays or express longings for Sunday church services, nor does she quote scripture, even when the going gets rough: a Cape Horn passage at Christmastime when eight months pregnant would have prompted many of her sister sailors to prayers, if not lamentations, but Susan kept her thoughts off the page. Perhaps it was too rugged to write.

The *Nauticon* rounded Cape Horn on schedule and sailed up the coast of South America, arriving at Talcahuano, Chile, on January 4, 1849. The family all went ashore, and, as Susan recorded, they "soon arrived at the Consuls whare i shall stop for a while." American consul William Crosby had a household of nine when Susan arrived to make it ten: his wife, Lucinda; three children; a doctor named Troupe; Captain Stetson of the New Bedford whaleship *Trident*, who was recovering from illness; a maid; and a cook. In addition to its function as a consulate, Crosby's home appears to

St. Nicholas and St. Jago in the Cape Verde Islands, and Staten Island off Cape Horn, from Susan Veeder's journal of the *Nauticon*.

Gift of the Friends of the Nantucket Historical Association, Ms. 220, Log 347

have been an American whaling refuge and convalescent clinic, as evidenced by Captain Stetson's residency and Susan's maternity stay there. Susan was not impressed with the consul's house, however, not approving of the high stone wall that blocked her view of the street; such an obstruction would be unthinkable on Nantucket, where houses in town were closely flanked and watching passersby was a traditional pastime. Although she never describes her quarters on the *Nauticon*, Susan did enumerate the furnishings of her room in the consul's house:

> *My room is quite retired and very plainly furnished. There is an English carpet, high post bedstead, one common table, three chairs, a lounge and two trunks.*
> (January 6, 1849)

The family suite on the *Nauticon* may have been more appealing to her, and, in her four months at sea, it had already become home. Captain's quarters were in the rear, or "aft" cabins, and included a tiny stateroom with a bed, built-in storage in every available nook, and probably a trundle bed for David. A private head adjoined, tucked into the side of the ship next to an all-purpose after-cabin with amenities like an upholstered settee against the rear transom, whose windows let in light, something the crew living in the dark forecastle would not have had. This room served as parlor, office, library, schoolroom, and sewing room. With a carpet on the floor and a comfortable chair, it was where Susan spent most of her time, although there was the deck for fresh-air strolls when weather permitted and when the crew weren't cutting-in and boiling whale blubber. She would have stayed below then, away from the grease and smoke and carnage.

> *Nothing of any note occurred until the 29th and then I was confined with a fine daughter weighing 9 lbs which was very pleasing to us both and so things went along about as they should . . .*
> (January 29, 1849)

One of the most startling entries in Susan's journal is the record of the birth of her daughter. She never mentions her pregnancy, nor does she hint at the reason for her stay in Talcahuano until January 29, when the simple birth announcement is recorded. What becomes immediately apparent is that the journal keeper was pregnant when she left Nantucket, well aware that her child might be born aboard the *Nauticon* if their voyage around Cape Horn was delayed. Her prolonged seasickness is understandable, as is her courage. Not only was she the first woman to depart on a whaling voyage from Nantucket, she was pregnant when she made her decision. Rather than hindering her plans, it may have increased her desire to be with her husband. When she sat in the Starbuck parlor with the ship-owners' wives, she probably kept the information to herself.

Susan was delighted to find another whaling wife in town, Caroline Munkley of the ship *Emerald* of New Bedford, who had been at sea a year longer than Susan and would have a son later that year. Talcahuano was a busy port for whalers, and Susan had a number of callers, captains who came for tea and a touch of domesticity, a reminder of the niceties of female companionship they had left behind. Charles chose to stay in Talcahuano with Susan, sending the ship to sea with Mr. Archer in charge, an unusual move, but understandable when Susan finally revealed that she had given birth to their fine nine-pound daughter. Several days later they received news that Mr. Archer and crew had taken their first sperm whale, a large one yielding eighty barrels of oil. A fortuitous day for the Veeders on all accounts, although not so for the sperm whale, the creature that attracted the *Nauticon* and all those other ships into the Pacific Ocean.

* * *

In the early years of Nantucket whaling, from the late seventeenth century to the early eighteenth, whales were sighted by lookouts posted in stations—wooden towers with viewing platforms—dotted along the southern and eastern shores of the tiny island thirty miles south of Cape Cod. Although today it is rare to see whales sporting in the waters so close to Nantucket, they were plentiful enough in the early years of the colony to turn the heads of the settlers from sheep farming and agriculture to a more promising industry. Whaleboats, approximately twenty-two feet long and manned by a crew of six, were launched into the surf to give chase when a whale was spotted. Before the native population of the island was decimated by disease in the late eighteenth century, Wampanoag men supplied the bulk of the manpower in the whaleboats, but they were not always there by their own choice and they seldom profited from their participation. Victims of a cultural misunderstanding of ownership of property—from land to liquor—many of the local Indians were involved in debt peonage situations that forced them to pay what they owed their English creditors with their hard labor at sea. Without them, onshore whaling could not

Illustration of a whale hunt from the journal kept by Captain James G. Coffin on the ship *Washington*, 1842–44.

Ms. 220, Log 252

have succeeded, since the population of able-bodied white men in the young island settlement was just not large enough to fill many whaleboats.

There were no whaleships and no whaling captains in the early days of onshore whaling, just companies of men who shared the expenses and the rewards of the endeavor. Whales were harpooned, lanced, killed, and towed to shore where their blubber was cut off and boiled down in large iron try-pots. As whales became scarcer near shore, the islanders went after them in their sloops, sailing north to Newfoundland and Davis Strait. They carried two of the whaleboats on the mother vessel and would launch them when a whale was sighted, the men rowing madly until they were practically on top of their prey. The boatsteerer, or harpooneer, balanced firmly in the bow of the boat, would hurl a harpoon—attached to a long coil of rope— into the creature. That it was a dangerous occupation is an understatement: it was not suited for the faint of heart or the physically weak. Once wounded and fastened to the whaleboat by the harpoon, the whale would often take off, towing the whaleboat behind in what came to be known as the "Nantucket sleigh ride," an exhilarating and terrifying high-speed trip that jarred the bones of the crew and made their teeth chatter. When the beast eventually tired, the boat crew once again rowed closer, and, in a delicate maneuver, the mate exchanged places with the harpooneer so he could heave a lance into the whale's vital organs. Spouting blood, the wounded creature thrashed around in a flurry that often damaged, or "stove," the boats and knocked the men overboard. Once the death throes subsided, the gore-bespattered men towed the whale's enormous carcass back to the side of the sloop where the blubber was stripped off, hauled aboard, chopped up, stored in barrels, and taken back to Nantucket or ashore on Newfoundland or environs for rendering in try-works set up for that purpose. This was the method of whaling practiced in the 1750s.

The bloody and furious battle between a boatload of men and a fifty-to-eighty-ton whale changed little in the next hundred years; it was the size of the ship, the number of crew members, and the length and scope of the voyage that kept growing until the mid-nineteenth century, when two dozen or more men would sail a 350-ton ship for four or more years, sometimes circumnavigating the globe. Mid-nineteenth-century whaling is described in wonderful poetic detail by Melville in *Moby-Dick*, a novel he was writing at the very time Susan Veeder was at sea in the *Nauticon*; no better portrait exists of the intricacies and profundities of the fishery, from sighting a whale to rendering the oil and contemplating leviathan than in that novel written by a man whose imagination never put a woman on board a whaleship.

The original prey of the Nantucket whalemen were humpbacks and right whales, the latter so named because they were the *right* whale to pursue; unlike other species, they don't sink when dead and are relatively slow swimmers, feeding on tiny organisms filtered through the two hundred or so strips of baleen that hang from their upper jaw. But the prey of choice was the sperm whale, discovered farther out in the Atlantic in the early eighteenth century. It was a different creature, a fast swimmer and deep diver, about the same size as the right whale but with teeth in the lower jaw, teeth that could crush a whaleboat (or take off Ahab's leg). Their oil was superior

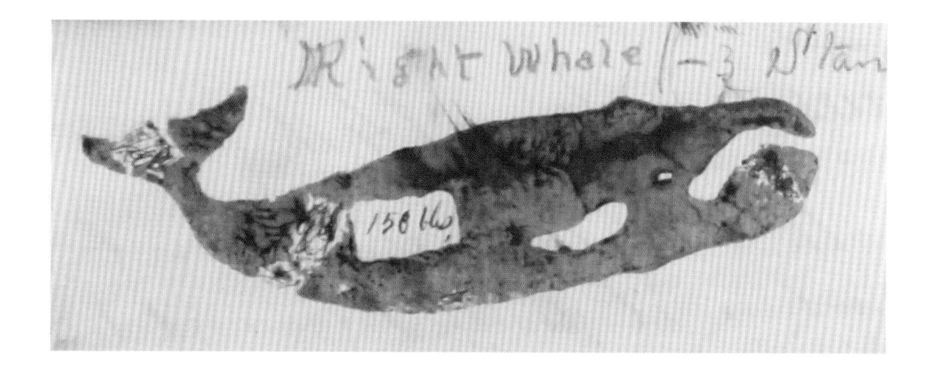

Right whale stamp from journal of the latter part of the voyage of the *William Gifford*, 1871–72, kept by seaman Edward J. Kirwin.

Courtesy of the New Bedford Whaling Museum, KWM Log 452

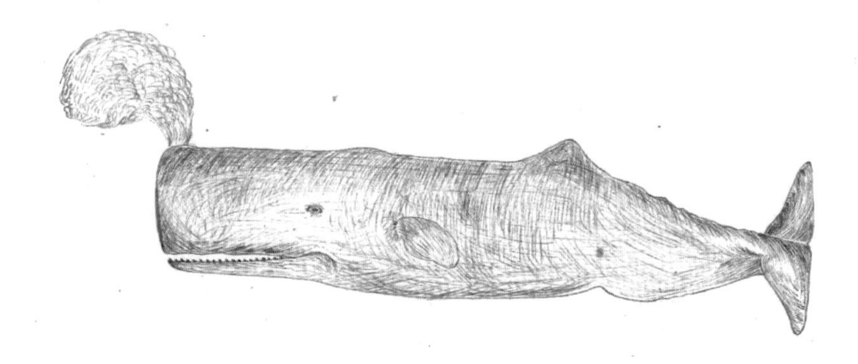

Sketch of a sperm whale from a British whaling journal kept by Eldred E. Fysh, surgeon, on the bark *Coronet*, 1837–39.

Ms. 220, Log 55

to that of other whales and their gigantic heads were full of an even richer grade of the product—it burned brighter and smelled better than any other illuminant in the world at the time. Sperm whales were also buoyant enough when dead to be towed back to the mother ship. As these creatures became scarcer in the Atlantic, Nantucket mariners began chasing them around Cape Horn and into the South Pacific, thousands of miles from home, often in uncharted waters. They took their try-works with them, assembling them on the open deck of their wooden ship—where, remarkably, the boiling took place—and storing the rendered oil in casks assembled by the ship's cooper. Instead of two whaleboats on board there were four or five on the larger barks and ships that replaced the sloops and brigs of the eighteenth century.

Susan Veeder's father, George Austin, was one of the intrepid mariners in the early years of what was called the "southern whale fishery," and so was Peter P. Veeder, father of her future husband. Their firsthand accounts of the drama of the chase, told by the hearth when they returned home, fueled the dreams and nightmares of their children. Young Charles Veeder imagined himself a captain; Susan Austin never dreamed she would go on a whaling voyage.

CHAPTER TWO

Paradise Lost

THE HAPPY NEWS of the first oil of the season prompted Captain Veeder to return to his ship with his sons, leaving Susan and their new daughter at the consul's house in Talcahuano for almost two months of recuperation and female companionship, which were not what Susan wanted; she wanted to be back on board the *Nauticon* with her family. On Saturday, February 17, she wrote, "To day the wind is fair. At 2 [o'clock] the Captn and boys left me and the ship went to sea and I am left alone." The next day she wrote one line only, "I feel quite feeble to be left among strangers." Although much is left unsaid, one can imagine Susan's trepidation, stranded in a foreign country with a new baby, her family sailing away. She rallied, however, as she always did. The New Bedford whaleship *Pacific*, with Captain Asa Hoxie and his wife, Mary, arrived in port and "it seems very pleasant to see some American ladies." Contemplating her situation and American ladies in general, Susan wrote,

> *I think Talcahuano is a bad place the longer I stay hear and the more I see of it the more disgusted I feel. I don't no what some of our ladys would say if they should be an eye witness as some of us are.*
> (February 22, 1849)

Artist that she was, and critical observer of the exotic Chilean port town, Susan did not paint any scenes of the place. Perhaps she was serious in her intention to record only "Islands Seen from the Ship Nauticon" the title she gave her journal. Perhaps she was too busy with the baby and her active social life, or maybe her painting was a private amusement, something not shared with strangers. More likely, she didn't want to paint a place she was disgusted with, exotic or not.

Susan's humor gradually improved as she spent more time with Mrs. Crosby and the other American women in town, and she began to feel like her old self; she went for a horseback ride, by her account her first time, which is not surprising. Nantucket was an island of walkers, its town small enough in area for easy strolls to most places, and, if one didn't walk, the general mode of transportation was the calash, an open, horse-drawn two-wheeled cart in which people often stood instead of sitting. Riding a horse sidesaddle for three miles six weeks after delivering a rather large baby was a feat to be recorded.

On March 11, Susan got her first packet of letters from home and noted that her friends were all well. For six months she had had no news of her family, and the news she finally received was already months old; even though there was relief that all was well at the time, there was still uncertainty about what might have occurred in the intervening months. And there was the ever-present uncertainty about the *Nauticon*. Where *were* Charles and the boys?

On March 16, the whaleship *Globe* of Mystic, Connecticut, arrived at Talcahuano with Captain William A. West, his wife, and their sick thirteen-month-old baby, who died four days later. Susan attended the funeral and saw the child buried far from home, all the ensigns on the ships in the harbor at half mast, Mr. Crosby reading a few prayers. It made a lasting impression on her. Finally, the *Nauticon* returned to Talcahuano on March 23 and Susan began packing her trunk, eager to be back on board, but first she and Charles went for a horseback ride with Mr. and Mrs. Crosby, Susan happy to show off her newly acquired equestrian skills. When they returned to the ship, a fifteen-year-old Spanish girl accompanied them to help with the baby; Susan justified the luxury by stating, for the record, that her health was not very good. Hard to believe, considering her excursion on horseback. Charles was probably being indulgent; he knew that her mother and sister and a whole community of women on Nantucket would have been available to lend her a hand, to coo over the new baby and bring her booties and caps and blankets, to compare her to aunts and grandmothers and to admire the bulk of her. No Spanish girl, however helpful, could begin to fill that void, but it was something.

In the bosom of her family with her healthy daughter, Susan wrote no comments in her journal for ten days. It was now all about whaling, which they had begun in earnest, chasing humpback whales in Mejillones Bay north of Talcahuano, warming up for the deep-sea sperm whale hunting to come. On April 7 they had success, so they stayed in the area for a few days and Susan got to go on shore to collect shells and go fishing, but the novelty wore off and she commented that there were no inhabitants, and "not a green bush to be seen." Her husband's tales of the verdure of the South Pacific must have seemed suspect. As the humpbacks became more elusive, the *Nauticon* headed up the coast of South America; off Peru, Susan sighted her first sperm whale, the primary object of their pursuit, the creature her husband spent his life battling, and it was not a pretty sight:

> *Today we saw a dead sperm whale but it was not good. This is the first I have seen. I am in hopes they don't all smell quite so bad as that did.*
> (April 24, 1849)

Susan did not reveal any sympathy for the whale, nor did most of those involved in the industry at that time. Today, we listen to whale songs and read about the intelligence and social characteristics of the species, admire their familial bonds, and go on whale-watching tours just to get close to them. Some intrepid photographers even swim with them and are treated respectfully by the species once ravaged by humans. Those who have looked a whale in the eye or seen them cavort with their calves have an appreciation of the animals that was not a nineteenth-century attitude, certainly not among those involved in the whaling industry. Whales, and the sperm whale in particular, were simply cash cows. Susan doesn't exhibit compassion for the tortoises they later captured on Chatham Island in the Galápagos Group, either:

> *All ashore for the last time today, as we shall leave tomorrow. I have been on shore twice since we have been here. There are a few trees and bushes. Some of the men brought off some prickly pears and while they was on shore I did them up in molasses for the people. Another day while here I made ginger bread and sent it on shore to them about 150 cakes.*
> (May 1, 1849)

Her feelings may have been too complex to record, and she was not one to philosophize. She had never seen a tortoise on Nantucket, and to witness boatloads of them gathered like pumpkins must have been shocking. Susan doesn't even mention them, aside from the fact that they collected a hundred and eighty, nor does she describe how the men lugged the giant, slow-moving creatures back to the ship and stacked them up in the hold. Galápagos tortoises were a favorite food of whalers and an easy bounty to collect if you had a strong back. They survived for months with no food or water, and were eaten along the way. Fresh meat was a true delicacy on a whaling voyage, and tortoise meat was described as tender and delicious by men weary of salt pork and beef. The shells made handy bowls, too. When the Nantucket ship *Essex* was rammed and sunk by a sperm whale in 1820, each of the three whaleboats full of survivors was allotted two tortoises salvaged from the wreck. After devouring those, they must have used the shells to collect rainwater and to hold portions of their dead comrades, which they also consumed. Like all Nantucketers who went whaling, Susan was aware that she might find herself in a similar predicament, yet there she was in the Galápagos Islands, baking ginger cakes.

Heading north from the Galápagos, the *Nauticon* sailed to the Bay of Panama, where there were a number of whaleships actively pursuing sperm whales. On the first day of June, the *Nauticon* got its first one since Susan

***Turtle Catching on Land,* delineated by John Heaviside Clark, engraved by Matthew Dubourg, 1813.**

From the Edouard Stackpole papers, 1995.290.7

rejoined the vessel. She does not describe the hunt or the butchering and boiling that must have been a hellish sight, the long strips of blubber cut from the whale's body as one would pare an apple, blood and gore making the decks slick and sticking to the men, the stench and smoke of the boiling-down process; she only comments that the whale made twenty-five barrels of oil. She stayed out of the way in her cabin below deck with David and the baby, listening to the commotion overhead and holding her nose.

Although care of her baby and David were her primary concerns during the voyage, Susan rarely mentions them, saving her comments for what she found "noteworthy"; being a mother was not anything to write about. It was her role in life and she found it unnecessary to note her daily child-tending chores. On June 11, after days of cruising unsuccessfully for more whales, she recorded one of her few remarks about her infant: "the babe grows nicely and is very cunning." For the next month or so the *Nauticon* stayed in the vicinity of the Galapágos Islands where they spied lots of other New England whaleships: *Roscoe, Catawba, Daniel Webster, Alfred Tiles, Mary, President, Martha,* and *Mary Frances,* the latter suggesting a name for their daughter. Susan found no sister sailors aboard any of them, but several of the captains gammed with the *Nauticon,* drinking tea and probably discussing the scarcity of sperm whales. One of them provided some recent newspapers, but Susan received no letters until August 1, when the *Harvest* of Nantucket brought her a missive from home—written nine days after she sailed, almost a year previously. A disappointment, surely. But she carried on, going fishing on August 3; it was a sport she enjoyed, something she noted with pride and pleasure throughout the voyage, even after the worst tragedy. She also painted scenes of *Chatham Island, Dist. 1 Mile* and *Albemarle, Dist. 4* miles, both in the Galápagos group; Albemarle is what the English called the island, the Spanish called it Isabela, the name it retains today. Late in August, the *Nauticon* returned to the mainland of South America, stopping first at the island of San Lorenzo, off Callao, Peru:

> *Today we sent a boat on shore at Port Lorenzo to see if we could get anything. At 2 o'clock p.m. the boat returned with 4 of the residents. They brought off a number of hats to sell but they was not such ones as we wanted so we could not trade much. We bought 3 for the boys.*
> (August 21, 1849)

Finally, Susan made reference to the fact that she had *three* sons, although one was in Nantucket. Even if the hat for Charles Edward survived another three and a half years, it might not have fit—his entire family gone for a quarter of his lifetime and all he got was a straw hat from Peru! Susan never writes about her older son, George, either, but it becomes apparent after the journal ends that he was one of the crew of the *Nauticon*. Shortly after the family returned to Nantucket in 1853, he shipped out as fourth mate on the *Young Hector*, his position an indication of his rapid progress from seaman to boatsteerer on his first voyage, under his father's tutelage. Susan must have watched from the deck when boats were lowered to chase a whale, her heart in her throat as her oldest son risked his life in hunt after hunt, each a terrifying drama of man versus beast versus ocean. Or maybe she sat silent below deck and sang lullabies to Mary Frances and attempted to persuade David that the life of a farmer could have exciting moments, too.

Near Callao on August 24, the *Nauticon* spoke the bark *Kirkwood* of Nantucket, Captain Charles C. Alley, who informed them that he had been at sea twenty-two months and had 420 barrels of oil. The *Nauticon* had been at sea almost a year and had 250 barrels, so they were on a par. On Captain Veeder's most successful voyage ten years earlier on the *Christopher Mitchell*, he had returned with 2,700 barrels of sperm oil after only three years, or an average of 900 barrels a year. The comparison must have been disheartening, although no one really expected to get 2,700 barrels anymore; 2,000 barrels would be a very good haul. Still, they had a long way to go.

On August 30, they anchored in the port of Tombez, Peru, and there they found Captain Consider Fisher of the ship *Peru* of Nantucket, and his wife, Hannah. Although in charge of a Nantucket ship, Fisher and his wife were from Edgartown, on Nantucket's sister island Martha's Vineyard, and like the Munkleys in Talcahuano had set sail a year before the Veeders. It had been months since Susan had seen another woman, and the captains indulged their wives: the Fishers visited the Veeders on the *Nauticon* "and brought aboard some cakes, melon, oranges, tamarind, etc." for what must have been a congenial meeting and meal, and the next day, a local feast day, the two couples went ashore to a plantation for festivities and music. Later, Susan visited the town of Tombez and found it even less appealing than Talcahuano:

> *I have often heard of Tombez but could not form any idea of the place until I saw it, about all that is to be seen is a few bamboo houses and a lot of half naked children.*
> (September 4, 1849)

Chatham Island and Albemarle Island in the Galápagos, from Susan Veeder's journal of the *Nauticon*.

Gift of the Friends of the Nantucket Historical Association, Ms. 220, Log 347

Susan and the captain had been on shore a few times since their arrival in the port, but the crew was not allowed liberty since desertion was an ever-present possibility for men who endured cramped quarters, bad food, grueling labor, physical punishment, and the promise of the same for several more years. Captain Veeder had been eager to send the *Nauticon* to sea when he was in Talcahuano with Susan awaiting the birth of their child because four men had deserted there, and he was not about to let that happen again. But on September 6, after a week of looking at the land, the crew rebelled: "To day there has been quite an excitement on board with some of our crew. They came aft and demanded liberty but the fuss was soon stopped by putting the ring leaders in the rigging and giving them a dozen or two." Although Susan had baked ginger cakes for these men when they were tortoise-gathering in the Galápagos, she showed little sympathy for their desire to go ashore, and she expressed no disapproval of her husband's method of quelling the demand with a whip. It was a business decision, a necessary show of force to keep the crew in its place, submissive to the demands of the captain who held their lives, and the success of the voyage, in the palm of his hand.

The *Nauticon* left Tombez a week later and sailed to Paita, "about the same as Tumbus, full as dirty," Susan wrote, but from the sea it looked charming. She painted the harbor from one mile out; her style was changing, her painting curves as if she were looking through her spyglass and was influenced by the circular view. She depicts "Payta Harbor" with eight ships in the foreground, two scudding along with their sails full, the others at anchor, sails furled tight. The town in the background features a cluster of one-story white houses, each with two windows separated by a door, like a little face; a pair of two-story blue buildings with white scalloped ornament above the second-floor windows; two large windowless buildings with prominent chimneys, and above the settlement on the hill three masts, or crosses. This is the most complicated scene yet painted by Susan and the detail, particularly the rigging of the ships, is intricately depicted.

From Paita, they steered west in search of whales. Susan remarked on September 26, "Sis grows like a Pig and is very cunning." So far, the baby's name is not recorded by her mother, but she was dubbed Sis by her brothers, who must have had a fine time with her now that she was eight months old and sure to be gurgling at them and perhaps even crawling around the cabin—the darling of the *Nauticon*, better even than young David's short-lived pet monkey, who had been buried at sea. With the comfort of family around him, his wife suckling their thriving daughter, David darting from one end of the ship to another to listen to the stories told by the crew and grab a biscuit from the cook, George becoming a promising mariner,

The harbor at Paita, Peru, from Susan Veeder's journal of the *Nauticon*.

Gift of the Friends of the Nantucket Historical Association, Ms. 220, Log 347

Captain Veeder was experiencing a different kind of voyage. No longer did he worry about what might be happening to his family at home, and he was confident he could keep them safe while sharing the Pacific with them.

* * *

CRUISING OFF THE GALÁPAGOS once again, Susan spied a volcano erupting on Albemarle Island, not a rare occurrence in that hotspot of volcanic activity, but nevertheless a sight to behold: "I could see the lava running down very plain with my glass" she recorded on September 27, 1849. There were few whales to be found, and when they finally raised a shoal of sperm whales a week later, the boats lowered and chased all day, but had no luck.

On November 1, Susan wrote, "We have had to bake our bread about 30 casks over, it was very weevilly and I think it has killed them." The common alternative employed by whalemen was to dip the ship's bread, or hardtack, in hot tea or coffee, if they were lucky enough to get it, and wait until the bugs floated to the top of the beverage where they could be scooped off. Fine food, or even decent food, was not a benefit of a whaling cruise. Months could pass between provisioning trips and fresh food soon ran out: salt pork, salt beef, tortoises, beans, and hardtack along with potatoes and onions sufficed, until the potatoes and onions were eaten. Susan must have been so happy when later in the day they spoke an Australian merchant brig bound to California; the captain and ship's doctor came on board the *Nauticon* and brought her a jar of plums, a tin of soup, a cheese, and a few bottles of wine, some delicacies to add to her table. Susan was delighted by these small gifts that offered variety to her shipboard fare, and she carefully noted whenever someone brought her a treat at sea.

While the captain and doctor were aboard Captain Veeder's ship, some of the *Nauticon* crew were allowed to go aboard the brig for a gam of their own, with interesting consequences, considering the conduct of Captain Veeder on a later voyage:

Some of our crew got intoxicated and brought liquor on board of the ship with them and got more of them drunk and by this bad conduct two of them got punished: Cornelius Rust and Barney Jones.
(November 1, 1849)

A complete crew list of the *Nauticon* does not exist; along with first mate James Archer, we now know a couple more of the two dozen or so men on board. Controlling those men, keeping them from deserting, rebelling, getting drunk, and generally ruining the voyage required strong leadership. Captain Veeder asserted his by using corporal punishment and not allowing his men liberty where they might choose to disappear. A dozen years earlier a young whaleman had jumped ship on Nuku Hiva island in the Marquesas and survived to write a rousing tale of Polynesian life called *Typee*, published in 1846, and perhaps read by the captain and his wife; it was a popular book. That young man, Herman Melville, was one of hundreds of men who found the whaling life extremely distasteful, horrible enough for them to risk their lives on what were then known as cannibal islands. David Whippy of Nantucket, a castaway in Fiji in the 1820s, befriended a local chieftain whose daughter (or daughters) he married, grew wealthy as an entrepreneur and trader, and became progenitor of a line of Whippys in Fiji that is still strong today. There are many similar stories of lives of deserters and castaways, some written about, many more lived in obscurity. Captain Veeder was not entirely unsympathetic to the needs of his crew. He gave his men an opportunity to gam at sea, to go on board a different ship and meet some other sailors and share a pipe or two and tell stories. They abused the privilege and were not offered the opportunity again for a very long time.

The *Nauticon* was in the vicinity of the Washington Islands, or Marquesas, on November 11; from there they turned toward the Tuamotu Archipelago and Tahiti. "We are stearing to the South where I am in hopes we shall git some sperm oil. We are all well. It is a year today since I have heard from home." Susan didn't count the letter received in August, because it was written earlier than those that reached her in Talcahuano in January, the ones

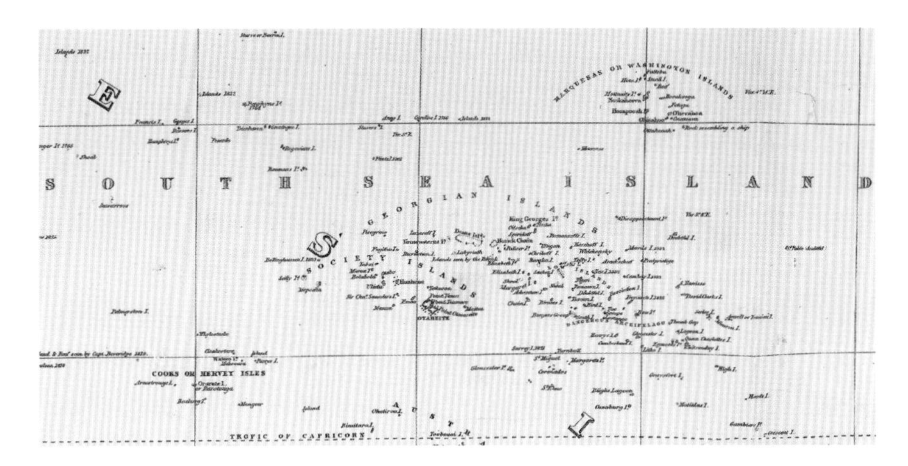

South Sea Islands, detail from *A New Chart of the South Pacific Ocean, including Australasia, the East India Islands, Polynesia and the Western Coast of South America.* London, R. Blachford & Co., 1842, corrected to 1845.

Gift of John Becker, Ms. 1000, no. 1

that were full of news already months old. She was experiencing a different kind of time, its progress unmarked by the regular report of the church bell, the tides in the harbor, the first frost; she kept track of the date in her journal, it was her landmark.

Cruising in November in the Tuamotu Archipelago, or what Susan and others of her day called the Paumoto Group, the captain had his first look at a string of atolls that would seduce him in a later voyage, particularly a tiny ring of islets known now as Raroia, but then as Barclay's Island.

> *Today we saw the Island of Wolskonsky. We went within a mile of the shore and saw some of the residents. They came down on the beach and waved for us to come on shore but the Captain did not think it best as he did not know anything about them. So we left the island. This Island is in the Latt 15.40 Long. 142.10. We have also seen today Barclay Island. This island is SW from Wolconsky 10 miles distance.*
>
> (November 19, 1849)

The changeable names of the islands in this part of the world present some challenges when it comes to locating them on a map, as does the less-than-perfect spelling of our journal keeper, but Susan did clarify where they were in the Tuamotus by adding latitude and longitude to her description. Wolconsky and Barclay islands were named for the Russian military heroes Prince Sergey G. Volkonsky (1788–1865) and Michael Andreas Barclay de Tolly (1761–1818), but they were also known by their local names, Takume and Raroia, and called Napaite, "The Twins," by the ancient Paumoto people. To further confuse matters, Barclay's Island can be found labeled Tolly Island on some nineteenth-century maps of the Pacific islands of Oceania. The Tuamotus, each a ring of closely spaced low-lying islets surrounding a lagoon, have often been described as a string of pearls in the South Pacific, and they were home to expert swimmers, divers, and fishermen. On this voyage, Captain Veeder was wary of the native population. He sent a boat to Peacock Island, now known as Ahe, but, as Susan records on November 25, 1849, "they saw some of the natives and did not

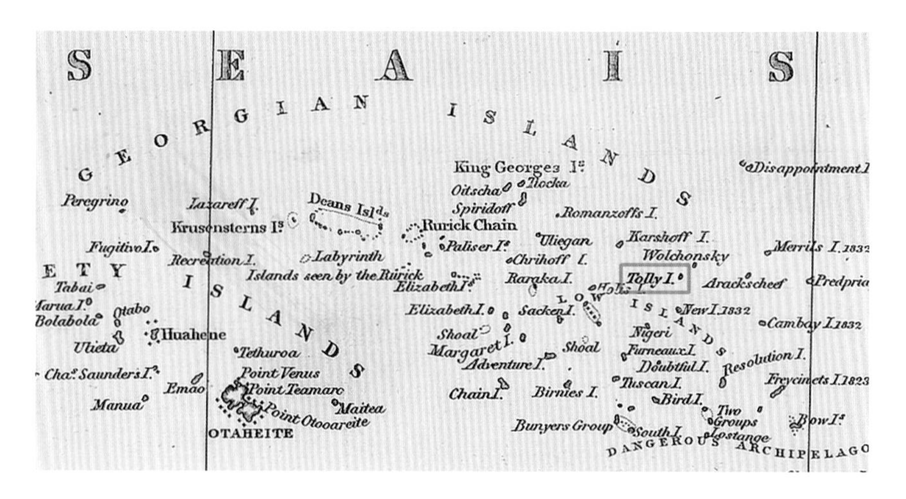

Tolly Island and vicinity, detail from *A New Chart of the South Pacific Ocean, including Australasia, the East India Islands, Polynesia and the Western Coast Of South America*. London, R. Blachford & Co., 1842, corrected to 1845.

Gift of John Becker, Ms. 1000, no. 1

like the looks of them so they soon returned." After so long at sea she must have longed to go ashore, unless the scantily clothed brown bodies of the inhabitants of the cannibal islands made her a little nervous.

Susan filled one page of her journal with a watercolor scene titled *Some of the Paumotu Group*, giving us two different perspectives in this panel: the atolls as seen from sea level—a long, low strip of land fringed with coconut palms—and another view looking down on two of the atolls from a height, so that the entire circle of isles can be seen as well as the calm lagoon within. She must have climbed up to the lookout's cross-trees on the mast, the captain showing her where to put her feet and helping her hang on. There, from the gently swaying vantage point, she could see for miles: endless aquamarine water, bleached sand and coral islets, coconut palms. Here was the vista she had been waiting for, as different from barren, windswept, gray Nantucket as possible. Color! She could feel it. She went gingerly down the ropes to the deck for her journal and paintbrushes to record the idyllic scene. The Veeders must have been as happy as they would ever be—the family healthy, whales in sight, warm weather, incredible beauty.

The Tuamotus proved to be a rich whaling ground, even though the whales were fast and elusive and squalls were frequent. Susan remarked on November 25 that it was all she could do "to take care of myself and little one." Finally, on December 6, they lanced a large sperm whale that made ninety barrels of oil. On December 25, they traded on one of the atolls, bringing on board coconuts, pigs, and chickens, celebrating Christmas and their good fortune: the hold was filling with oil, and they were in a balmy blue world. Susan was pensive on New Year's Eve, penning one of her longer journal entries, a summary of the year:

> *Today is Monday and the last day of the year 1849. We are all well, the weather very warm. 15 ½ months out, 350 sperm, and it is 13 ½ months since my last letter was rote that I received from home. I feel anxious to hear now. Mary Frances is 11 months old, has 7 teeth, creeps all about the ship and is very cunning. She is now on deck taking a ride in her wagon.*
> (December 31, 1849)

Paumotu, or Tuamotu, Group, from Susan Veeder's journal of the *Nauticon*.

Gift of the Friends of the Nantucket Historical Association, Ms. 220, Log 347

Little Mary Frances got a wagon for Christmas, and what a wagon it was, if it is the same one that surfaced at Northeast Auctions in Portsmouth, New Hampshire, in the summer of 2008, attributed to Captain Veeder of the *Nauticon*: carved from whalebone, "with pinned construction, functional wheels and steering, length 11 inches" according to the auction catalog, with an estimated value of $10,000 to $15,000. It is a fairly small toy, easier to pull, one would think, than to ride in for the child who was growing like a pig according to her mother. But if Captain Veeder carved a wagon on the *Nauticon*, it was for Mary Frances and she could sit in it if she liked. What a doting father, surely happy to watch his daughter grow up and to know that he wouldn't be a stranger to her.

January 1850 was a banner month for the *Nauticon*, cruising along Peacock Island where the captain was now comfortable sending boats ashore for coconut collecting and fishing expeditions. At Wilson's Island, or Manihi, they brought a "resident" on board, and a few days later two boats went on shore and brought back three "residents" who were on the ship for a week. Who these mysterious people were and why they were

Scrimshaw toy cart made aboard the *Nauticon*, circa 1850.

Courtesy of Northeast Auctions

on board so long is not known. Susan doesn't say, but on a later voyage Veeder frequently took on inter-island passengers. It was also common for officers, and sometimes men in the forecastle, to entertain native women, who were not shy about trading sexual favors for a bit of calico or a bauble.

Seven smallish sperm whales were harpooned in the Tuamotus, each making about twenty barrels of oil, enough to satisfy the captain, who steered toward Tahiti in February, with a stop along the way at Krusenstern Island (now known as Tikehau), where they got sixteen pigs, and Metia (Makatea), where they collected twenty-two more. A visit to the noisy pig pen on deck must have been a treat for David.

* * *

Tahiti, the largest of the Society Islands which lay east of the Tuamotu Archipelago, was first seen at a distance on January 14, 1850. Five days later, the *Nauticon* anchored at Papeete, where the captain and his family planned to stay for a while, renting "a nice house formerly occupied by the United States Consul." Finally, Susan found a foreign town she liked:

> *Today we have been out walking. I like the place very much some very fine buildings.*
> (February 23, 1850)

Papeete was a bustling port in 1850, with ships from all over the world in the harbor. Contemporary writer and former whaleman Edward T. Perkins observed that along the shore were wooden houses for foreign consulates and two-story stone buildings for the French government recently imposed on the island. Tahiti still boasted a royal family, led by Queen Pomare IV, and, although an impressive figure around town, she was only a titular head of state with little power. Lush gardens surrounded open-air native houses made of lattice topped by thatches of pandanus palm, and, beyond the town, impenetrable green forests rose on mountains dripping

Otaheite, or Tahiti, from Susan Veeder's journal of the *Nauticon*.

Gift of the Friends of the Nantucket Historical Association, Ms. 220, Log 347

with waterfalls. After months at sea, it looked like a fairyland, where there was not only magical beauty but comfort and fresh fruit and a breeze scented with tiare flowers. Encircling the island was the old Broom Road, where Susan could walk with other American ladies, or Charles and his fellow ship captains, Mary Frances tottering along pulling her little wagon and David and George racing down the road.

The Veeders socialized with the American consul and his wife and other whaling captains who were on shore, and Susan relished the company:

> *This morning Captain McCleave took breakfast with us, and at 10 o'clock we went on board of the Roscoe and stopped a short time, had a very pleasant visit, received a number of presents, this afternoon the ship Minerva Smith, Capt. Childs arrived. He came to our house as soon as he arrived and it seems very pleasant to us to have them both with us.* (March 4, 1850)

Happy shore time, unfortunately, was soon over. After six idyllic weeks, it was time to get back to whaling, but Mary Frances was fussy with teething and her parents sought local medical advice. In the longest, most heartfelt entry in her journal, Susan recorded the first of a long line of family tragedies at sea:

> *Tuesday morning our babe did not seem very well and as we expected to go to sea the next day we thought we would call in a physician as she was teething and have her gums lanced. So we called in a Dr. Johnson. He came and said nothing was the matter but a little cold, and he gave her a powder to take then and left one for me to give her at bed time which I did and put her in a warm bath, but at 3 o'clock in the morning she was taken convulsed and we very soon see that there was no hope for her recovery, we sent immediately for a physician and everything was done that could be done but all in vain. She was poisoned no doubt by taking the second powder. What can be done what can be done was all that we could say. The thought of losing our babe was more than we could bear to think of. She was a fine child too good*

to live, and at 11 o'clock a.m. she breathed her last. What shall be done with our darling was the next question with us both. Could we think of burying her at Tahita? No we could not. We must take her with us away, so we have had a lead coffin made and the corpse embalmed to take home with us. (March 5, 1850)

CHAPTER THREE

The Billows Rolled as They Rolled Before

THIRTEEN-AND-A-HALF-MONTH-OLD Mary Frances Veeder was embalmed and laid in a lead coffin, "our little one taken on board and we are ready for sea." Susan does not comment on the family's grief and Mary Frances is never mentioned again in the journal. The funeral of the child of Captain and Mrs. West that Susan attended in Talcahuano in January 1849 had horrified her; she could not imagine burying a child in a foreign land and sailing off, so the small lead coffin found a place in the hold and made its own quiet voyage home, rocking away for three more years.

Susan's fortitude is soon obvious:

> *Saw the Island of Lazareef. At one o'clock the Captain and myself and boys went on shore. We found the island was not inhabited. We got a fine lot of coconuts and caught a nice mess of fish as we all went prepared with hooks and lines. I caught as many as anyone in the boat.*
> (March 16, 1850)

A bereft woman completely out of her element, sailing from one Pacific island to another, she could still hold her own with a fishing pole. And she was proud of it.

A little over a week later the *Nauticon* was back at Krusenstern Island, or Tikehau, in the Tuamotu Archipelago, where Captain Veeder and some of the crew went ashore; there two men deserted—Cornelius Rust, who had been punished earlier in the voyage for bringing liquor back to the ship, and Thomas Barnard. The captain dealt with the situation in his usual severe fashion, as Susan records:

> *Today the Captain went on shore to see if the men had been apprehended but he did not hear anything from them. The island is small and but 12 natives on it so he told the natives he should return in a few days and if they had not caught them he should take away their pigs and burn their houses. Accordingly, in three days he returned. As soon as they see the ship they set a flag and made a fire to let us know that they had caught them. One boat went in and took Thomas Barnard, the other one the Captain did not want, it was the second time that he had run away and got others to go with him.* (March 27, 1850)

Susan describes the captain's threatened punishment of the native men in the cadence of mythical stories, as if her husband were an omnipotent being imposing his demands on mere mortals and "accordingly" waiting the prescribed three days. In fact, whaling captains *were* omnipotent, in charge of all the lives on board their ships and superior in technology and resources to the inhabitants of the remote Pacific islands. The native people of Tikehau complied with the captain's demands, capturing the deserters and offering them in exchange for mercy. Their pigs and houses were spared, but they also acquired Cornelius Rust, who was discarded by the captain. The disruption of the peace of their tiny village would not have endeared them to the American whaleman, who was at best one more mouth to feed among people who were barely subsisting. At worst, he may have become a meal; the Tuamotuans and other Polynesians had a fairly recent tradition of ritual cannibalism that had not been completely eradicated by the message of Christian missionaries. With the desertion crisis settled and an example made of Cornelius, the *Nauticon* sailed away. His crewmates had mixed feelings as they watched the rebellious figure diminish on the shore of Tikehau, wondering if he was a doomed man or a fortunate escapee soon to dine on roast pork and enjoy the attention of an island girl.

The Veeders needed to notify their family of the death of Mary Frances, and Susan was desperate for news of home, so the captain steered east for the South American continent to send and collect letters, making a slight detour to Pitcairn Island, a thousand miles to the southeast, to visit the descendants of Fletcher Christian and the other mutineers of the *Bounty*. It was both an educational and recreational diversion that Captain Veeder may not have made if his family was not on board, but he was eager to show his wife the island that Nantucketers had put on the map when they discovered the mutineers decades earlier, and he knew they could re-provision there.

> *We landed on the opposite side of the Island from where the village is on account of its being so rough. We landed on the rocks and had to go up a precipice almost perpendicular. Two of the residents assisted me in getting over carrying me part of the way. We arrived at the village about 4 p.m. we went to the house of Fletcher Christian and there we stopped. We had not been there many minutes before the house was full of people; everyone in the place came to see me. I think they are the kindest people I have ever met with.*
> (April 24, 1850)

The Veeders stayed in the village three days and the gracious treatment continued:

> *They all called to see me every day while there, and when they found we was a comeing away they all got together and collected many things, some fowl, others oranges and coconuts, and some other things, they all followed us down to the boat and waited our departure. We had the pleasure of naming a little one while there, son of Henry and Albina Young. The number of residents is 164.*
> (April 27, 1850)

Susan named the child Charles Carleton Veeder Young.

Nantucket whaling captain Mayhew Folger, commanding the ship *Topaz* of Boston, stumbled upon the mutineer enclave on Pitcairn in 1808, eighteen years after their revolt against the notorious Captain Bligh on the British ship *Bounty*. Other Nantucket whaleships had stopped there in the intervening years, marking Pitcairn as a hospitable English-speaking island, pretty much in the middle of nowhere, which was why the mutineers had chosen it. Just six months after the Veeders' visit, Eliza Swain Palmer, wife of Captain George Palmer of the whaleship *Navigator* of Nantucket, died on the island, and on Christmas Eve, 1850, the son of Captain Charles and Nancy Grant, of the *Potomac* of Nantucket, was born there. Despite the difficulties of approaching the rocky shore, Nantucket whaling captains were intrigued by the notoriety of the place and it was a fertile fruit-basket in the Pacific. Pitcairn residents had been subject to the concerted efforts of English missionaries for several decades; by the time Susan and family visited they were reputed to be—at least in the reports of the clergy who were stationed there—a harmonious community engaged in daily praying and singing, sending their children to school, and tending to their farming. One observer from the period described some dangerous sport, too, an early form of surfing on a three-foot long board with a small keel, "carried along on the very apex of the surf at a prodigious rate right upon the rocks, where you think nothing can save them from being dashed to pieces the surf seems so powerful; but in a moment they are on their legs, and prepared for another slide."

Susan painted *Pitcairn Island as Seen bearing S. W. Dist. 2 Miles*, clearly demonstrating the inaccessibility of the mountainous, harbor-less protrusion in the sea. She depicts men in whaleboats rowing in toward the cliffs of the shore and a cluster of houses in the crook of the hills, their square white faces staring out to sea. Her illustrations appear more frequently now; without the care of her baby she had more time to herself and she began to paint more. Perhaps it was therapeutic.

Bowl from HMS *Bounty,* commandeered by mutineers in 1789. Nantucket captain Mayhew Folger, in charge of the Boston sealer *Topaz,* discovered the small community of descendants of the mutineers on Pitcairn Island in 1808. The bowl was presented to him by the only surviving sailor of the *Bounty*, John Adams.

Gift of Margaret Folger, 1956.36.1

A souvenir of Pitcairn Island, this box was made in 1850 by Arthur Quintal, first child born on the island after the mutineers of HMS *Bounty* settled there. Quintal presented the box to Frederick S. Raymond of the Nantucket whaler *Peruvian* in 1851, a year after the Veeders visited the island.

Gift of Sarah C. Raymond, 1911.22.1

Pitcairn as depicted by third mate James F. Roberts in his journal kept on board the *Nauticon*, 1848–51.

Courtesy of the Nicholson Whaling Collection, Providence Public Library

* * *

Six weeks after leaving Pitcairn, the *Nauticon* arrived in Paita, Peru, "for the purpose of leaving letters, and there we was fortunate enough to get two from home. We found Mrs. Hoxie there with a little one a week old." Mary Hoxie was Susan's friend from Talcahuano, wife of Captain Asa Hoxie of the *Pacific* who had been in that port when Susan was pregnant. Now Susan had to share the news of her loss, difficult to do with the new mother soon to take her own infant to sea. The contents of the letters that awaited Susan at Paita are not disclosed, but they may have been congratulatory notes on the birth of the daughter who now reposed in the dark hold of the ship.

Repeating the circuit of the spring of 1849, the *Nauticon* steered for the Galápagos Islands in June 1850, the crew having already consumed the one hundred and eighty tortoises previously collected. The men captured thirty-three more on Chatham Island and from Albemarle Island hauled off twenty-eight boatloads of wood, fuel for the galley and for the tryworks that they hoped to fire up soon. On June 27, while sailing around Albemarle Island, they discovered the wreck of the whaleship *Lafayette* of New Bedford on a reef nearby; Captain Sisson of the *Callao* had seen it, too, and he and Captain Veeder worked together to salvage what they could. According to

Pitcairn, from Susan Veeder's journal of the *Nauticon*.

Gift of the Friends of the Nantucket Historical Association, Ms. 220, Log 347

Susan, they each took a hundred and twenty barrels of oil, along with bread, flour, sails, iron hoops, rigging, and spars. The men of the *Lafayette* had taken to their whaleboats when the ship sank: Captain Samuel Lawrence's boat and that of the second mate were rescued by the New Bedford whaleship *Golconda,* but the boats of the first and third mates had become separated from the other two, eventually landing on Albemarle Island where thirteen men were stranded. Bedraggled and starving, they were wretchedness embodied, another troubling reminder of what could happen to anyone sailing among the islands and reefs of the Pacific. Veeder signed four of the shipwrecked men as crew; he needed one to replace Cornelius Rust, and a few extra hands to fill in for the occasional sick or injured man would help when they were actively hunting and processing whales. He gave other survivors a ride to Chatham Island, and the *Callao* did the same.

The *Nauticon* sailed along south in company with the *Callao* and another Nantucket ship, *Susan*, whose captain, Charles B. Ray, had been at sea almost four years and had only seven hundred barrels of oil. On July 29, they reached what was called the Offshore Ground, beginning at latitude 5 south, longitude 100 west, and from there worked their way westward hoping to find whales somewhere in the miles of open ocean that lay between them and the Marquesas Islands, the easternmost group of French Polynesia. They were on what was once a sperm whale highway, near where the *Essex* was sunk in latitude 4 south, longitude 119 west, and where the *Ann Alexander* would meet a similar fate the next year in latitude 5.5 south, longitude 102 west. In early August, Susan wrote:

> *It is now a week since I have wrote and even now I have not anything of any note to write. We are cruising on the off shore ground as they call it here. It is quite rough and we have not seen anything but Finbacks and Porpoises. It is now over 6 months since we have seen S. whales. I shall now put away my book and hope the next time I write we shall have more oil.*
> (August 4, 1850)

As if her pen drew the very creatures she wished for, sperm whales appeared the next day, and the attack was all on the side of the humans: no whales fought back. Boats were lowered and the men struck two, but the line parted on one and it got away. The remaining whale yielded fifty-eight barrels of oil. Cruising for the next two weeks brought no results, except for the company of another ship, the *Sharon* of Fairhaven, Massachusetts, whose captain, George C. Rule, had begun the voyage in 1848 as first mate, but had recently taken over for an ailing Captain Nathaniel Bonney who had returned home to recuperate. They gammed several times in the course of a week, and Captain Rule brought Susan "a number of presents." She must have loved to spot another ship on the horizon, in anticipation of news, visits, and comestibles—cheese or jam or a newspaper, any diversion from tortoise soup, twice-baked hard tack, and the routine of a day at sea in the middle of a vast watery nowhere.

On August 22, 1850, the *Nauticon* left the Offshore Ground bound for Cocos Island for water, a necessity that, ironically, could not be procured in the middle of the ocean. It took them almost three weeks to reach the uninhabited island—four miles long by two miles wide—three hundred and fifty or so miles off the coast of Costa Rica and about four hundred miles north of the Galapágos Islands, but it's not surprising they went there: the island has an annual rainfall of eighteen to twenty-four *feet.* With dozens of waterfalls, filling barrels with fresh water would be a simple task; Cocos was literally a water spigot. Susan arrived on what must have been one of the rare sunny days, and in the midst of huge trees dripping with moss, gigantic ferns, coconut palms, eighty-seven species of birds, three hundred and sixty-two of insects and arthropods, sixty species of animals—all accounted for by contemporary naturalists—she writes about her laundry:

> *Today we went on shore to wash our clothes. I think it is one of the best places to wash clothes I ever saw. The Captain has had a tent put up so we can wash comfortable.*
> (September 11, 1850)

Cocos Island, from Susan Veeder's journal of the *Nauticon*.

Gift of the Friends of the Nantucket Historical Association, Ms. 220, Log 347

As adventurous as she was, the domestic sphere was still Susan's most familiar environment. An opportunity to freshen the families' clothing and linens, eradicate some of the stench of whale oil and immerse herself in some real physical exertion was a welcome activity. The fresh water falling in cascades, the spongy ground and verdure were all part of the pleasure. The next day she happily went back:

> *Today went ashore to look at my cloths and to wash more. I have got the grass full a whitening.*
> (September 12, 1850)

One of the most charming illustrations in Susan's journal is her *Cocos Island as Seen from the Bay*. The *Nauticon* appears at anchor in front of the mountainous island that sports a line of palm trees from shore to peak and all along the ridge like a crew cut of fronds. Two waterfalls can be seen to the left of a large white tent surrounded by sheets on the hillside, bleaching in the sun. The next day Susan remarked "on shore today and had a fine shower." If she was referring to a rain shower, she would probably have complained that her laundry wasn't drying. In all likelihood she found a secluded pool under a waterfall, rinsed her salty clothes and body in the noisy cascade and allowed herself a moment of private luxury, soothing her tired arms, washing her long dark hair and marveling at the profusion of botanical pulchritude around her. Cocos Island was the green, natural opposite of the island she called home. It was alive with birdsong and insect hums, dripping leaves, and the roar of waterfalls. When the sun shone, everything—from palm fronds to moss-wrapped rocks and coconut husks—sparkled and steamed. Charles and the boys may have found their own bathing pool and attacked the grime in their hair and under their nails, David and George diving and cavorting like porpoises, happy to use their sea legs in another element. With damp hair and scrubbed skin, the family dressed in their clean clothes and returned to the ship, fortified by the clear water of Cocos, and that night Susan and Charles lay on clean, sweet-smelling sheets.

Sailing south along the coast of South America the *Nauticon* encountered blackfish, or pilot whales, not really what they wanted, but they gave chase anyway and caught four, which altogether produced only ten barrels of oil. Hardly worth the effort since it was a grade of oil inferior to sperm oil and much less valuable, but it kept the crew active and broke up the monotony. On October 12 their luck changed when they raised a shoal of sperm whales and got one that added forty barrels to their hold; but the next three weeks they saw nothing but finbacks and blackfish as they sailed to Callao, the port town adjacent to Lima, Peru, arriving November 12: "Today I went on shore found a good hotel, engaged a room. I think I shall like the place much." For ten days Susan had a bed that didn't sway with the waves, although she spent time on the *Nauticon* and visited other ships in the harbor. She also took the stagecoach to Lima with her landlady. She approved of the city; "I think Lima a fine place. There are many fine stores and much to be seen." A three-hundred-year-old city founded by Spanish conquistador Francisco Pizarro, Lima was the hub of a newly independent Peru with a thriving economy based largely on the exportation of guano. Spanish colonial architecture and public parks gave it a European feel, and a lively international trade brought a variety of goods to the market. For a woman long confined to a whaleship, it was a visual delight and a slop chest extraordinaire. Susan enjoyed it so much she went back again

Cocos Island, from James F. Roberts's journal of the *Nauticon*.

Courtesy of the Nicholson Whaling Collection, Providence Public Library

with Captain MacDonald of the ship *Mersey* of New York, and his wife, a sister sailor. Also in port were a couple identified as Captain Hooper and his wife, who accompanied Susan to the *Nauticon* at 5 p.m. on November 24 and returned to shore the next morning; there must have been room for guests on board, although it's hard to imagine where.

Susan had been at sea for more than two years and had recorded meeting six other captain's wives, all in ports in South America; so far she had not encountered another wife out on the maritime oil fields. Within the next decade, however, many more women accompanied their husbands and it became a more social scene on the high seas. On July 21, 1853, Charlotte Coffin Wyer of the Nantucket ship *Young Hero* penned in her journal, "There are three ships in sight and I anticipated another visit, so I took a nap for the occasion." For Susan, however, Tahiti, Hawaii, and the port towns of South America were the only places to find American women.

On November 25, the *Nauticon* headed south to Juan Fernandez Island off the coast of Chile, where Susan was fortunate to go ashore and pick strawberries, a rare indulgence. From November 31 to New Year's Day 1851 her pen was silent, not recording the summation of the previous year like she had for 1849; 1850 had not been a good year for whaling, or for her family. Another reason for her absence from the page is the possibility she was pregnant again and that she lost a child; nine months had passed since the abrupt weaning of Mary Frances. Susan characteristically would not have mentioned a pregnancy or a miscarriage or stillbirth.

She had little to report in January 1851, either, as they cruised off the coast of Chile with other ships, including the *Zenas Coffin* of Nantucket. Captain Charles G. Arthur of that ship brought her a letter, but since he left Nantucket in 1848 just two months after the Veeders, the news was stale, unless he had picked the letter up along the way. It's hard to believe any mail reached recipients at sea, but it sometimes did. Nantucket's newspapers, the *Inquirer* and the *Nantucket Weekly Mirror* frequently ran ads announcing the date a ship was due to sail and the location where letters could be left for the ship's letter bag. Some of those letters would be delivered when ships met at sea, or they would be left with American consuls or other officials in South America or the Pacific islands, but many never reached the addressee. Perhaps the appropriate paths never crossed, or the letters were at the bottom of the ocean. At a cove called Post Office Bay at uninhabited Santa Maria Island in the Galapágos Group, a barrel covered with a giant tortoiseshell and nailed to a post served as a letter drop. There, whalers could leave and pick up letters; perhaps Captain Arthur had seen a letter there for Susan, heard that the *Nauticon* was sailing to Juan Fernandez, his destination, and brought the letter to her, or her mother and sister may have placed their newsy correspondence in his letter bag back in November 1848. She may have been getting letters from home in response to her sad news of March that had traveled from ship to ship, and captains were doing their best to pass along letters of condolence to her. Susan soon received two more letters via Captain Long of the ship *Charles Carroll* of Nantucket, who had left their home island in December 1848. Tied with a ribbon and carefully stashed in a special letter box, those missives from Nantucket were Susan's most prized possessions, read and reread as she waited for the next installment.

The men of the *Nauticon* spied sperm whales twice in January, lowered their boats and chased for hours but could not catch them. Numerous whaleships were in the vicinity, and they all exchanged news of their success, or lack thereof, and Susan recorded how long each ship had been out and the number of barrels of oil in each: *Oregon*, Fairhaven, seventeen months out, 500 bbls; *Zenas Coffin*, Captain Arthur, twenty-six months, 650 bbls. On February 3, she and Captain Veeder went on board the *Robert Edwards* of New Bedford for a gam with Captain Nathaniel Burgess. The wind was so strong they had to stay until 3 P.M. the next day when the wind finally moderated—another whaleship sleep-over not described, and Susan does not mention the captain's wife, but she and two children were on board, information that whaling wife Azubah Cash records in her journal after she and Ann met at sea on February 8, and Ann told her she had had a good time with Susan Veeder just a few days earlier.

The consul's quarters were as popular as ever. Dinner parties were held there and aboard various ships in the harbor, plus an excursion to Concepción for Susan, a nearby town where Charles had purchased gifts for her, and their new daughter, in 1849. With Mrs. Burgess, Mrs. Crosby, and Mrs. Russell in town, Susan found Talcahuano more pleasant than when she first visited, although the memory of her time there with newborn Mary Frances weighed heavily on her, especially after she went on board the *Robert Edwards* to help Mrs. Burgess with her sick baby, Helen, born in 1849.

* * *

AFTER TWO WEEKS OF SHORE TIME, the *Nauticon* set sail for a new whaling ground: the Arctic Ocean. Sperm whales had become so scarce and elusive in the South Pacific that the ever voracious whalers turned to a different beast, the giant bowhead whale that lived close to the Arctic icepack; it was not the Nantucket whalemen's first choice, however, as they were the longtime masters of the sperm whale fishery, but the news of the new whaling grounds shared by New Bedford whaling captains at Talcahuano intrigued Captain Veeder, and he was willing to take a risk if it might contribute to a profitable voyage and expedite the return home. The arduous labor involved in pursuing a bowhead amid ice floes and fog in a strong wind, with cold hands gripping frozen oars, water so frigid that if your boat was stove and you had the misfortune to find yourself "sadly puzzled under the water" as eighteenth-century Nantucket whaleman Peleg Folger put it, chances are you would not live to talk about it—well, the crew must have been apprehensive. It is doubtful that the slop chest had an inventory of warm clothing since it appears that Captain Veeder had not initially planned to sail so far north; while in Talcahuano he must have added more wool monkey jackets, the common coat of mariners, and oil-cloth suits to protect against the frigid water. If the men wanted to stay warm, they would have to pay for it; the cost of additional clothing would be deducted when the accounts were settled at the end of the voyage.

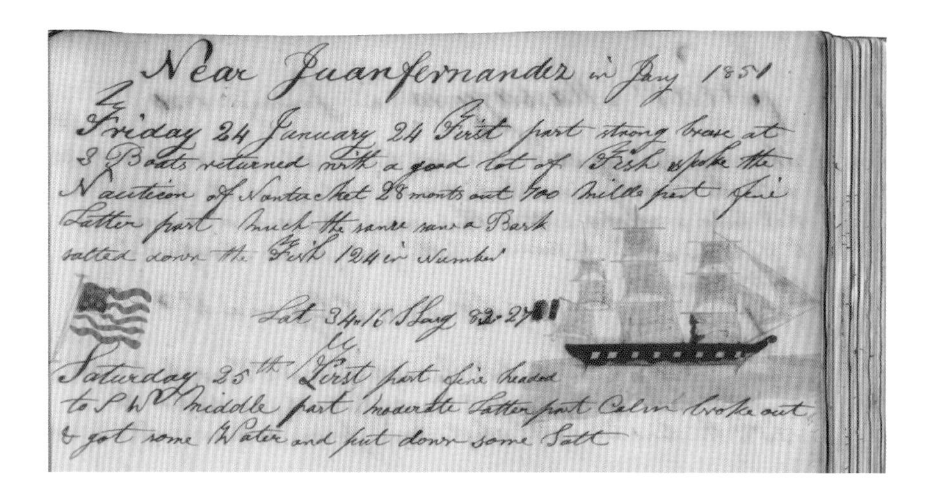

Near Juanfernander in Jany 1851
Friday 24 January 24 First part strong breese at
3 Boats returned with a good lot of Fish spoke the
Nauticon of Nantucket 28 months out 700 Middle part fine
Latter part much the same saw a Bark
salted down the Fish 124 in Number
Lat 34.16 S Long 82-27 W
Saturday 25th First part fine headed
to S W middle part moderate Latter part Calm broke out
& got some Water and put down some Salt

Sketch of the *Nauticon* from a journal kept on board the *Charles Carroll* by Captain Josiah C. Long, January 24, 1851.

Gift of the Friends of the Nantucket Historical Association, Ms. 220, Log 413

Bowhead whales, named for their immense heads that could come up under two feet of ice and blast right through it, were different animals from sperm whales—gigantic, fifty to sixty feet long when mature and weighing more than sixty tons; sperm whales, by comparison, were at least ten feet shorter, generally, and twenty tons lighter, although thirty years earlier there were tales of much larger sperm whales, eighty or more feet long. Slow swimmers compared to sperm whales, bowheads were easily frightened, diving under the ice for protection, and floating islands of ice were all around the whaleships that ventured into those waters. As valuable for their long strips of baleen—the ten-foot-long fibers in their mouths that filtered their food—as they were for their oil, bowheads were new prey for American whalemen who had begun to venture into the Arctic whaling grounds just two years earlier. The intrepid whalemen might not fill their holds with the preferred pure product of the sperm whale, but there was a market for whalebone, as baleen was familiarly called, and bowheads had a mouth full of it, strong and flexible and moldable, perfect for corset stays, parasol ribs, skirt hoops, and buggy whips, the ubiquitous accoutrements of the era. A strong, flexible, natural product made of keratin, baleen did the job that thin steel and many plastics do today.

Another sperm whale was added to the *Nauticon's* tally on her way north, but one of the crew, Jack Right, "got badly hurt overboard" according to Susan. Any number of scenarios might account for Jack's injury, from tumbling out of the whaleboat during the hunt and nearly drowning, or becoming entangled in the line and pulled from his post. Details are not provided, but he survived. Three weeks later, however, there was another accident, a tragic one. While Susan was sitting at the officers' table writing a letter home, the ship's motion over the wind-whipped waves making it challenging work to write at all legibly, she heard a loud thump on the deck above, followed by the sounds of men running and a general commotion.

> *Today strong wind and while I sat writing Mr. Roberts our 3d mate fell from the main top gallant head and killed himself almost instantly only breathing a few times. It has cast a gloom over the whole ships company.*
> (April 23, 1851)

The next morning there was a burial at sea, another reminder, if anyone needed it, of the perils of their occupation. With his bloody head and broken body wrapped in a piece of sailcloth, Mr. Roberts was prepared for his descent into the cold sea. The sound of his body splashing in the water echoed in everyone's soul.

> *Light wind. At 8 o'clock a.m. all hands was called to bury the dead. The head yards was hauled aback and the ensign was set half mast. Prayers was read and the body committed to the deep and a solemn sight it was to us all. He was a very active fine young man and his death will be lamented by all of us on board.*
> (April 24, 1851)

A bowhead whale *(Balcena mysticetus)* hunted by French whalers. An engraving by Amable-Nicolas Fournier after an illustration by Édouard Traviès from Charles d'Obigny, *Dictionnaire Universel d'Histoire Naturelle* (Atlas, vol. 1, plate 21, 1849).

Twenty-four-year-old James F. Roberts, third mate of the *Nauticon,* may have been a particularly congenial shipmate for Susan. As an officer, his berth was near the stern of the ship, and he would have had meals with the captain and Susan and the other mates. In such close quarters there was opportunity to get to know a person well, whether you wanted to or not. In Mr. Roberts's case, however, their friendship would have been based on shared interests: Roberts kept a journal, too, and he illustrated it with a few tiny ink and watercolor sketches of islands and ships. He and Susan may have painted together on deck on occasion, or written their brief entries in their journals in the evening, pen and books side by side on the table. Mr. Roberts only mentions Susan once in his journal, when he recorded on March 6, 1850, "Died at ¼ before 11 Mary Frances, only daughter of Charles A. & Susan Veeder aged 14 months," but he would have been as familiar to her as a younger brother. His journal is in the style of a typical logbook, indicating that he was practicing for his duties as first mate on his next voyage, or the one after. His entries are headed with the title "Remarks on Board ship Nauticon" on the left page, and on the right "Cruising on the Line" or "In the Gallipagos" or occasionally something a little more telling, such as "off on a pleasure cruise" or "15 months out living on bread and water," penned in early January 1850. He wrote only one personal comment in his journal, as if he foresaw the tragedy ahead: "Hard Times and Worse Coming," scribbled across the bottom of the page on December 17, 1849. His last entry described the main tasks of April 23, 1851, "Employed in bending new ForeTopSail & MainTopGallant sail . . ." and in completing that last task, he fell to his death.

The following pages of his journal are filled with lists of whales spotted, rows of whale stamps in four columns indicating which boat crew was responsible—starboard, larboard, waist, and bow—and a selection of sea chanteys, including, at the very end, "The Sailor's Grave":

Our voices broke, our hearts turned weak
Hot tears were seen on the honest cheek
And a quiver played on the lips of pride
As we lowered him down the ship's dark side
A plunge, a splash, and our task was o'er
The billows roll'd as they roll'd before
But many a rude prayer hallowed the wave
That closed above the sailor's grave.

The sea burial of James F. Roberts was not a pretty prelude to a trip into unknown waters, but Captain Veeder was not afraid of new territory, and he must have been an excellent navigator. His portrait, painted before the voyage by James S. Hathaway, shows us a handsome clear-eyed man with a square face and carefully combed brown hair, cradling a spyglass in the crook of his left arm. Like his wife, he looks entirely capable of rising to any challenge.

He sailed the *Nauticon* up the west coast of North America and looked for

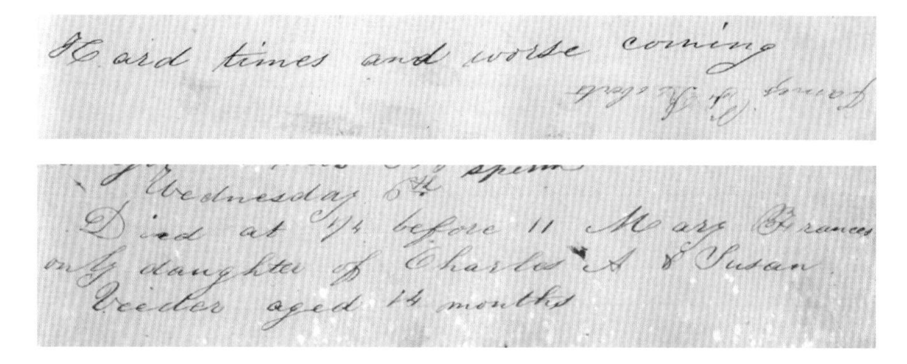
Hard times and worse coming

Wednesday 6th
Died at 1/4 before 11 Mary Frances
only daughter of Charles A & Susan
Veeder aged 14 months

Excerpts from the journal of the *Nauticon* kept by third mate James F. Roberts.

Courtesy of the Nicholson Whaling Collection, Providence Public Library

a passage through the Fox Islands, part of the Aleutian string that reaches arm-like from the south of Alaska and points southwest. He couldn't find one, so he changed course and sailed due west across the North Pacific, fifteen degrees latitude below the Bering Sea. Arriving in the Kamchatka Sea on May 20, 1851, on the east coast of that peninsula of Russia, he then steered north toward Bering Strait. The *Nauticon* was not alone. On May 25, they spoke the ship *Governor Troup* of New Bedford and on May 26 the *America*, Captain Seabury, of the same port, who sent Susan "a nice ham and some candy for the boys." The next day they spied *thirty-two* ships in the near vicinity, and there was a flurry of exchange of news as captains gammed throughout the day. Susan's heart leapt when she saw Captain Hoxie's ship, *Pacific,* but she noted in her journal that his wife was not on board. She was somewhere warm with the baby. Captain Veeder returned from one of the whaleships with two stoves, and, although where he placed them is not disclosed, Susan certainly warmed herself by one of them, as did the mates. Susan welcomed Captain Dallman of the Fairhaven ship *Mary Ann* on June 7, disappointed to

---

***Following pages:* James F. Roberts kept a record of whales taken by each boat—starboard boat, larboard boat, waist boat, and bow boat—using a stamp in the shape of a sperm whale. He also kept a record of his purchases from the ship's "slop chest."**

Courtesy of the Nicholson Whaling Collection, Providence Public Library

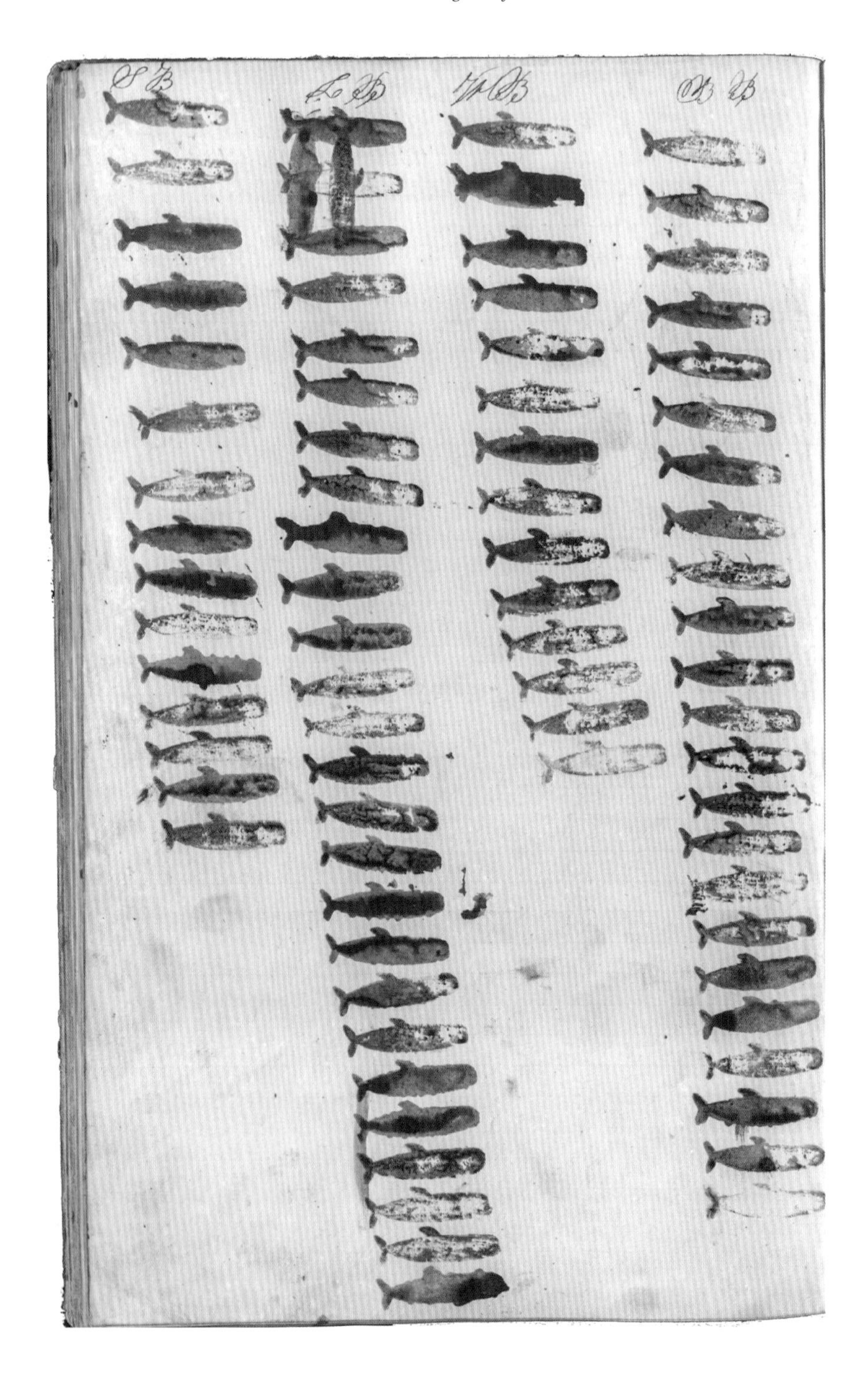

James B. Roberts Dr. to Ship Nauticon

To Cash in Talcahuana	8.75
" 2 pr Shoes at 1.10	2.20
" 2 straw hats at 37½	0.75
" Cash in Tombez	1.50
" Postage on letters sent from Payta	2.00
" 4 Payta hats (baskets) at 31¼	1.25
" 1 Jack Knife	0.50
" 1 Pr. shoes a 1.00	1.00
" 1 lb Tobacco at 25¢	0.25
" 1 Jack Knife	0.50
" Cash in Tahita	9.00
" 2 Calico shirts at 1.00	2.00
" 2 lbs Tobacco	.50
" 1 Pr Shoes.	1.10
" 4 lbs tobacco	1.00
" Postage on letters sent from Payta	2.00
" Cash in Payta	1.87½
" 1 Pr shoes	1.00
" 6 lbs tobacco	1.50
" 1 Pr shoes	1.00
" 4 lbs Tobacco	1.00
" 1 Pr pants	2.00
" 1 Vest	3.00
" 2 thick Shirts a 2.00	4.00
" 1 Pr drawers	1.50
" Cash in Callao	34.00
" Letter sent from Callao	2.00
Cash in Talcahuano	11.00
10 lbs tobacco	2.50
" 2 prs Shoes	2.00
" 1 thick Shirt	2.00

learn that he had left his wife in Talcahuano, but glad to receive gifts of fresh meat, cranberries, and pickles. Did she wish she were back in Talcahuano with some of the other wives? Maybe not. It was a sight to behold: dozens of ships in among the ice, and, finally, in the Arctic Ocean, bowheads!

> *Today clear and cold. A plenty of bowhead whales around and our boats lowered but could not catch them as they would go under the ice—there is a number of ships about here and two we have seen today with the ice all around them.*
> (June 14, 1851)

When it was foggy it was too dangerous to chase whales because the men needed to have the *Nauticon* in sight in such dangerous conditions, and it was often foggy. Susan must have been frustrated, too, because it was too cold to sit on deck and paint. Fine weather a few days later gave the men their first real opportunity:

> *At 10 this morning lowered our boats for a whale and fortunate enough to get one and get him to the ship. At 1 p.m. we was amongst floating ice all of the time. It is a very large whale, suppose it will make 200 bbls.*
> (June 19, 1851)

In fact, the whale made 230 barrels of oil and 4,600 pounds of whalebone. All around them ships were boiling their catch of the day, as the bowheads were not so hard to chase when the sun was shining. A few days later their friend Captain Burgess arrived in the *Robert Edwards*, and, lo and behold, his wife, Ann, was with him. After almost three years at sea they finally met—offshore—another ship with a woman on board. Captain and Mrs. Burgess came on board the *Nauticon* and spent the day, Susan Veeder entertaining in the Arctic, sharing some jam, pickles, and ham with her guests. She was more descriptive about her time in the Arctic than anywhere else they had been, writing faithfully every day about the ice

***Charles Veeder*, by James Hathaway, circa 1842.**

Gift of the Friends of the Nantucket Historical Association, 1999.30.2

and the fog and the number of ships—as mesmerized by the cold, foggy otherworldly seascape as she was terrified of being iced in.

Sailing close to the shore of Siberia on June 26, the *Nauticon* attracted native visitors. When all the boats were out chasing whales, leaving the captain, Susan, younger son David, and most likely the steward, cook, and cooper on board, they were approached by canoes:

> *At 1 p.m. saw whales and the boats lowered. The starboard boat struck one but being very near the ice the whale run under and they had to cut the line having lost about half of it. While the boat was off there was two canoes came along side with about 30 natives. They brought a few fish and teeth and some skins to sell. They appear to be very harmless and honest. All they wanted was tobacco, needles and knives.*
> (June 16, 1851)

It must have been a little disconcerting to be outnumbered by these strangers, but Susan was unperturbed. It was the ice that was the real threat, and by evening the next day they were surrounded by it.

> *This morning we have had the misfortune to get our ship in the ice. We let go the anchor in 25 fathoms water but it did not stop her. The ice is coming down very fast.*
> (June 30, 1851)

As far as they could see, ice, with a few blue spots of open water in the distance where bowheads, out of reach, could be seen spouting their heart-shaped spray. Soon that distant blue turned white too.

> *Today no water to be seen. We made all sail on the ship in hopes that we could start her a little, but she would not move. The ice is close to her. When we shall get away from here I know not.*
> (July 3, 1851)

> *Fine weather. No water to be seen. The ice is around as far as we can see from mast head. All hands been out cutting the ice around the ship. All well. No prospect of getting out.*
> (July 6, 1851)

It was terrifying. The ice could crush the ship, and then they would be forced to attempt to reach land across miles of frozen sea, most likely pulling their whaleboats full of supplies with them, cursing their luck, and looking forward to survival on the far northeast coast of Siberia, if they could reach it. They were in what Susan called the Anadir Sea, or the Gulf of Anadyr, just south of the Arctic Circle. No one would want to desert there.

> *Fine weather. The ice seems to loosen some so at 3 p.m. we got the ship around heading the other way. At eight o'clock this morning we saw a white bear close to the ship, but his hearing a noise he started off the other way very quick. We have seen a number of whales since we have been here. They often come up in the air hole and spout near the ship and we have lanced two of them off the ice. No doubt if we was clear of the ice we should be able to get some of them.*
> (July 9, 1851)

What an extraordinary sight: a polar bear lumbering across the ice to investigate the ship, while bowhead whales, taking advantage of the open water near the vessel, surfaced to catch a breath and were stabbed by the ineffectual humans, who found themselves dwarfed by creatures at home in the icy ocean. Finally, the men managed to work their way free of the worst part of the frozen sea, but it wasn't easy:

> *At 10 this morning commenced cutting the ice around the ship and with exertion they succeeded in starting the ship and by getting out lines they could haul her ahead a little and feeling encouraged they continued cutting and hauling the ship ahead and at three the next morning we got through the heaviest of it, being now in floating ice.*
> (July 11, 1851)

The *Nauticon* was trapped by ice in the Arctic for thirteen days in the summer of 1851. Two decades later, thirty-three American whaling ships were lost in the same icy waters. *Abandonment of the Whalers in the Arctic Ocean, Sept. 1871*, is one of a series of five lithographs memorializing the loss of the Arctic whaling fleet, by Benjamin Russell of New Bedford, 1872.

Gift of Mrs. George W. Allen, 1896.234.2

And then, clear water, "to the great joy of all on board, having been in the ice thirteen days." Susan had witnessed a freeze-up of the harbor in Nantucket in the winter of 1836–37, forty days without mail from the mainland and no steamer from Christmas until the end of February. Although there was a shortage of provisions that winter, she got along fine, and everyone knew that spring would come. A freeze-up in the Arctic was a different kettle of fish; being unfamiliar with the territory made for no comforting predictions. Even so, she trusted her husband, and after her long maternity leave in Talcahuano she had made the decision to always stay with ship and family, even if it meant giving up a comfortable bed, fresh oranges, and warm weather. Open water appeared along the coast, but the captain was looking for a passage out into deeper water where they might find bowheads, or escape altogether. Siberian natives, most likely Chukchi, visited their ship several times over the next few days, bringing fish and other items to trade for the metal objects that would replace the ones they carved from ivory: needles, hooks, and knives. As the crew of the *Nauticon* attempted to extricate the ship from the icy shoreline, the wind died completely, so they lowered one of the whaleboats to tow the ship; a good way for some of the men to work up some heat, rowing the twenty-eight-foot whaleboat that pulled the heavy ship. Still within sight of land, they soon saw other whaleships in the area, two of them from Nantucket: the *Constitution*, trying to top off an unsuccessful four-year voyage chasing sperm whales, and the *Columbia*, less than a year from home port. Captain William Cash of the latter ship would send home 19,400 pounds of baleen, worth $22,000, from his bowhead catch, making it a profitable voyage; the Veeders would see him again in Hawaii where his wife, Azubah, and sons were waiting. Although it must have been reassuring to see ships nearby, especially two from home, they learned that nine ships had been destroyed, some by ice, others by a gale of wind. No lives were lost, but profits were.

On the second of August, as they made their way toward Bering Strait, Susan noted her husband's forty-second birthday. Six days later they arrived back in the Arctic Ocean and soon saw ten ships; Captain Veeder went on board one of them, the bark *Cossack* of New Bedford to get the news. He discovered that they had not gotten any bowheads yet and didn't know of any ship that had, but that would change: statistics show that the *Cossack* racked up 18,700 pounds of bone, almost as much as the *Columbia*. It had been almost two months since the *Nauticon* got its first, and only bowhead, and with so much competition for what appeared to be few whales, plus the dangers of the ice, the captain must have wondered if he made the right choice. Susan, sitting by her stove, reading to her son or knitting something warm, must have wondered, too.

The *Nauticon* did discover something else valuable in the sea—a wreck, the second one they had spotted so far on their voyage.

> *At 4 p.m. we discovered something that we called a ship's hull and going a little nearer we found it to be a wreck—and the Captain went to her with a boat and found it to be the Mary Mitchell of San Francisco. We found the bark Russell of San Francisco to work on her. We got 4 boat loads of wood from her last evening, [so] rough we had to quit for the night. In hopes to see her again in the morning. At 7 p.m. Captain Cootey of bark Russell came on board to spend the evening.*
> (August 8, 1851)

The *Mary Mitchell* was formerly a Nantucket whaleship, recently sold to San Francisco. Unfortunately, the next morning, her last remains had sunk, but at least the *Nauticon* acquired a little more wood for the stoves and the try pots, should they ever need them. On August 9, Susan's birthday, a clear day with a heavy swell, she wrote, "steering south . . . aged 35 years, enjoying good health." Two days later they spoke the ship *Arctic* of Fairhaven, Massachusetts, a vessel named for the new whaling ground. She was only eight months out, having headed directly for her namesake; from her Captain Veeder bought fresh mutton, sausages, clams, and lobsters, perhaps for a late birthday celebration for Susan, and an even later one for himself. In latitude 64.42 north, longitude 172.25 west they anchored in Cinnamon Bay, or Chukotka, at the far northeast corner of Russia and went ashore for water—the first they had taken on board since Cocos Island.

> *We found the Stepany [Stephania] of New Bedford here and the Friends of New London, likewise a brig from San Francisco. The natives came on board but did not bring anything to trade, they are very poor—hardly clothes to cover themselves. They appear very civil and harmless.*
> (August 16, 1851)

The next day news of the loss of the ship *Globe* of New Bedford in the Bering Strait was relayed to them: ten ships down so far and the season had barely begun. The crew may have heard the news as well and were increasingly discouraged as well as cold. The captain had recently bought sixteen barrels of meat from the *Columbia* of Nantucket, fuel for the unhappy men who had not expected to find themselves in the Arctic. Crew members on a whaling voyage were paid according to a "lay" system, wherein each member got a certain percentage of the profits, if there were profits. The ship-owners got the biggest cut, then the captain, the officers, the boatsteerers (harpooneers), and then down the line to the green hands, who might end up owing money if they took tobacco and clothing on credit during the voyage. So the longer they were fruitless in their search for oil, the more disgruntled the men might become. A little meat would help, especially after they had seen the fresh mutton and lobsters going to the aft cabins.

The stress of their recent imprisonment in the ice must have been a contributing factor to Susan's headache on August 28, the third she mentioned so far in her journal. This time, she applied a blister—a mustard poultice—to the nape of her neck; the proper method was to remove the poultice before it caused an actual blister, because that was not the point, the point was to draw the blood away from the source of pain. It worked for Susan, so she must have done it correctly; the next day she reported that her headache was much better. Her nursing skills extended to her family and probably to every man on board who suffered a minor complaint or injury.

On August 30, David S. Veeder, now eight years old, accompanied his father on his first gam, to the ship *Samuel Robertson* of Fairhaven; they were near Copper Island, off the coast of the Kamchatka Peninsula. The captain and his son visited for three hours, returning with potatoes, onions, and a jar of tamarinds—only the second time to date that David is mentioned by name in his mother's journal, even though she must have spent most of her time with him, teaching him to read and write and to keep his wits about him on the ship. The last we heard of David was when his pet monkey was buried at sea, in the fall of 1848. The fact that he was leaving her supervision and making the tricky passage from ship to ship in a whaleboat in the icy sea made it a notable event, one Susan faithfully recorded. David was becoming a mariner.

Although there were no whales in the vicinity, the men of the *Nauticon* caught codfish, thirty of them on August 31, a hundred on September 1, forty the next day—in sight of Bering's Island—and another hundred two days later. Everyone must have been well fed as the *Nauticon* turned tail in the North Pacific and headed to the Sandwich Islands, their Arctic experiment a near disaster, oil and baleen from one bowhead whale the harvest of a summer at the top of the globe.

CHAPTER FOUR

That Old Road Home

Three years at sea, and they were still in the Pacific Ocean, with whales to catch and months ahead of them before their ship was full. According to brief notes made by Susan, the *Nauticon* now had approximately 550 barrels of sperm oil, not counting the 120 barrels from the wreck of the *Lafayette*, plus 230 barrels of whale oil from their giant bowhead and 4,600 pounds of whalebone: not a lot to show after all that time. Sailing south, she must have been so relieved when the weather warmed enough to take the stove out of their cabin on September 18, 1851. Ten days later "all hands in swimming," finally washing off the grease and grime of their Arctic labor. On October 5, the Veeders gammed with Captain and Mrs. Burgess again, entertaining them on board the *Nauticon*, another offshore visit with another whaling wife who survived the Arctic experience but, unfortunately for us, did not write about it. None of the women Susan met in her years at sea left us a description of her; if she had not kept an account, her own voyage may have been noted only as a curious comment in the journal of doomed Mr. Roberts, that the child of Captain Veeder and his wife had died in Tahiti.

Mid-October, the *Nauticon* anchored in "Mowee" in the Sandwich Islands, and the captain and his family went ashore for two weeks:

> *Dined at Mr. Cartwrights, made up our minds to stop on shore—and we took a house, sent on board the ship for our bed and some other things—and took our tea by ourselves—had it sent from the hotel—got along nicely.* (October 14, 1851)

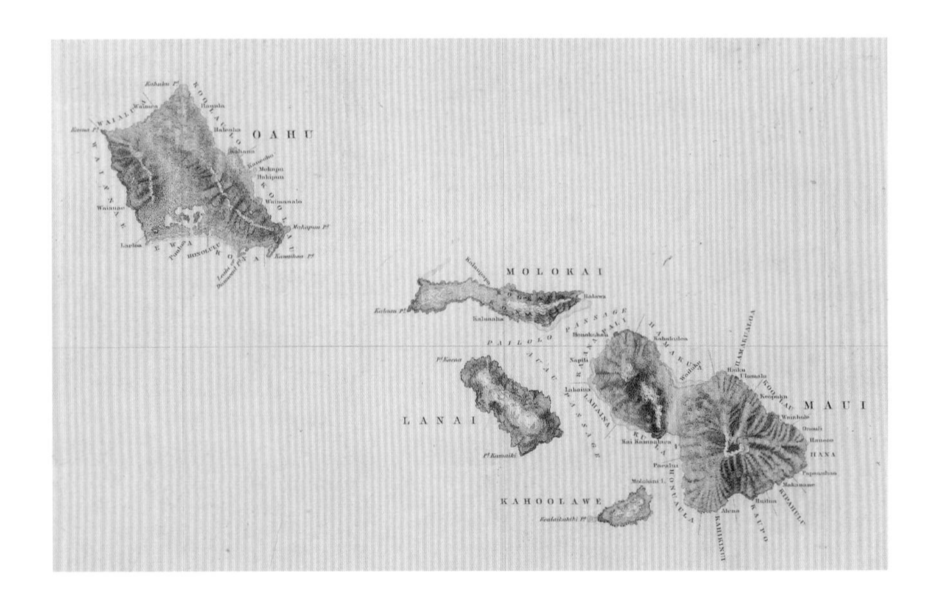

Detail from *Map of Hawaiian Group or Sandwich Islands by the U. S. Ex[ploring] Ex[pedition], 1841.*

Ms. 1000.4.2.8

There were a lot of American women on the island. Susan had tea with ladies referred to as Mrs. Baldwin, Mrs. Parsons, and Miss Bunker, and she got tickets for a ball scheduled for the next evening, but perhaps she should have consulted the captain, or maybe she decided she was lacking the proper attire, or the captain forgot his dancing shoes—at any rate, they didn't go because, as Susan notes obliquely, they were "not prepared." It was one thing to arrive in a port and have tea with a few captains and their wives but quite another to dress in one's best clothes and dance in a crowd of strangers: That took more courage than trading with thirty Chukchi off the coast of Siberia. Instead, they spent the evening with Captain Charles B. Swain II of the Nantucket ship *Enterprise* and his wife, Eunice. What a pleasant time Susan had in Maui, constant visitors—Captain Joy and wife, Captain Gwen and wife—and walking excursions with her new pals. In fact, she was too busy to write a word in her journal for the next ten days.

When the Veeders returned to the ship, Susan learned that five men had deserted—hard to blame them after months in the Arctic and years away from home. The captain shipped five new hands in their places, in the changing crew of the *Nauticon*. As they were preparing to sail from Maui, their friend Captain Cash of the *Columbia* arrived with his wife, Azubah, who had been in Hilo Bay on Hawaii while her husband was trying his luck in the Arctic. Captain Veeder postponed sailing so he and Susan could spend the day with the Nantucket couple, who had left home on October 13, 1850. Their two-year-old news of Nantucket would be fresh enough for Susan, and she and Azubah had a lot in common. Both had been pregnant when they left home. Azubah's son, William Murray Cash, born August 20, 1851, was still a babe in arms when his mother took him on board the *Nauticon*: an older son, Alexander, was along, too, a companion for David for the day. Prior to sailing from Nantucket, Azubah had shared twenty-six weeks with her husband in eleven years of marriage, not enough time to create a large family or much of a relationship for that matter, but she would end the voyage pregnant with daughter Fidelia, born on shore in

Left: **William Cash (1816–1882), 1855, photograph by Nichols & Warren, Fall River, Massachusetts.** *CDV1043*

Right: **Azubah Cash (1820–1894), 1882.** *GPN1537*

Nantucket in 1854. She and Susan remained lifelong friends, as revealed in a journal Susan kept at home twenty years later.

From Maui the *Nauticon* sailed to Oahu, or "Woahoo" as Susan spelled it, and, most likely at Susan's insistence, they stayed overnight:

> *About 9 a.m. went ashore. We have made up our minds to stay all night—have tickets to attend a ball this evening—have made up our minds to go to the ball.*
> (October 31, 1851)

She reported the next day,

> *Last evening went to the ball. Had a fine time. About 350 there. Today it is rather rough and we shall not go on board till tomorrow morning. Chas has shipped a third mate, a Mr. Baker. This evening went to the Circus. It rained hard.*
> (November 1, 1851)

With a ball on Halloween and the next day Rowe's Olympic Circus—featuring acts of fine horsemanship—Honolulu must have been overstimulating for the Veeder family. Home of the royal family on the island of Oahu, it was a town of ten thousand in mid-century, far bigger and more prosperous than Papeete, Tahiti, where Susan had admired the architecture and ambience the previous year. And there were more amusements: "school festivals, agricultural exhibits, ladies' fancy fairs, moonlight rides on horseback, sea bathing at fashionable watering place Waikiki, balls and parties for those who wish them . . ." according to contemporary writer Laura Fish Judd.

Susan must really have regretted missing the ball in Maui and did not let another opportunity pass. And now, for the first time in three years, the man she has referred to all along as "the Captain" is called Charles in her journal and will be for most of the rest of the voyage. Something in their relationship shifted in Honolulu. Perhaps it was the realization that the captain was not almighty, that she could wield a little power, even if it was just insisting that Charles take her dancing. Or maybe he had promised they would be home by now, and if not, well, she could call him Charles.

The *Nauticon* now steered for the Paumoto Group, or the Tuamotus, where they had had luck in the fall and winter of 1849–50, and on November 30 they were there again, chasing sperm whales in familiar seas:

> *This morning quite pleasant. At 9 a.m. raised breeches. At half past 9 see that they was sperm whales—and got the boats ready to lower but a squall came about the same time and they waited till over—and at 10 lowered the boats. The bow boat struck but the iron drawed and that whale went off. The larboard and waist boat struck and each got a whale, rather small.* (December 25, 1851)

The names of the whaleboats refer to where they were hung by davits on the side of the ship: the starboard boat on the right side and the larboard boat on the left side, both at the rear of the ship; the waist boat in the middle on the larboard side, and forward of that the bow boat. The middle of the ship on the starboard side was where they hoisted the blankets of whale blubber aboard. Each of those boats was headed by one of the mates: first mate, second mate, third mate, fourth mate. Since there were four mates, Captain Veeder probably refrained from joining the hunt unless an extra boat was needed, but George, now seventeen, was in one of them. The crew of the *Nauticon* was back in the game, cutting and boiling, stowing the oil, and cruising again. On the fourth of December they saw Lazareef, where Susan had shown her mettle fishing with the boys a month after Mary Frances died in 1850. Two boats went ashore for coconuts, wood, and fish, but it wasn't a family fishing party this time—on to Peacock and Wilson's Islands, or Ahe and Manihi in the northern Tuamotus. The captain was no longer wary of the native people, as he had been on their first visit. He sent boats ashore for pigs and fish, and they brought back some shells for the captain's lady—tuns, marlinspikes, spider conchs, and beautifully patterned little cone shells.

The Veeders were in the Tuamotus for Christmas, as they had been in 1849 when they stopped at Wilson's Island for a few pigs, fowl, and coconuts. The location and menu were similar in 1851:

> *Today fine weather. This morning saw Peacock Island. At one the Starboard and Larboard boats went in to see if they could get some fish and coconuts—at 4 returned with 1 boatload of wood. Today is Christmas and we have dined on roast pig and haslet—it was very good.*
> (December 25, 1851)

Susan was referring to haglet, a name the whalers gave petrels—pelagic birds with odd-looking tubular noses atop their beaks. They must have been tasty: eighteenth-century whaleman Peleg Folger looked forward to meals of haglet pie in the North Atlantic in 1752, a hundred years earlier. Any change from the usual diet was a treat, and the plump Tahitian petrel was a nice addition to the table.

In early January, the men raised sperm whales and lowered three boats: the starboard boat, the larboard boat, and the waist boat. The larboard boat, headed by first mate Mr. Archer, appears to have been the most successful overall, once again getting the prize:

First mate of the *Nauticon*, James Archer (1810–69), 1860s.

GPN1282

Today fine weather. This morning saw a shoal of sperm whales. At 8 o'clock the boats lowered. The larboard boat got one, the waist struck but lost his line, the starboard boat struck, the iron came out.
(January 6, 1852)

Eleven days later, still cruising in the northern Tuamotus, the men of the *Nauticon* had a banner day:

At 8 o'clock this morning raised a shoal of sperm whales. The boats lowered and struck 5, got 3 of them. At 4 the boats got to ship and commenced cutting. Cut in two of them, let the other lay alongside.
(January 17, 1852)

Two more days were required to finish cutting up the whales and boiling down the blubber, and at the end they had sixty more barrels of oil. Captain Veeder appeared to give no thought to the fact that killing small whales meant there would not be large ones later; his shortsighted attitude was based on the demands of the ship owners to get as much oil as possible, as quickly as possible. As soon as the decks were clean they spied another shoal of whales and got three more for another sixty barrels. Unlike in the Arctic Ocean, where there were dozens of whaleships in sight, the Tuamotus appear to have been virgin territory for whalers, as the *Nauticon* was alone; it was a tricky area to navigate, a submerged volcanic mountain range that had imploded eons earlier, leaving only the coral necklace of each peak above the water. The archipelago was home to juvenile sperm whales and their mothers; in four months in the area the men of the *Nauticon* took twelve small whales whose yield was a total of two hundred and thirty barrels, equal in quantity to the one bowhead they killed in the Arctic the previous summer but worth three times more.

Susan made no trips ashore, remaining on board as boats collected pumpkins, potatoes, and watermelons from "Metia" (Makatea), one of the few true islands in the Tuamotu group and the only one with any kind of agriculture.

On the atolls, villagers subsisted on fish, pigs, and coconuts, a simple diet; and they lived more primitively than anywhere else Susan had been except the Arctic, where the people were poor but obviously clothed. In the subequatorial Tuamotus, little or no clothing was needed, and there was little to make it from except palm fronds. Tapa cloth, frequently made elsewhere in Polynesian and Oceania, was made from the bark of mulberry or banyan trees, neither of which grew on the little coral atolls. The lack of attire may have shocked our journal keeper, who makes no comment about the physical appearance of the local people, nor does she include the human figure in any of her paintings.

On February 13, Susan finally got some shore time with her husband on one of the atolls—Krusenstern's Island, or Tikehau, where Cornelius Rust had been abandoned almost two years earlier. She remarks that that the residents had left, probably moving to another of the islets surrounding the lagoon. They found no trace of the former troublemaker or anyone else. Susan would have had an opportunity for a dip in the lagoon if she dared or for a little exploring before another of their boats came ashore a couple of hours later. She merely notes that everyone collected coconuts and "had a nice time." From Peacock Island a few days later, more coconuts were gathered and fish caught; the atolls offered nothing more in the way of fresh food, but it felt good to walk on solid ground, even if the ground was coral.

After killing a sperm whale on February 26 and fastening it alongside, the *Nautic*on sailed back to Metia for fresh food for the crew, who had been exerting themselves more than usual during the recent bout of whaling activity. Arriving with their latest whale in tow, they were met by the local people, who were fond of whale meat and willing to trade:

> *A number of canoes came along after whale lean [meat]. At 8 the Captain went on shore to see if he could [get] any vegetables as we have not any potatoes on board. At 10 returned with a number of fowl, some bread fruit, a few potatoes and pumpkins. A 1 p. m. the larboard boat went in—at 5 returned with a few fowl, potatoes etc. At 5 commenced boiling the whale—fine weather, all well.*
> (February 27, 1852)

So Makatea for vegetables; Lazareef for wood; coconuts and fish everywhere—Captain Veeder was weaving his way around the Tuamotus and becoming familiar with the islanders, who turned out to be friendly and eager to trade what little they had. On March 18, they dropped off a crewman named Harry Wilson on Wilson's Island (Manihi) where, according to Susan, they had picked him up three months earlier. Like many Pacific islanders who signed aboard American whalers, Wilson worked under an assumed Western name for convenience, adopting (or being assigned) a surname that identified his place of origin. He may have signed on for short-term work, or needed transportation from one atoll to another. On a later voyage in the archipelago, Captain Veeder would spend more time ferrying passengers around than whaling, but in the spring of 1852 he attended to the business at hand. Another whale was snagged on March 24, thanks to the larboard boat again and as Susan mused, "one is better than none." The next day they raised yet another shoal and spotted a large sperm whale, one who knew the score when a whaleboat approached: "got very near a large whale but his seeing them he started to windward, and that started the rest." The full-grown sperm whales were wary, not such easy prey as young ones who needed an experienced adult to get them out of harm's way.

In April, Susan gives us a brief, and rare, glimpse into domestic life aboard the *Nauticon*. "This forenoon I have been busy ironing. This afternoon sewing on a pink calico shirt." She must have had sewing projects going the whole voyage, clothes for the baby, for her boys and husband, and for herself, but this is the first time she has shared information with us. Was the pink calico shirt for David? George? For herself? She is so formally attired in her portrait that it is hard to imagine her in pink calico, but it was hot and she *was* on a whaleship, so she dressed as simply as possible in an era when women's dresses featured tight bodices, full petticoats, and long sleeves. The next day she notes that Charles was making a pair of shoes for David—how else was a growing boy to get a new pair of shoes at sea? Charles appears to have been a talented constructor of things, from the ivory wagon he made for Mary Frances, with its functional wheels and

Detail from Susan Veeder's *Ohtahiete as Seen from the Harbor.*

Gift of the Friends of the Nantucket Historical Association, Ms. 220, Log 347

steering, to a pair of boy's shoes. He could work with his hands, navigate, trade with Pacific islanders, explore new whaling grounds, maintain discipline, protect his family, and fill the hold with oil: so much responsibility on his shoulders, the monarch of a floating kingdom. He was a man to be admired, and Susan was by his side, making it possible for him to be a real member of his family for the longest period of time in their marriage.

Their cruise in the northern Tuamotus ended, the *Nauticon* sailed south for nearby Tahiti, arriving on April 14. There they found the ship *Hector* of New Bedford with 2,900 barrels of oil, a stupendous amount. A note in Alexander Starbuck's *History of the American Whale Fishery* states that the *Hector*, which left New Bedford in June of 1848, three months before the *Nauticon*, had dropped anchor only four times in the entire course of the voyage.

Susan did not go on shore the first day they sat at anchor in Papeete, so there was time for her to find her watercolors and paint her most complex painting: *Otaheite as Seen from the Harbor*. Her feelings about Tahiti were probably equally complex—she had loved it in 1850, but it was where her child died, and that child was still awaiting a permanent resting place on Nantucket. She depicts a number of vessels in the semi-circular harbor, ranging in size from three-masted whaleships to smaller barks and little skiffs, as well as two French ships flying their national flag. Houses line the shore and back up into the green and brown mountains whose many peaks form a dark meringue atop the confection of the town. How many times did she turn to that page later as she sat by the fireside in her Nantucket house and remember how warm it was, how fragrant, how foreign? In the harbor a week, Susan and Charles went on shore several times for tea with various captains, and they entertained on shipboard, too: Captain Cathcart, Captain Smith, Mr. Gray, the usual social rounds of visits and conversation among the transient American whaling aristocracy.

On April 21, back to sea heading to the coast of Chile and beginning their long voyage home, with nothing noted by our journalist but wind and weather and the occasional details of ship-keeping: her cabin was cleaned, painted, and varnished in mid-May, and after a week of strong winds she managed to do laundry and dry it quickly. Laundry references occur regularly—it was hard work and consumed a day, but it was something she knew how to do, a contribution, and she took pride in it, although accomplishing the task at sea was entirely different from an idyllic day on Cocos Island, surrounded by waterfalls. As they neared the coast on June 10, they surprised a shoal of sperm whales: the waist boat got a huge one that made 134 barrels of oil, as much as from six or more of the little sperm whales of the Tuamotus. For the next two weeks the litany in Susan's diary is "moderate wind, seen nothing," "strong wind, seen nothing," "light wind, seen nothing"—no whales, no ships, no islands, nothing but the ocean in every direction—a thousand leagues of blue. Finally, "saw the island of Juan Fernandez," a familiar sight, where Susan had picked strawberries the previous November. They caught some fish there but didn't dally long, soon steering for Valparaiso, where they went ashore to sell some of their oil. Susan's description of the town is less than enlightening:

> *We have been out walking and taking a view of the place which I find is about the same as all other Spanish ports that I have been to.*
> (June 25, 1852)

From Valparaiso they were bound to Talcahuano, arriving on July 17, when Susan went ashore and found her friend from the high seas, Ann Burgess, the only other whaling wife in the Arctic the past summer, who had also gammed with Susan offshore near Maui. "Mrs. Burgess and family here and well," she wrote, surely relieved. Susan packed a trunk and headed to Mr. Crosby's hospitable abode. She put away her journal for almost three weeks, but we can imagine the teas, excursions, horseback rides, and good times she had there, knowing it would be her last visit, ever. Once again we are left wondering if she was pregnant and what went wrong if she was.

On August 6 they put to sea, and Susan noted that one man ran away, the final deserter from the *Nauticon*. The weather was rough as they approached southern Chile, but ten-year-old David was perfectly happy hanging out on deck "catching speckled haglets during a moderate wind," as his mother noted. All he needed was a hook and some salt pork, and the petrels would dive underwater and take the bait, according to Francis Allyn Olmsted, a Yale graduate who went on a whaling voyage for his health in 1839. Olmstead presents a wonderful description of a bird whose behavior would surely entice many ten-year-olds: "The speckled haglet is a beautiful bird, but like all other aquatic birds of this region, emits a most disgusting effluvium from its mouth when captured." A messy sport, indeed, but haglet for dinner.

Sperm whales were sighted once more before the *Nauticon* steered north into the Atlantic, but they were too fast for the boats to catch. At noon on September 8, 1852, Susan saw Cape Horn, and six hours later they were in the home ocean: the only way to look now was north to Nantucket, months away but pulling her like a fishhook to a magnet. For four years they had been at sea, so much must have changed at home. Charles Edward would be a teenager; her parents were elderly, possibly dead for all she knew. Anything could have happened.

Cruising for whales off the Falkland Islands was fruitless, so they pushed on. Susan found nothing to remark except wind and weather, an occasional finback or porpoise, and on October 11 "fryed kelp for supper, found it good." The sea was rough and the wind cold, and five men were sick, perhaps the five men newly shipped in Oahu. Two weeks later Susan remarked that the sick men were about the same. When they spotted right whales on October 28 off the mouth of the River de la Plate—a large estuary between Argentina and Uruguay—only two boats were lowered, since there were not enough healthy bodies to man three, and they couldn't get close enough to strike. But the next day the trusty larboard boat got one, and the available crew cut and boiled. The oil looked dark, especially so after all the sperm oil they were used to, but something was wrong and they stopped the boiling. A session of trouble-shooting the tryworks no doubt occurred, because the next day, as Susan relates "commenced boiling again, the oil looks much better."

On November 6, the *Nauticon* spoke the ship *Constitution* of Nantucket—the same ship they had met in the Arctic in July 1851. Having returned home after a poor voyage, the *Constitution* was now two months out again from the home port, this time under Captain Joseph Winslow, who came aboard the *Nauticon* for a visit. He had just left his wife, Sarah, who was six months pregnant, and his three-year-old son, George, and must have been impressed to see Susan and her boys, now completely seaworthy, on the *Nauticon*. So impressed, that on his next voyage in 1857 Sarah and their two daughters joined him, and two more daughters were born during their five years at sea. (George, alas, died of typhoid fever on Nantucket in 1854, age five.) Sarah loved being at sea, writing to her sister-in-law, "it is a great deal more pleasant than being at home."

Cruising off the River de la Plate for six more weeks, the crew of the *Nauticon* saw lots of right whales but couldn't catch them, and the ship still didn't have a full working crew. On November 12, Susan noted that the sick folk were a little better; she was more than likely in charge of their recuperation, nursing them to the best of her ability. And then, an injury in the midst of a sperm whale hunt:

Point de la Galera, St. Lorenzo, La Plata, and Pelado, from Susan Veeder's journal of the *Nauticon*.

Gift of the Friends of the Nantucket Historical Association, Ms. 220, Log 347

> *Today fine weather. At 9 a.m. saw 3 sperm whales. At 10 two boats lowered. About 11 the larboard boat struck, the whale sounded and took the line, the boat returned to the ship and got another line but see no more of that whale. About 1 p.m. the waist boat struck another whale. The line got foul, took the second mate out of the boat and dragged him under water some minutes. When taken out found him quite exhausted and he vomited considerable blood and another boat lowered and took him to the ship and got him quite comfortable. The larboard boat went on and killed the whale. At 5 took him to the ship and got the fluke chain and head rope fast to him and got ready to cut him in in the morning. He is a noble whale. Should think he would make 80 or 90 barrels.*
> (November 21, 1852)

A noble whale! Is Susan merely referring to his grand size, or does she find him admirable in some other way? Maybe she developed a respect for the species after four years of pursuit and felt regret that the beast failed to escape the bloodthirsty men, that he missed an opportunity to travel back to the Pacific and sport among the Tuamotus and Tahiti. It took the men five days to finish processing the noble one, who yielded a hundred and ten barrels of oil. In the interim, Susan reported the condition of the sick and injured: "Mr. Simpson (second mate) getting along nicely, just gone on deck. The rest of the sick ones better so that they are around with the exception of Charles Swain, a boatsteerer. He is quite sick." For the next few weeks they caught nothing but a green turtle and a porpoise, and Susan tended to her laundry. One last fruitless attempt to get a sizable sperm whale the day after an unremarked Christmas: "the whale took the line and went off to windward very quick," giving the boat crew a Nantucket sleigh-ride for the holiday season.

Having had enough of whaling in that latitude, Captain Veeder steered north for St. Catherine's Island off the coast of southern Brazil. They had had no fresh food, except for kelp, in a long time, and they needed water. David went ashore with his father on December 31, and on January 2 Susan had a day on land, too, at a hotel where she could take a bath and have a nice meal.

She and Charles visited the Governor at the "Fort," although she doesn't indicate which of the three forts on the island they saw, and they visited the American consul. It must have seemed a safe place to let the crew loose, so the captain allowed one watch on shore on liberty; he must have known whom to trust at this point, who really wanted to go home to Nantucket and wouldn't abandon ship at this late date in the voyage. On January 8, Susan informs us that the captain made up his mind to take a freight of coffee. Determined to make the *Nauticon*'s years at sea as profitable as possible, he loaded her with a thousand sacks of coffee—an executive decision since he could not have communicated with the ship owners about the prospect of investing in the beans. He may have bought the cargo in the name of G. & M. Starbuck, or it may have been a personal investment.

Ready for sea on January 12, Captain Veeder agreed to take on four passengers: captain, mate, carpenter, and steward of the bark *Alabama* of Baltimore, which had sunk off the River de la Plate loaded with a cargo of coal. It was warm in the South Atlantic as they sailed toward the equator and Susan doesn't note much else, except for an occasional sail on the horizon, but the top of her journal page now reads "Ship Nauticon Bound Home." They raised two sperm whales in latitude 14 south on February 8, and both the waist boat and the larboard boat got lines in one of them, requiring the assistance of a third boat, so the starboard boat was lowered and struck and killed him, a ninety-seven-barrel whale. Four days later, the boiling finished, Susan wrote, "washed ship and all snug." She must have been *so* anxious to get back to the island as they zipped along north, writing February 17, "A'going along nicely towards home, O hasten the time when we may arrive there."

A last shoal of sperm whales may have seemed like an impediment to her, but they appeared the next day, so boats lowered and struck one, a juvenile, making only twenty-five barrels and slowing the ship down for a day or two as they processed and stowed and cleaned again. Susan notes that she spent two days painting, but what? Her cabin? There are no more watercolors in her journal. She began packing up some of her things on

March 5, 1853, the three-year anniversary of the day Mary Frances was given that first infamous powder by the doctor in Tahiti, and on March 11 they threw the tryworks overboard. No more whaling—they were almost home, working their way against gales, stopping once to speak a schooner and get "a barrel of beef, a few potatoes, some butter," and on the March 22, the Gulf Stream, that old road home. Susan wrote the next day, "Light wind, one sail in sight. All well, quite cold." Her last entry begins "Thursday 24th," but she put down her pen, home at last, her voyage over.

CHAPTER FIVE

Nantucket in Decline

> *PORT OF NANTUCKET*
>
> *Sunday, March 27*
>
> *ARRIVED.*
>
> *(At Edgartown) ship Nauticon, Veeder, Pacific Ocean, 70 days from St. Catharines with 1000 bbls sp oil, to G. & M. Starbuck & Co. She has also 1000 bags of Coffee on freight fm St. Catharines, for New York. . . . Passengers in the Nauticon, Mrs. Veeder, (Capt's wife) and child, also Capt Myers, master, and Mr. Landeman, 1st Officer, and part of crew, of bark Alabama of Baltimore, picked up and carried into St. Catharines.*
>
> (*The Inquirer*, March 28, 1853)

WELL, SUSAN WAS *ALMOST* HOME. The shallow entrance to Nantucket's harbor made it impossible for large, heavily laden ships like the *Nauticon* to gain entry, so it was common procedure by the 1850s to unload cargo at sister island Martha's Vineyard, in the more accommodating harbor at Edgartown. Susan and family took passage on the first packet to Nantucket, just a few miles away as the gull flies, but in order to avoid the shoals and islands between the two harbors—Gravelly, Tuckernuck, and Muskeget—a longer sail in a less direct route was required. As they approached the north shore of Nantucket, the old familiar landmarks were visible: Great Point Light at the far northeastern tip of the island, Brant Point Light marking

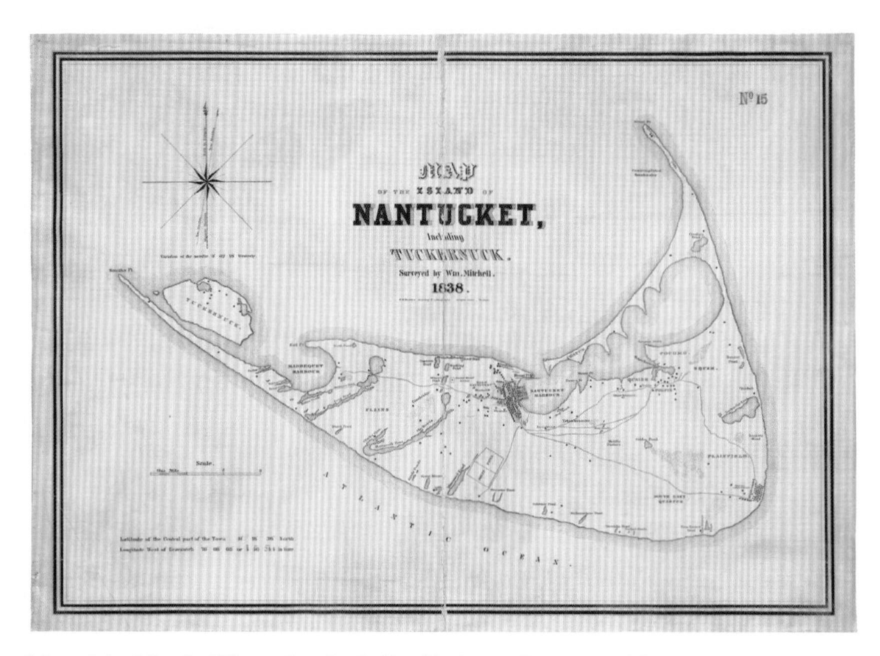

***Map of the Island of Nantucket, Including Tuckernuck,* surveyed by William Mitchell, 1838.**

Courtesy of the Norman B. Leventhal Map and Education Center, Boston Public Library

the entrance to the harbor, the church towers and windmills above the compact little town, the five wharves reaching their fingers into the harbor. Nothing mountainous and green like Pitcairn, or dirty and exotic with tropical torpor like the South American port towns Susan disparaged. Nantucket *was* an anthill in the sea, as Melville so perfectly described it, bustling with human activity, but barren except for the brick and wooden built environment. The author had visited Nantucket for the first time the previous summer, a year after his major opus, *Moby-Dick*, failed to capture the imagination of the reading public. He accompanied his father-in-law, Lemuel Shaw, chief justice of the Supreme Court of Massachusetts. While Shaw was hearing cases in the local court, Melville explored the town, home to his fictional Ahab and Starbuck and the very real Captain Pollard, whose ill-fated ship, the *Essex,* inspired Melville's tale of Ahab and his albino adversary.

***Southeastern View of Nantucket, Mass.*, drawn by John Warner Barber and published in his *Historical Collections, Being a Collection of Interesting Facts, Traditions, Biographical Sketches, Anecdotes, &c., Relating to the History and Antiquities of Every Town in Massachusetts, with Geographical Descriptions* (Worcester: Dorr, Howland & Co., 1839).** *1992.418.1*

Although there were changes to the town immediately obvious to Susan and her family, much remained unchanged; even today the town has a nineteenth-century appearance: the cedar-shingled houses silvery or drab, depending on the weather and the season and one's state of mind; the Greek Revival mansions of Main Street as imposing as they were a hundred and fifty years earlier; the cobbled streets as bone-rattling and beautiful. What was most apparent was what was missing: men. While Susan and her family were at sea, gold fever had infected the town and more than five hundred men had sailed to California; five hundred from a total population of about 8,700, of which the majority were women and children. The men formed mining companies, bought old whaleships, loaded them with supplies, and headed around Cape Horn on the slow route to San Francisco; or they sailed to Panama, crossed the isthmus in wagons and on mules, and sailed north from there. The hope for a quick fortune was enough to tempt mariners and tradesmen alike, who gambled that their chances of success were better in the Californian soil than in the depths of the Pacific Ocean. In fact, while Susan was plowing the Pacific in the *Nauticon* in 1849, her brother, Edward, was sailing the Nantucket ship *Montano* to California, with his wife, Phebe, along for the ride.

At the wharf to welcome them home were Susan's parents, George and Susan Austin, who were sixty-six and sixty years old, respectively, accustomed to the heart-rending departures and joyous arrivals of the men in their maritime clan, now relieved that their *daughter* was home. In the Austin household lived Charles Edward Veeder, age sixteen, practically grown up now and a little awkward at the reunion with his brothers and parents who had become strangers—this family who had been through so many adventures and tribulations together, arriving with his unknown baby sister in a lead casket. Susan's younger sister, Eliza, married to Clement C. Foster, a mariner from New York, lived with Susan's parents, too, while her husband was at sea. Holding her hand was four-year-old Susie Veeder Foster, named for her aunt. Susan's older brother, Edward, back from California, may have been at sea again, but his wife, Phebe, a close friend of Susan's, was undoubtedly present and eager to compare notes about her trip around Cape Horn; Phebe and Edward did not have children of their own. This was the extent of Susan's immediate family; her brother, William, had died at sea when he was twenty, in 1832. They were a family of mariners, coming and going all the time from their island home.

Edward C. Austin (1811–1879) and Phebe Parker Austin (1815–1880), 1850s, brother and sister-in-law of Susan Veeder.

Gift of Ginger Andrews, SC905-21

Charles Veeder's childhood home at 3 Bear Street, by Paul LaPaglia, circa 1990.

Bequest of Andy Oates, 2013.19.18

Charles grew up on Nantucket, too, but his family left the island in the mid-1830s under circumstances tinged with scandal. In 1818, his father, Peter P. Veeder, bought the house at 3 Bear Street where his wife and five children—Charles, David, Amie Ann, Mary Ann, and Ann Maria—lived. Charles was the oldest, born in 1809, followed by David, born in 1812, and the three Anns born between 1814 and 1819. It's not entirely clear when Peter made Nantucket his home, but his wife, Rachel Allen, was a local woman, a young widow he married sometime around 1808. Peter was captain of the Nantucket whaleship *Peru* from 1821 to 1824, evidence that he had a long history in the whaling industry; what his career was like between 1824 and 1830 is not known, as there is no record of his voyages during that period, but when he was fifty years old he went to sea as first mate on the Nantucket ship *Loper*, under Captain John Cotton, and something went seriously amiss on that voyage. Obed Macy, the first historian of

The ship *Peru*, built in 1818, made fifteen whaling voyages out of Nantucket and two from New Bedford before it was broken up in the early 1880s. Peter P. Veeder was captain of the ship, 1821–24. This ship portrait is attributed to Nantucket artist James Walter Folger, circa 1880.

NHA purchase, 2000.76.1

Nantucket and a faithful diarist, recorded in his journal, August 19, 1832:

> *Ship Loper, John Cotton, arrived. 5 or 6 days previous to her arrival an affray took place between the Capt. & Peter P. Veder [sic] the mate which ended by the Capt, with the help of the crew in putting Peter in irons, in which situation he remained until the Ship arrived at which time the Capt. lodged a complaint against him for assault & battery with an intent to kill. A court of inquiry was instituted, and was adjourned in order to have the crew from the bar [sandbar at the entrance to Nantucket harbor where the ship was anchored] as evidences. In the intermediate time a second complaint was lodged against him for committing murder on the body of a Negro in the*

> *course of the voyage. Finding himself in a bad situation, he absconded from the island, leaving his bondman to pay the reckoning, who he secured with making over all his property, which [has left] his family [in] a destitute condition.*

Nantucket's local newspaper, the *Inquirer*, does not note the incident, but it does record a death associated with the ship: "On board of ship *Loper*, laying at the Bar, Mr. Andrew Gater, aged about 27, of Philadelphia—in a fit of insanity he cut his throat with a razor." Whatever was going on, the *Loper* was an unhappy ship. There are no court records to substantiate Macy's account, but the fact is Peter P. Veeder fled Nantucket and never returned. On August 22, he sold a parcel of land in the Newtown section of the island for $100, and with that cash in hand he made a quick exit. He relocated to Rochester, New York, and eventually settled nearby in North Greece, where he established a farm. His family joined him, all but Charles, who married Susan Austin on Nantucket in 1833. The historian of a weekly newspaper in North Greece wrote about founding father Peter P. Veeder in 1973:

> *We will never know why Captain Veeder came to the mainland from his island home thirty miles at sea and eventually migrated to North Greece. It is difficult to contrast a life at sea to that of a farmer, yet the fact remains that he became a settler and was successful in his new venture of husbandry.*

Somehow, Charles Veeder's father escaped the long arm of the law, as Charles would do later in his life by vanishing into a different kind of wilderness. There was no one from his side of the family to greet him upon his return from four and a half years at sea. Nantucket was perhaps Susan's home more than his; she had family around her and had spent most of her life on the island while he was chasing whales. Her own heritage paralleled his, however, because neither the Austins nor the Veeders were part of the Nantucket whaling gentry, families who were descended

Looking south on Orange Street from the corner of Main Street, Charles H. Shute & Son, photographers, 1870s.

GPN-Shute-26

from the first English settlers of the island—like the Starbucks, Coffins, Gardners, and Macys—whose ranks included ship owners and whale-oil merchants as well as mariners. Although there had been other Austins on the island for more than a hundred years, Susan's father, George, was not related to them; George's father, John, is referred to in local genealogies as a "stranger" (i.e., someone not native to Nantucket) who married a local woman in 1775.

Charles and Susan and the boys made their way from Steamboat Wharf to Main Street and up that wide boulevard, lined with substantial commercial buildings and dotted with the island's first elm trees, planted just a few years earlier, to Orange Street, long known as the street of whaling captains. Although there was hardly a street in town that had not been home to a whaling captain or two, Orange Street boasted more than a hundred in the nineteenth century, some already, in 1853, long dead, others retired, and a few, like Charles Veeder at forty-four years of age, still very much in the game even if the game was almost over. Heading south on Orange Street they passed the South Church, or Unitarian Meeting House, one of the landmarks of the town, with its massive bell from Portugal ringing the hours. They crested Quanaty Hill and began the long descent to Newtown, the moniker for a densely populated neighborhood on the edge of town.

The Veeders' house stood at 91 Orange Street, around the corner from where Susan's parents lived on Warren Street and just two blocks south of her brother, Edward Austin, at 77 Orange. In October 1837, Charles had purchased the newly built house from John B. Nicholson, one of the island's most prolific house carpenters, establishing Susan and his young family in their snug dwelling before sailing as captain of the *Christopher Mitchell* in 1838. Perched on a high brick basement, the two-and-a-half story shingled dwelling was one of Nantucket's "typical" houses, with a standard floor plan dictated by the large ridge chimney that was the backbone of the structure. A parlor, stair-hall, and buttery, or closet, were in front on the first floor overlooking Orange Street, and a bedroom and kitchen were in the rear. Three bed chambers hugged the chimney on the second floor, and a large attic provided storage space for sea chests and old furniture and could serve as extra sleeping quarters. The basement would have allowed for a second, or summer, kitchen, and because of the height of the brick foundation walls, five or six exterior stairs were required to reach the landing at the front door.

It was a fine house, well-crafted, and worth the $1,650 purchase price. Hundreds of these iconic houses with the same plain cedar-shingled exteriors and similar interior layouts still line the streets of Nantucket, which is one reason the island is called the Grey Lady. The sometimes grim winter

91 Orange Street on the right, with figures at the door believed to be Susan Veeder and either her niece Susan Veeder Foster (b. 1848) or daughter Marianna (b. 1860). Half of a stereograph by Josiah Freeman, 1860s.

SG6541

weather adds another layer of grey, and in March of 1853, it may have seemed particularly colorless to those who had seen the islands of the South Pacific.

Home at last, they unloaded the trunks and treasures from their long sea voyage, lining the parlor mantle with shells and putting Susan's journal on a table, unpacking the straw hats from Peru, and starting a fire in the stove on that cold spring day, brewing some tea. Susan's mother and sister brought supper and gathered round to gam at *home*, hardly knowing where to start, so many stories to recount, friendships to renew, and family to embrace.

No longer in the cramped confines of her sea cabin, Susan could move from room to room and not lose her balance; the house was solid and fixed and permanent and full of people she loved.

After settling in, one of the first tasks was to bury Mary Frances in the Newtown cemetery, a burying ground on the outskirts of town, southeast of the eastern windmill on the Popsquatchett Hills. Susan and Charles ordered a small headstone carved from white granite, decorated with a medallion of flowers reminiscent of their brief idyllic time in Polynesia. It was inscribed, "Here lie the remains of Mary Frances, daughter of Charles A. and Susan C. Veeder, who died at Tahita, Society Islands, March 6, 1850, age 13 mos. & 6 days."

The story of Susan's long voyage, although in some parts a tale of woe, may have inspired at least two Nantucket women to follow her example and join their husbands on voyages that left shortly after her return. The *Lexington*, with Captain Peter C. Brock's wife, Eliza, on board, sailed on May 17, 1853; and the *Phoenix*, with Betsey Morey accompanying her husband, Captain Israel Morey, sailed on July 19. There must have been gatherings of women at 91 Orange Street, updating Susan with the latest news and leafing through her journal and examining her paintings, eager to hear

Headstone in Nantucket's Newtown Cemetery. "Here lie the remains of Mary Frances daughter of Charles A. & Susan C. Veeder, who died at Tahita, Society Islands, March 6, 1850. Aged 13 mos. & 6 days."

Photograph by Georgen Charnes, 2005, NTC-G4

her story of life on a whaleship and at exotic ports and islands, imagining themselves adventurous and hardy sailors who would no longer have to endure years of separation from their husbands. Of course not everyone minded the separation, as evidenced by the jaunty poem "Nantucket Girl's Song," recorded in the journal of whaling wife Eliza Brock:

I have made up my mind now to be a Sailor's wife,
To have a purse full of money and a very easy life,
For a clever sailor husband is so seldom at his home,
That his wife can spend the dollars with a will that's all her own,
Then I'll haste to wed a sailor, and send him off to sea,
For a life of independence is the pleasant life for me,
But every now and then I shall like to see his face,
For it always seems to me to beam with manly grace,
With his brow so nobly open, and his dark and kindly eye,
Oh my heart beats fondly towards him whenever he is nigh,
But when he says Goodbye my love, I'm off across the sea
First I cry for his departure, then laugh because I'm free,
Yet I'll welcome him most gladly, whenever he returns
And share with him so cheerfully all the money that he earns
For he's a loving Husband, though he leads a roving life
And well I know how good it is to be a Sailor's Wife.

Brock, who was at sea three years, would have preferred to be the land bound sailor's wife of the poem. Her journal reveals an extreme distaste for shipboard life and a passionate yearning for her Nantucket home.

Susan was undoubtedly a local celebrity, subject to polite interrogation and scrutiny by her maritime community. Living proof that a woman could live shipboard for four years and survive quite nicely, she was an example for her fellow whaling wives, and they were lining up, some more willingly than others. In conversations with his cronies, Captain Veeder must have espoused the pleasure of having a wife on board, regaling the other captains with stories of Susan and his sons by his side, touting the advantages of a shared cabin and shared concerns, no longer the worry that something awful had happened to one's family thousands of miles away, that while you were harpooning a whale your young son back on Nantucket was dying, or your wife was getting restless. Better to lose a treasured child in Tahiti, both parents there to comfort each other. Better, too, to avoid entanglement with the perfectly willing women of the Polynesian islands and avoid bringing home a disease that would be evidence of betrayal.

Even if Susan's adventure was a catalyst propelling other wives to sea, once was enough for her. She had three up-and-coming mariner sons to think about, two of them soon to take off on their own, and it was time for David to get some serious schooling. He was now eleven years old and full of his recent exploits—a schoolroom might seem more confining than a whaleship, and he would need her guiding hand. She must have felt so good to be in her own home, *her* kingdom, not her husband's, a place she could keep clean and orderly, her own kitchen and familiar food and a door that opened onto solid ground. What a comfort to be near her aging parents and her friends, in a community she understood and was embraced by.

Although today it is apparent that a major economic decline was beginning on the island, in 1853 it was harder to discern. Nantucket was still a vibrant town, freshly rebuilt after the Great Fire of 1846. Main Street had been widened and lined with new storefronts, while Centre, Broad, and Federal streets had a mixture of Greek Revival houses and two- and three-story commercial buildings with large halls above, where meetings and entertainments of all kinds were held. The Nantucket Atheneum, the first public building constructed after the fire, rose on the ashes of its predecessor in less than six months and was soon hosting talks by Ralph Waldo Emerson and other luminaries of the age who spoke to audiences of well-educated women, world travelers, and social activists. Although Nantucket was thirty miles from the mainland, it was no backwater town. One could purchase all the necessities of life and many of its luxuries: silk plush caps, muslin and lace chemisettes, cashmere shawls, gold and silver thimbles, cigars, the latest sheet music (songs, polkas, waltzes), and English gooseberry bushes for the garden.

Walking up the long hill to Main Street from her house on lower Orange Street, Susan passed her brother Edward's house and, across the street, the house of Owen Chase, former first mate of the whaleship *Essex*—he was known as a hoarder, with an attic full of provisions to protect against any future starvation. Not far past Chase's house was that of her maritime friend Azubah, wife of Captain William Cash, on the corner of Cash's Court. After cresting Quanaty Hill with its stellar view of the harbor, it was an easy stroll down the slope to Main Street. No more empty stretches of ocean for Susan, although if she missed the maritime vista a short trip to the shore in any direction would give her a view of the Atlantic. With her feet safely planted on the home turf, she planned to stay put, but it was impossible to ignore the pull of the sea on her husband and sons. None of the boys had learned another trade. They were born mariners—George had spent the equivalent of four years of high school experiencing the whaling business from the bottom up, and young David grew up on a whaleship. Even Charles Edward, who was land-bound on Nantucket during the four years his family was gone, became a mariner.

At the end of the journal she kept on board the *Nauticon*, Susan devoted a page to the record of voyages of the Veeder men in the 1850s. Since every entry is in pencil, in the same script, it seems likely that she decided to record the information all at once, sometime after they all sailed. The first notation on the page is dated October 4, 1853: "Sailed ship *Young Hector*, George A." Only five months after their return to the island, eighteen-year-old George shipped out as fourth mate, indicating that he had proven himself more than worthy on the *Nauticon*. Although the lowest-ranking officer, he was a notch above boatsteerer, or harpooneer, and decidedly removed from the forecastle hands, who included four other young men from Nantucket, and he was in company with thirty-year-old third mate Franklin S. Barnard, also from the island. Along with Barnard and the two other mates, George would now be in charge of one of the whaleboats on the *Young Hector*, a New Bedford whaleship under the command of Captain Peter G. Smith, who had arrived in Tahiti in April 1852 with a full cargo when the *Nauticon* was there. One wonders how many whales George harpooned when he was on his father's ship, whether he was a chip off the old block, with a chance at becoming a captain in the next decade. He sailed away and did not return to the island for three and a half years. The voyage was modestly successful, garnering 1,170 barrels of sperm oil, earning George a little money.

Although Captain Veeder must have been quite proud of the son he had mentored, he was not ready to abdicate his position as the preeminent mariner of the family, and his employers, the Starbuck brothers, were glad to have the experienced and trustworthy captain back in town and prime for another voyage. So confident were they of his abilities in the whale fishery, they contracted with Josiah Holmes Jr. and his brothers, shipbuilders in Mattapoisett, Massachusetts, to build the *Ocean Rover,* a 417-ton ship, 119 feet long—larger than the 372-ton, 106-footlong *Nauticon*—for

Ship believed to be the *Ocean Rover* in Hong Kong harbor, 1858, by a Chinese artist.

Courtesy of William T. Vinal

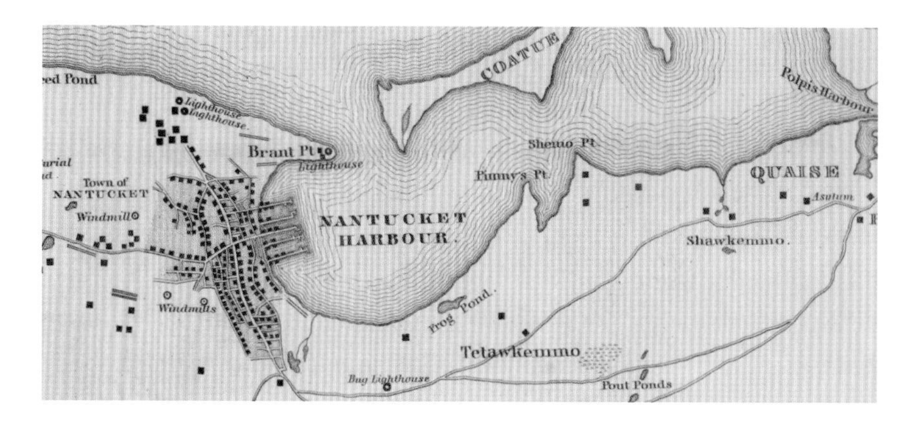

Detail from *Map of the Island of Nantucket, Including Tuckernuck*, surveyed by William Mitchell, 1838.

Courtesy of the Norman B. Leventhal Map and Education Center, Boston Public Library

Veeder's next voyage. Admiration of Veeder may not have been universal, however. Nantucket Captain Joseph Marshall, who was at sea on the *Sea Queen* of Westport, Massachusetts, commented in a letter home to his brother-in-law in 1855 that he had heard that the Starbuck brothers were going to build a new ship for Captain Veeder: "they must have a quantity of money on hand and do not know what to do with it." Whether that barb was directed at the chosen captain, or the ship owners, or both, is not entirely clear; it may also have been a comment about the whale fishery in general. Marshall, who had been at sea since 1851, expressed his eagerness to get home to Nantucket "in its flourishing state—new Steam Boats, streets lighted with gas, and folks riding with splendid grays."

Awaiting his new ship, Captain Veeder was ashore with no occupation, and he was not a man to be idle. Like many other master mariners on the island, he owned a farm in the fertile crescent of the island that extended from Monomoy to Pocomo on the south side of the Great Harbor. In 1841, he had purchased a fifteen-acre tract in Shimmo, a name meaning "a spring" in the Algonquian language of the local Wampanoags. Before the family sailed on the *Nauticon* in 1848, he acquired several more adjacent parcels of land in the area near Shimmo Spring, increasing his plot to twenty-eight acres. Salt meadow and farmland along the harbor was not expensive in the 1840s; the combined purchases cost less than $200. When the property was sold almost twenty years later, it included a farmhouse, barn, and outbuildings, indicating that a considerable amount of time and energy and money had been expended on the farm project. It is a stunning piece of property. Standing on a rise at the south end of the acreage, one has a view of little undulating hills, a tidal inlet bordered by rushes, a strip of beach along the harbor, and, from the beach, the town is clearly visible, rising from the wharves up to Quanaty hill where the gold dome of the Unitarian Meeting House presides. The natural grasses that grew in the area made hay for cattle, which was probably Veeder's primary concern there. Some of the wealthier gentleman farmers of the island experimented with fancy fruits, growing quinces, peaches, and multiple varieties of pears, while others raised purebred livestock in an era of agrarian reawakening necessitated by an increasingly impoverished island population. Shimmo was a prime location for an agricultural endeavor, but it's doubtful that Veeder's heart was in it. Before he sailed on the new *Ocean Rover* in 1855, he advertised "four good cows for sale." Better to liquidate livestock than to invest in a farmhand, if one could be found on an island with a diminishing population of men. Although the farm might not have been productive agriculturally, Susan and family enjoyed an occasional outing to it, a three-mile carriage ride from their house on Orange Street—through the Newtown gate near the present rotary and out to Milestone One on the seven-mile-long Siasconset Road, then northeast on the Polpis Road through the rolling hills south of the harbor, and north on what is now Gardner Road out to Pimney's Point, directly across from the first point of five-pointed Coatue, the serpent of sand that forms the barrier beach on the north side of the harbor. An alternative, shorter, and decidedly preferable route was by boat up the harbor to the waterfront property that today is one of the choicest pieces of real estate on the island. Charles had the opportunity to teach his sons the finer points of rowing a whaleboat on their trips up harbor, how to put their backs into it and dig in with the oars, and then as they approached an imaginary whale to make a shallow, quiet dip of the oar, glide, whisper, and brace themselves for an encounter.

The Veeders weren't the only ones to own a farm along the harbor: in the 1850s there were more than a hundred farms on Nantucket, six of them in Shimmo and more than two dozen farther down the Polpis Road. It's curious that Veeder sold his farm in 1859, just a year after his return from sea on the *Ocean Rover*, at a time when he had no other prospects for a livelihood. The Nantucket Agricultural Society had been founded in his absence in order to encourage the cultivation of crops and improvement of livestock by the growing number of farm-owners on the island. Prizes were awarded at annual fairs, which drew not only local crowds but visitors from the mainland. Veeder's investment in the land had matured; carpenter William B. Gardner paid a thousand dollars for the Veeder farm, which included "all those tracts, parcels, and pieces of land and the dwelling house, barns, and outbuildings standing thereon." The Shimmo farm may have been an investment all along as there is no indication that Captain Veeder participated in the annual Agricultural Fair in the period 1856 to 1859, or, if he did, that his livestock garnered any prizes. Perhaps he refused to align himself with the motto displayed on a banner during the first fair: "If no harvest of oil, let us return to the soil." His preferred pasture was the Pacific.

* * *

In 1853, Charles Veeder's personal and real estate were assessed by the town at $7,000, and the tax due on that amount was $63.12, sums that were published in the Inquirer, along with the assessments of 164 other men who owed fifty dollars or more in taxes—in other words, the wealthiest men on the island. Veeder was at the bottom of the list, ranking about one-hundred-thirty-fifth, but many other well-known mariners of the era didn't even make the cut. It was the whale-oil merchants and ship owners who reaped the profits in the whaling industry. The real and personal property of the Starbuck brothers was ten times that of Veeder, and their father, Joseph Starbuck, was the richest man on the island, with an estate worth $222,104. William Hadwen, who built the two Greek Revival mansions on Main Street just a few years earlier, was a close second at $209,775.

A man of substance, with a house and a farm and a ship under construction for him to take to sea, Veeder made a rather odd decision in the fall of 1854; he decided to run for the office of state representative. It was a time of political upheaval on Nantucket and elsewhere in the country, the end of the old two-party system of Democrats and Whigs, who were now joined locally by the Know Nothing and People's Ticket parties. Six hundred and eighteen men voted for state representative on the island on November 15, 1854; 310 votes were required for a win, and nobody won. There were three Whig candidates, three Democrats, three People's Ticket, two Know Nothings, and one candidate who claimed to be both Know Nothing and People's Ticket. This last man had the highest number of votes but not enough to claim victory; a second vote two weeks later elected him and a fellow Know Nothing candidate to the state assembly. Veeder garnered seventy-five votes the first go round, and his two Democratic co-candidates polled similarly, with eighty and seventy-five votes. Two weeks later, the Democrats lost about thirty votes each to the winners, and Charles was denied a political career that would have taken him to the State House on Beacon Hill in Boston in 1855. Instead, the forty-six-year-old captain took the *Ocean Rover* to sea.

Before he sailed, the captain drew up a legal document that would be put to good use by his wife many years later; it was a power of attorney, granting Susan the right, among other things, to "sell and convey any and all real estate now belonging and which may belong to me." The good captain probably did not consider that his wife might use that document to protect herself financially from his follies. In the local press on July 11, 1855, the day of his departure, Veeder was referred to as "one of our most successful and energetic shipmasters." In a brief entry in her diary that day, Nantucketer Hepsabeth Russell Bunker recorded that the *Ocean Rover* sailed from Hyannis, with Captain Veeder, mate Peter Raymond, and David S. Veeder on board. Did Susan allow her youngest son, now thirteen, to accompany his father on another whaling voyage, this time without her supervision? It's not clear, since Susan recorded other information about David, who may have only temporarily been on the *Ocean Rover*.

For a year or two, Susan and Charles Edward, and perhaps David, too, were home together on Nantucket, and eight-year-old Susie Veeder Foster joined the household in 1856, when her mother, Eliza, died of consumption at the age of twenty-nine. The loss of her younger sister was a blow to Susan, following the deaths of her mother in December 1853 and her father in February 1856. The 1850s were abundant in tragedy for the Veeder family, but having her niece and namesake in the household was a comfort; had Mary Frances lived, she would have been almost the same age.

If his mother's notation is correct, young David Veeder got his opportunity to go to sea in 1857, when he was fifteen, sailing on the New Bedford ship *Gladiator* with Captain Peter Cromwell of Martha's Vineyard. Susan noted that the ship arrived at Honolulu on November 4 "in charge of the mate, the captain having died off Cape Horn." In a gale in that notorious passage, Captain Cromwell fell headfirst from the main rigging onto the deck, sustaining injuries that led to his death a day later. If David was on board, he witnessed a sobering accident, reminiscent of Mr. Robert's fall to the deck of the *Nauticon* in the Bering Sea. Hard to know which was worse, to hit the deck and maim yourself, or to fall into a watery grave. Each tragic accident observed was a cautionary tale in the mariner's personal anthology. Luckily, David returned home unscathed in 1858, just a day after his father. Susan recorded their arrivals in her diary in October:

> *Tuesday, the 19th: today is a very pleasant day. This afternoon called on Mrs. Cash also on Mrs. Fuller—this eve have been into Aunt Deborah, at half past eight we was agreeably surprised by the arrival of my husband not knowing anything until he rapped at the door. Happy news. His health not very good.*

> *Wednesday, the 20th: today fine weather expect my son David S. from Edgartown this afternoon. Invited to a party to Edward's. My husband not able to go. This evening at 9 o'clock David S. arrived well rejoiced to get home. Happy meeting.*

She must have been ecstatic—husband and youngest son home safe and sound! That David arrived just a day after his father brings up the question of the boy possibly having been with Captain Veeder on the *Ocean Rover* the whole time. But why would Susan have noted his sailing on the *Gladiator?* A logbook kept on the *Ocean Rover* by an unidentified crew member, most likely the first mate, makes no mention of the captain's son on board, but it is primarily a record of wind, weather, and ship duties, so the lack of evidence is not proof. Perhaps David left the *Gladiator* and joined the *Ocean Rover* in Honolulu. It is not an impossible scenario. The *Ocean Rover* arrived in Maui on November 7, 1857, and remained there until the twenty-sixth, then sailed to Oahu on the twenty-seventh, so there was ample opportunity for Captain Veeder to meet up with the *Gladiator* and collect David from a ship that had lost its captain.

The spanking new *Ocean Rover* proved to be a fine ship for Captain Veeder, and he managed to fill it with sperm oil in a little over three years. He revisited Pitcairn Island, cruised again in the Tuamotus, and spent time in Tahiti where three men ended up in the local calaboose for bad behavior and three others deserted, the usual problems encountered when crew had liberty on a South Pacific island. The *Nauticon*'s dismal hunting and near peril in the Arctic on his previous voyage was a lesson learned; this time the captain headed to the Bonin Islands, near Japan, and from there to the Carolines, where the crew had liberty on Strong's Island. Instead of three men deserting, they gained three stowaways. From the Carolines the *Ocean Rover* sailed to the Sandwich Islands, where the captain may have found his son, David. Crisscrossing the vast expanse of the Pacific, the ship arrived in Hong Kong in February 1858, and, while the carpenter and blacksmith were at work caulking and painting the ship, Charles Veeder went ashore, carrying with him an image of his wife. He found a suitable artist and commissioned the portrait of elegant Susan in her Mona Lisa pose.

George Veeder had arrived back on the island in June of 1857, soon after the *Young Hector* sailed into the busy New Bedford harbor, but he was more than likely at sea again in October 1858 when David and the captain returned. Although a complete record of his voyages does not exist, it would have been customary for him to seek employment fairly soon in order to advance his position as a mariner. The only member of the family definitely not home was Charles Edward, who managed to be on Nantucket when his family was at sea, and at sea when his family was on Nantucket. According to Susan's brief journal entry, he had sailed on the ship *Flying Eagle* under Captain John Warren Bates on a trading voyage from Boston to San Francisco in 1856. Compared to a whaleship, the *Flying Eagle* was huge—1,094 tons—and reputed to be the fastest sailing vessel afloat at the time. In the "Marine News" section of the *Inquirer*, December 8, 1856, there is notice of the departure of the ship for San Francisco, and two lines down in the same column "Heard from July 20th, on Kodiak Ground, ship *Ocean Rover*, Veeder, Nant, 250 sp[erm]."

The length of the voyage that Charles Edward began in 1856 was relatively short because he was on another clipper ship, *Midnight*, under Captain George H. Brock of Nantucket, also on a passage from Boston to San Francisco, in December 1858, when he was lost overboard. The *Midnight* had proved her speed in 1854, when she made the run from Boston to San Francisco in 117 days, attaining a sailing speed that would have made it impossible to retrieve someone who had the misfortune to be swept from the deck in rough seas or to fall from a climb into the rigging. With Captain Brock on the *Midnight* were his wife and six-year-old daughter, Susan Emma, who later in life wrote the story of her trip to the Pacific in a little book called *Doubling Cape Horn*. The ship sailed from Boston, and, on the first night at sea, in a heavy squall, Charles E. Veeder fell overboard. Brock relates that someone trying to assist the drowning man had removed the steps that led from the upper to the lower deck and thrown them overboard, where they might serve as a life preserver.

Unaware of this, her father fell down the stair-less passage and knocked himself out cold. "Youth and a strong constitution were on his side, and he soon recovered but the unfortunate seaman (a native of Nantucket) was never seen again." Brock's memoir focuses on her father's frightening injury, rendering Veeder an unnamed aside in her tale of parental mishap. News of twenty-year-old Charles E. Veeder's death in December 1858 was not reported in the local newspaper until May 1859. Although the telegraph had been invented and was used along the East Coast and into the Midwest, it was not yet transcontinental, so months passed before the Veeders on Nantucket knew their son had been lost not far offshore from his home island.

Susan's relief that David and the captain had returned in October 1858 was indeed short lived. When David went back to sea is not known, but he did, and, like his brother, never came home. "Lost at sea" is all that is written beside his name in local genealogies: no date, no record of ship or circumstances for the boy who had grown up on a whaleship. The editor of the *Inquirer* expressed the sentiment of the maritime community when he wrote about three young men, all victims of accidents at sea, in January 1860:

Susan Emma Brock (1852–1937), carte de visite by E. T. Kelley, 1850s.

Gift of Grace Brown Gardner, CDV1018

> *. . . these casualties on shipboard never fail to strike us with extreme sadness. From sudden death "Good Lord deliver us," says the eloquent liturgy of the Church; and when the news comes from some vessel alone on the ocean, that an ingenuous youth has been plunged into a watery grave, with no requiem but the wailing of the winds through the tense cordage, away—far away from home, we would fain respond- Good Lord deliver us! It may be our boy next! Kelley, Veeder, Swain, all three ingenuous youths, within a short period have been snatched away, never more to respond to parental affection, till the sea shall give up its dead.*

The editor may have been referring to Charles Edward, or news of David's death may have been recently received. All that is certain is that David met his fate before the Civil War, that other devourer of young men; his name never appears in lists of those Nantucketers who served nor on local draft lists. He last appears in the 1860 U.S. Federal Census of Nantucket, listed as a mariner, and assumed to be living.

* * *

THE 1860S BEGAN with some long-overdue happiness for the Veeder family. Susan, who was almost forty-four years old, gave birth on April 11 to Marianna, and five months later, on September 11, twenty-five-year-old George married Sarah Starbuck Winslow, two years his junior. The young Miss Winslow was the daughter of Shubael and Ann, one of twelve children in a large family that included nine-year-old brother Thomas, who would go to sea with Captain Veeder eight years later. Winslows had been on Nantucket since the late eighteenth century, and although many of the men in the family worked as mariners and ship captains, Sarah's father was a butcher. He more than likely provided the main course for the wedding feast while George's middle-aged parents showed off their baby girl.

In July 1860, between the birth of his daughter and the marriage of his son, Captain Veeder traveled to New York on the steamer *Island Home* with six other local whaling captains to see the largest vessel afloat at the time, the *Great Eastern,* a gigantic British steamship made of iron and equipped with five steam engines and six masts. After several years of trial and mishap, the *Great Eastern* had made her maiden voyage to the United States. An explosion on a previously attempted voyage may have deterred greater participation, but the trial voyage was completed successfully in ten days. The Nantucket whaling captains marveled at the 682-foot-long ship with a capacity of almost nineteen thousand tons, longer than five or more whaling vessels combined. And they had much to discuss about the future of ocean travel. In fact, during their junket to New York they came up with the idea of forming the Pacific Club—a social club for mariners who had rounded Cape Horn or the Cape of Good Hope—in order to continue meeting and discussing and of course reminiscing about the golden days of Nantucket whaling. The seven men are the founders of the club and all of them but Veeder were among the twenty-four shareholders who purchased the surviving Rotch warehouse at the foot of Main Street for a permanent home for their club. Why Veeder chose not to invest is a mystery; he had recently sold his farm in Shimmo and had money in the bank. He was never one to follow the herd, however, and a future that included sitting around a coal stove and talking about the past may not have been that appealing.

One of the best descriptions of the island at this fallow period between whaling and the advent of the next all-encompassing industry, tourism, appeared in *Harper's New Monthly Magazine* in November 1860, as part of a series titled "A Summer in New England," written and illustrated by Porte Crayon, the pen name of New York artist and travel writer Henry David Strother.

> *On entering the harbor of Nantucket one is impressed on every hand by the signs of decadence. A few battered and dismantled hulks of whale ships sleep alongside the lethargic old wharves; quiet listless seeming people saunter about with an aimless air very uncommon in New England; grass-grown streets and dingy warehouses all combine to complete the picture of departed*

glory. No not of departed glory: I mean, simply, "old decadent commercial prosperity"; for the fame of Nantucket is historic, and the glory of having given birth to the boldest and most enterprising mariners that ever furrowed the seas is hers, imperishable and forever.

Also remarkable to the New York journalist was the "great preponderance of women and children," which gave the town a "cheerful and homelike air." From a population of almost ten thousand in 1840 to less than half of that twenty years later, women, children, and old men were left to make a life on Nantucket, and Captain Veeder, for one, did not like being

***Old Custom House, Nantucket,* by Hubert G. Ripley, 1922. The founders of the Pacific Club purchased the eighteenth-century Rotch warehouse on Straight Wharf at the foot of Main Street as their headquarters. The building has housed many offices and businesses over the years, once serving as the Customs House, as pictured here.**

Gift of Mrs. A. E. Thurber Jr., 1975.56.8

one of the old men. At fifty-one years old he was virile and ambitious, but his future as a whaling captain was bleak. During the Civil War years, from 1861 to 1865, only eight whaling voyages were attempted from Nantucket, and only one was successful, the *Islander,* under the command of neighbor William Cash, husband of Susan's friend Azubah, bringing home an astounding 2,400 barrels of sperm oil from a Pacific voyage. Veeder must have been itchy to get back to sea, but ocean voyages of all kinds were in jeopardy, and the war was the final calamity that knocked the town of Nantucket off its feet. The Great Fire more than a dozen years earlier was the first harbinger of gloom for the whaling town, and even though there was a rapid rebuilding of the burnt commercial district and renewed effort to regain a foothold in an industry that was shifting to New Bedford, it could not be maintained. The entrance to Nantucket's harbor was just not deep enough for the bigger and bigger vessels built for the longer voyages necessitated by the scarcity of an overhunted population of sperm whales. After 1859, when it was discovered that petroleum could be procured by drilling in the ground, chasing gigantic cetaceans around the globe for years at a time in a treacherous pursuit requiring massive capital for an uncertain return was no longer seen as an intelligent investment.

The last able-bodied young men on the island desperate for work volunteered for the Union army and navy, for the $100 local bounty plus a $100 federal bounty and a regular paycheck. There was no denying that Nantucket was now dead in the water—no industry and a steady exodus to the mainland. George Veeder, twenty-seven and married, avoided service, but by the end of the summer of 1862 more than four hundred Nantucket volunteers, mostly teenagers or men in their twenties, had left the island for the battlefields of the continent, or to serve in the Union navy. By 1863, with the war dragging on and more men needed, George's name appeared on a list of men to be drafted if the town's quota was not filled by volunteers, but that was never the case. In recognition of its generous enlistments, Nantucket was known as a "banner town" of Massachusetts, but it was not patriotism alone that spurred the participation, it was poverty.

This sketch of New North Wharf (now Steamboat Wharf) in 1852 by George G. Fish shows a laid-up whaleship and three vessels that connected the island to the mainland at that time—the steamers *Telegraph* and *Massachusetts* and the packet sloop *Tawtemeo*.

Gift of George C. Fish, 1895.143.1

Susan found herself busy with girls for a change—her new daughter, Marianna, and niece, Susie, who was twelve years old in 1860. Around this time, another niece, Rachel Veeder, daughter of Charles's brother David, joined the family for a spell. Her mother had died in 1860, when she was thirteen, and Charles, visiting his relatives after his return from the *Ocean Rover* voyage, must have thought Susan would welcome another girl, almost the same age as young Susie. Rachel had a grand time on the island, entertained by her aunt's and uncle's "exciting tales and experiences, in the world's most strange and exotic ports and seas." Charles, ever the craftsman, carved an ivory cane for her, which became a family heirloom. If Rachel came to the island in 1860, she may have returned home with Charles when his father died three years later. Peter, who had evaded the criminal charges against him in 1832 and moved to North Greece, New York, died on December 4, 1863. The captain's mother had died seven years previously when he was at sea on the *Ocean Rover*. He inherited family property amounting to a hundred acres that was equally divided with his siblings, but all his father's personal estate, including livestock, was left to him. He had business to settle and family to reconnect with; it was probably the last time he saw them.

No longer the lone female in a household, or ship, full of boys and men, Susan could dote on her baby and rest easy that the close community of women would help her see the child through whatever illness or accident might arise. This time around she was not stranded in a strange South American port town, wondering if Charles and the boys would return. George and his family lived nearby; Charles was home; Susie, Rachel, and Marianna filled the house with laughter, and the others were beyond her care. In the summer of 1861, George and Sarah had their first child, Charles E., named for the brother who fell from the *Midnight*. Three years later they had a daughter, too, Mary Frances, named for his sister, the darling of the *Nauticon,* who died in Tahiti in 1851.

CHAPTER SIX

Song of the Siren

Whoever draws too close, off guard, and catches the Sirens' voices in the air— no sailing home for him, no wife rising to meet him, no happy children beaming up at their father's face.

— Homer, *The Odyssey*

For ten years Charles Veeder wondered if he would ever go whaling again; not since he was a boy had he remained on the island for more than two years at a time. Bored and restless, he was desperate to escape the whirlpool that was sucking the life out of Nantucket. The population of the island was still declining in the 1860s, as the economy suffered withdrawal pains from the demise of its all-encompassing industry. In 1865, fewer than five thousand people lived on the island and ten years later no more than thirty-five hundred. Nantucket was a ghost town in the making. One resident, the talented but lonely daughter of a retired whaling captain, wrote to a friend in Philadelphia, "There is nothing whatever for me to tell you about us here in Nantucket. We do the same things, and see the same people day after day and year after year and I suppose we shall until we die or blow away or something." The community had paid a heavy toll in the Civil War; more than four hundred men enlisted and seventy-four died, falling in battle, wasting away in prison, or succumbing to disease. Many who returned home were sick or wounded. Those men who were able-bodied and ambitious, who would have worked as mariners or tradesmen when the whaling industry was booming, left the island looking for work, while local girls flocked to the straw-hat factory on Main Street, the island's largest employer, albeit a short-lived one. In its last decade of whaling, from 1859 to 1869, Nantucket sent out only twenty-two ships, about the same number the island had launched yearly in the 1830s, and G. & M. Starbuck, Veeder's employers on his three previous voyages, had gotten out of the increasingly unprofitable whale oil business. Their last ship, *Hero,* sailed in 1860, and was wrecked in Algoa Bay, South Africa, in 1861.

Even as petroleum gradually replaced whale oil, New Bedford refused to give up whaling, filling the void left by Nantucket's disinclination with more than seventy ships in 1859 alone and forty a decade later. So, if you were a whaling captain and wanted work in the 1860s, New Bedford was the place to be. Nantucket had a surfeit of captains; most of them, like Charles Veeder, were in their late fifties and had retired from the business, content to try a little farming or local fishing. But Charles was not content. He had run for the state legislature before his voyage on the *Ocean Rover*; he had served as one of the town's selectmen when he returned, and in 1865 he was on a committee to investigate the future of Nantucket as a "watering place" or summer resort. But it wasn't enough. The man who was accustomed to ruling his floating kingdom with an iron hand and a lucky harpoon missed the power and responsibility, the *liveliness* of it all. One more day of walking up Orange Street to town, sitting with the prevaricating old salts at the Pacific Club, reading the newspapers and then walking home again to Susan in the house she managed very well without him, a house that sat in the same spot and offered the same view day after day—well, damn.

He needed a ship.

And somehow, he got one. The 320-ton bark *William Gifford* was built in Mattapoisett, Massachusetts, in 1858, named for the New Bedford merchant who owned her. Ten years later William Gifford was dead, but his son, Charles, and other heirs owned most of the shares of the vessel. On her maiden voyage under Captain Nehemiah Baker, she brought home a cargo of oil and whalebone from the North Pacific and then turned around for another voyage, this time to Hudson's Bay from 1863 to 1868, avoiding a transit through the Atlantic during the Civil War. In 1868, she was ready to go again, and Captain Veeder was selected to take her into the Pacific.

It's not clear how he managed to get the job; there were plenty of master mariners in New Bedford and dozens more in Nantucket. Although he had a solid reputation and years of experience, so did a lot of others. The market for whalebone was strong and bowheads were easier to find than sperm whales, but Veeder was a sperm-whale fisherman, determined to hunt down the remnants of that once thriving population. He must have talked a good game, convincing Gifford that if anybody could bring home a trove of spermaceti without the risk of losing a ship in the icy Arctic home of the bowheads, he could. His experience in the Arctic with Susan in 1851 was enough for him: if that's where all the other whalemen were headed, he would go elsewhere.

Sketch of the *William Gifford*, from Edward J. Kirwin's journal of the *William Gifford*, 1871–72.

Courtesy of the New Bedford Whaling Museum, KWM Log 452

And what an opportunity for some of the island's young men to go with him, to learn the business from one of the best, and to continue the tradition of excellence in whaling that was a Nantucket boy's heritage. The *Whalemen's Shipping List,* a New Bedford newspaper focused solely on the whaling industry, reported on August 4, 1868:

> *Bark William Gifford, Capt. Charles A. Veeder, of Nantucket, sailed from this port Aug. 1st, 1868, for the Pacific Ocean . . . .*

Thirty-one persons composed the crew of the *William Gifford,* including three Nantucket teenagers: the youngest, George A. Cash, was fifteen; Albert C. Folger was sixteen; and Thomas C. Winslow was seventeen. Their fates were in the capable hands of the captain.

In his portrait painted in the mid-1840s, before the voyage of the *Nauticon,* the captain looks kind, capable, and handsome. He was a man on the rise: prosperous, a homeowner with a growing family of boys on an island famous for intrepid sea captains. He had a hardy wife. In a photograph from the mid-1860s, he had devolved into a tired and disappointed-looking man, the corners of his mouth drooping, his eyes sunken and jowls sagging, the result of years at sea plus a decade at home on Nantucket, watching the decline. He had lost two sons and a daughter. And no one had yet been told to smile for a camera.

* * *

WHAT WE KNOW about the progress of the *William Gifford* between 1868 and 1871 we learn from Susan, who decided to keep a diary of her life on the island when Charles set sail. She would have a record of domestic events and local news to share with him when he came home, and they could compare notes: the day he got his first sperm whale she visited her sister-in-law, or when he was becalmed in the Pacific she was sweeping snow from the front steps.

Although she had written a few entries in her diary in 1858, she stopped

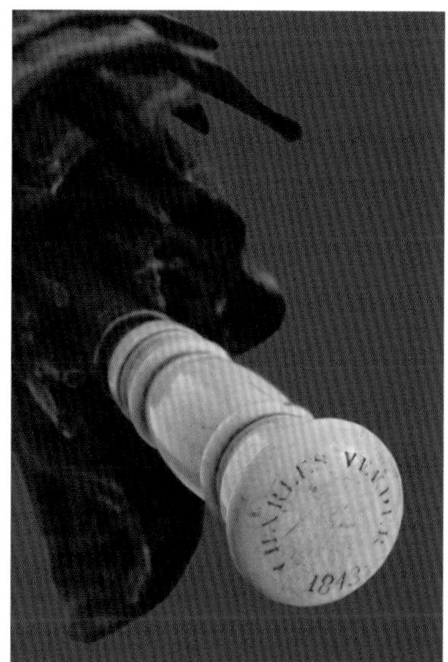

Left: **Charles A. Veeder (1809–1878), 1860s** *A86-29*

Right: **Whale-ivory handle engraved "Charles Veeder / 1843." Probably made as the handle of a cane, it was reused as an umbrella grip at an unknown date.**

Gift of Ariel Vinal, 2018.29.1

soon after Captain Veeder and David returned from voyages in October. Finding the almost-blank book ten years later, she decided to put it to use, to memorialize the noteworthy events of her life while Charles was away, first dipping her pen in the inkpot after she and eight-year-old Marianna accompanied the captain to New Bedford to wave goodbye. Charles Edward and David had both sailed away into oblivion and were, in Melville's words, "bundled into eternity." Mother and daughter wondered if the captain would meet the same fate. On August 1, 1868, Susan wrote, "my husband left home to sail on a whaling voyage in Bark *William Gifford* with a fair wind and fine weather."

In the period 1868 to 1871, Susan noted in her journal the receipt of a dozen letters from her husband. In October, she got letters from Fayal, in the Azores, where Captain Veeder had stopped for fresh fruit. Susan received her next letter on February 2, 1869, written from Paita, Peru. She noted that

Charles was well and had one hundred barrels of oil, whether whale oil or sperm oil she doesn't say, but most, if not all, of it (we know from other sources) was the latter—the kind that mattered. On May 11 she had "a good long letter" from Charles, and ten days later another one arrived, this one from Tahiti, where all was well. No more news until December 14, 1869, when a letter dated October 28 informed her that Charles had seen whales only twice, had gotten no more oil, and was on his way to the "Marquesan Islands."

From Tahiti to the Marquesas eight hundred miles distant, the *William Gifford* sailed through the Paumoto Group, or the Tuamotus, another locale Susan was familiar with, one she had painted in her *Nauticon* journal. Captain Veeder wrote his wife two letters from somewhere in the archipelago, "reporting him well with 320 [barrels of oil] all told and had discharged his mate sick." By March 1871 she knew that he had more than a thousand barrels of oil, and letters received in June assured her that all was well and he had shipped a new mate, Mr. Haughton. She had no reason to be concerned; her husband was healthy and the hold was filling with oil. She could easily imagine where he was and what he was doing, because she had been there.

Of course, the captain would not have enlightened her about the activities that one of the seamen on board the *William Gifford* found most interesting. Edward J. Kirwin, on his first whaling voyage, kept a daily account of the captain's activities over the course of Veeder's yearlong descent into alcohol-fueled desperation. When we meet the narrator of the journal of the *William Gifford* on May 17, 1871, he is twenty years old. After three years at sea he was a sailor who knew his ropes, sails, wind, and weather, and, from a poem he penned in his journal, we learn that he had a copy of *The Kedge Anchor, or Young Sailor's Assistant*, an often reprinted guide to all the parts and mechanisms of a sailing vessel:

When freshly blows the northern gale
Then under courses snug we fly
When lighter breezes swell the sails
Then royals proudly sweep the sky.

Maybe his mother gave him the book when he was seventeen and eager to go to sea, and he memorized the sails and rigging that by 1871 had become as familiar to him as his own shirt—he could splice a main brace, overhaul the davits' tackle blocks, send down a main topgallant yard, and loose a foresail. His journal is replete with the chores of the day, from basic sailing to wetting down the hold to keep the wooden casks of oil tight—but its real value for our story is his record of the downward spiral of Captain Veeder, whom he often refers to as the "Old Man," a common nickname for captains and, in Veeder's case, an appropriate one. Unlike Susan, Kirwin writes in his journal *every* day. He is observant of people but not descriptive of the seascapes and landscapes of the South Seas; instead, he records action. He must have been aware of the shock value of his narrative if read by the folks at home, or the trouble he would be in if the captain got his hands on the journal, but he wrote anyway, providing a rare record of South Seas shenanigans. The misbehavior of whaling crews and their captains and mates in that part of the world may not have been so rare, but detailed eyewitness accounts are.

The journal begins Friday, May 19, 1871, with the *William Gifford* lying in the blue waters off Tahiti. The captain is ashore at Papeete, and the mate's family is on board. Kirwin and "Ed" have been ashore, too, and "were aft this evening singing to the girls." Haughton's daughters, presumably. Innocent enough. In her journal, Susan informed us of Haughton's identity as a newly shipped mate, but we don't know why the captain was ashore until a few days later:

> *A boat went ashore this morning after the Capt. and he come off dead drunk. They raised whales from the ship while we were gone but lost run of them in stopping for the boat, seen them again at 2 ½ p.m. and lowered three boats, 2nd, 3rd, & 4th mates. They each got one. The Capt. knew nothing at all about it until the whales were nearly dead . . . .*
> (May 23, 1871)

The next day while the crew was cutting and boiling the blubber, "the stowaway Frenchman made his appearance" and the "after gang all drunk."

Thus begins the story of the voyage of the last year of the *William Gifford*, when, in the course of a year, the captain is noted as being drunk on eleven occasions, usually for more than one day and, in one instance, for more than twelve days straight. He is rivaled by the first mate, who is generally described as either half-drunk or so drunk he can't stand up, and, in one spectacular bout of inebriation that lasted sixteen days, the thoroughly besotted mate was spotted parading on the shore at Nuku Hiva in a woman's dress. This was not an ordinary whaling voyage, at least not as recorded by other logbook keepers and journal writers, who knew better than to describe what would not be well received by ship-owners—or wives, girlfriends, sisters, and mothers. The source of distraction for the captain and mates was not only alcohol, it was women, and, in particular, the captain's woman, variously referred to by Kirwin as the captain's

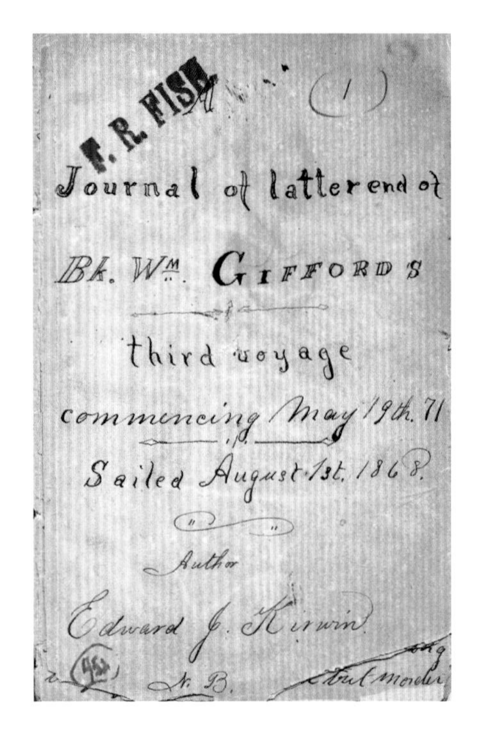
F. R. FISH (1)
Journal of latter end of
Bk. Wm. GIFFORD'S
third voyage
commencing May 19th. 71
Sailed August 1st. 1868.
Author
Edward J. Kirwin
452 N. B.

Title page of Edward J. Kirwin's journal of the *William Gifford*, 1871–72.

Courtesy of the New Bedford Whaling Museum, KWM Log 452

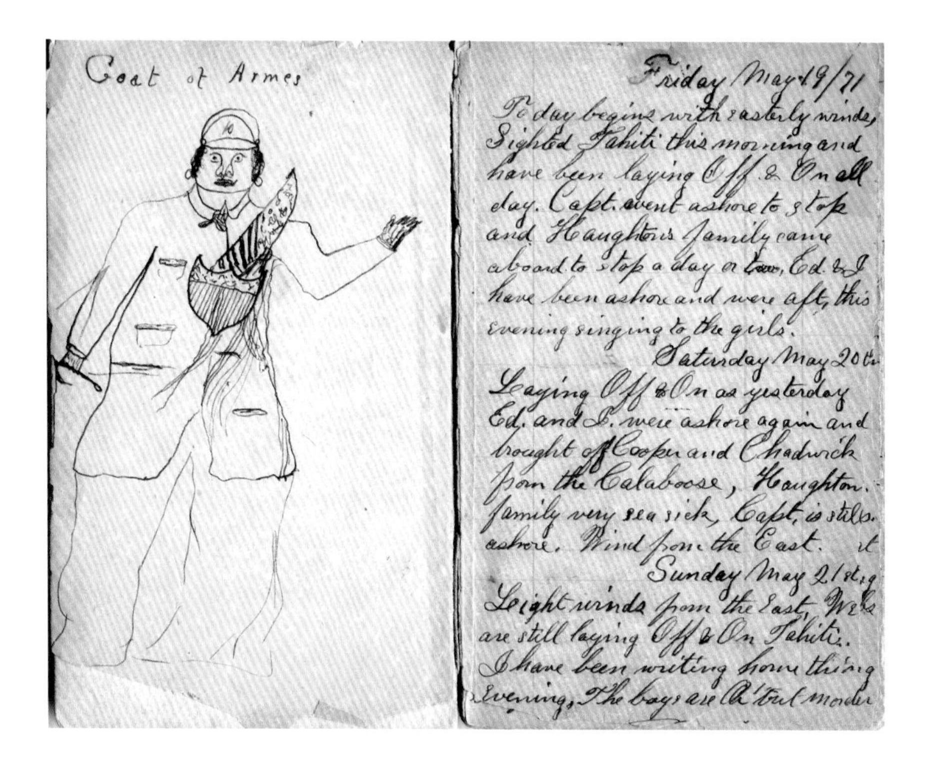
Coat of Armes

Friday May 19/71
Th day begins with easterly winds,
Sighted Tahiti this morning and
have been laying Off & On all
day. Capt. went ashore to stop
and Haughton's family came
aboard to stop a day or two, Ed. & I
have been ashore and were aft, this
evening singing to the girls.
Saturday May 20th
Laying Off & On as yesterday
Ed. and I. were ashore again and
brought off Cooper and Chadwick
from the Calaboose, Haughton
family very sea sick, Capt. is still
ashore. Wind from the East.
Sunday May 21st
Light winds from the East, We
are still laying Off & On Tahiti.
I have been writing home this
Evening, The boys are [illegible]

First page of Edward J. Kirwin's journal of the *William Gifford*, 1871–72.

Courtesy of the New Bedford Whaling Museum, KWM Log 452

mistress, concubine, or whore. We never learn her name. She made her appearance when she boarded the *William Gifford* as a passenger from her home, Barclay's Island, to sail on Veeder's ship to nearby Ticoma Island, the same coral atolls now known as Raroia and Takume in the Tuamotu Archipelago, where Susan sailed with her husband twenty years earlier, when he was initially wary of the native population. For a year, from May 1871 to May 1872, Captain Veeder's ship made the circuit from Tahiti to the Tuamotus to the Marquesas—Kirwin names more than thirty islands in the area, but their main cruising ground was off Barclay's Island, home of the unnamed paramour of the Old Man.

Engraved whale tooth depicting a Polynesian woman in a grass skirt, by George Hiliott, mid-nineteenth century.

Gift of Robert Waggaman, 1977.129.2

* * *

Barclay's Island, or Raroia, is one of seventy-eight atolls in the Tuamotu Archipelago, one of the largest archipelagos in the world. Tuamotu means "far-away Islands" in the local Polynesian dialect, the same designation that translates to Nantucket, the far-away island of the Wampanoag Indians, but there are vast differences between the two. Nantucket is only thirty miles from the mainland of North America, lying south of Cape Cod in the North Atlantic; the Tuamotus are *really* in the middle of nowhere, strung loosely between the Society Islands and the Marquesas in the South Pacific. When Susan visited the archipelago with her husband two decades earlier, she referred to the atolls as the "Paumoto" Group, a term that translates as the "conquered or finished islands," in reference to battles lost in regional conflicts. Residents of the area found the name humiliating and petitioned the native assembly in Tahiti in 1851 to change it to Tuamotu. Kirwin used the old term Paumoto in his journal, perhaps because that's what Veeder still called the area, or he may have been familiar with the chart drawn by Charles Wilkes of the U.S. Exploring Expedition in 1839, titled "Low

Archipelago or Paumotu Group," the first survey of area. The coral atolls in the group are each rings of islets, or motus, surrounding a large lagoon; only three of the seventy-eight Tuamotus are singular islands, without lagoons in the middle. The other atolls do not support agriculture, or have much potable water; coconuts, pandanus palms, and fish barely supply the human population. Barclay's Island, as Captain Veeder and his crew called it, is in reality an elliptical chain of two hundred and eighty mostly uninhabited motus, only three of which are sizable enough to support villages, although each is less than three miles long and barely half a mile wide. It is impossible to describe Barclay's, or any of the atolls, without resorting to statistics: in an area twenty-six miles long and almost nine miles wide, most of Barclay's Island is a two-hundred-and-twenty-three-square-mile lagoon, at its deepest one hundred and sixty feet, but full of submerged coral mountains, some barely beneath the surface. When Captain Veeder visited in 1871, a town flourished on Tetou, the largest islet on the east side of the lagoon, but it was destroyed by a massive cyclone in 1878.

* * *

ALTHOUGH THE *WILLIAM GIFFORD* was on a whaling voyage, little time was spent in pursuit of whales in the year that Kirwin recounts, and the sperm whales the crew did manage to kill were as small as they were in that area twenty years earlier. From Tahiti, where the journal begins, the *William Gifford* steered eastward for the Tuamotus, arriving off Barclay's Island and Takume by the middle of June but only stopping for wood; they traded at Tauere, Moller's, and Good Hope islands, and, at the latter, where it was too rugged to land, the islanders brought them 1,063 coconuts. Kirwin was particularly interested in food brought on board the ship; whether helping the steward keep accounts or just hungry, he devotes the better part of many of his journal entries to the number of barrels of beef, or bread, or molasses stowed in the hold or opened for consumption, and he comments bitterly about the difference in the fare of the captain, mates, and guests of the "after" cabins and the meager and often disgusting fare of the crew who lived in the forecastle.

On July 6, the ferrying of islanders began in earnest when Captain Veeder went ashore at Barclay's Island and "brought off two kanakas as passengers to take up to Ticoma Is. as the Gov. is very sick." Presumably the governor, later identified as Mana Mana, was one of those passengers. On July 10, the captain brought off a woman to take up to Ticoma, too, and the next day added a boatload more of Barclay's Island residents, but when the passengers disembarked at their destination on July 12, the woman stayed with Captain Veeder. On July 13, Kirwin informs us she is the captain's "mistress."

Captain Veeder was completely smitten with this woman who was probably a teenager. She was not yet permanently attached to any of the men on Barclay's, and she may not have been a stranger to Captain Veeder. On July 27, Kirwin wrote one of the most alarming, and mysterious, sentences in his journal: "Capt. is still stopping ashore burying a child in a flour bag the kanakas say, which belongs to him." The missing journal of the first three years of the *William Gifford's* voyage might give us a clue to what exactly was going on with Veeder and his woman—or women. Was it really Veeder's child buried so unceremoniously? Was his current mistress the mother, or had he had other liaisons? The captain had lost one child in Tahiti twenty years earlier; the memory of her death and Susan's agony could only contribute to his increasing instability. He and Susan had agreed that they could not bury a child so far from home, but now he was doing just that. And it was a child Susan knew nothing about.

The "kanakas" Kirwin refers to were native South Sea islanders, the term a Hawaiian word for "man" or "person." On many whaling vessels, as on the *William Gifford*, a crew member native to the area would be dubbed "Joe Kanaka." On Nantucket there was even a "Canaka" boarding house, located in the interracial New Guinea neighborhood where African Americans, Cape Verdeans, Azoreans, Sandwich Islanders, and other sailors from around the world found community and accommodation.

On August 1, 1871, Kirwin celebrated three years at sea with some doggerel:

Three years out and all hands well
Wind from the east and blows like H—

Back on Nantucket, Susan wrote in her journal the same day, "Tomorrow my husband's birthday being 62 years." The captain would celebrate by going ashore and bringing back to the ship his mistress and four other women, one for each of the mates. The "Old Man" spent an inordinate amount of time drinking and playing cards on deck with the women: Kirwin notes twelve times in the journal that the captain was playing cards "as usual." On one occasion he borrowed a deck from one of the crew, then threw the cards overboard when he had finished his game, stating he did not allow card-playing on his ship. When seaman Thomas Winslow of Nantucket, brother of George Veeder's wife, refused to let the captain

Polynesian man, or kanaka, holding a spear and a rifle, engraved on a whale tooth by George Hiliott, mid-nineteenth century.

Gift of Robert Waggaman, 1977.141.1

borrow his cards, they were promptly confiscated and thrown overboard. It was all work if you were in the fo'c'sle, all play if you were one of the officers aft. Kirwin began to grumble about the conditions on board:

> *Hauled aback off Nehiru Is. at 3 p.m. for a canoe to come off. Then lowered a boat and the mate and his woman went ashore after fish and coconuts, towing the canoe astern. They brought off a kanaka, his wife, and two children to take up to Ticoma Is. We broke out water, vinegar, and killed two pigs and got a soup forward made out of the bones and skins as usual. The women aft are all making dresses and get us many a job by communicating with them.*
> (August 3, 1871)

From Kirwin's reportage, it appears that while the crew were not allowed contact with the women on board, Captain Veeder gradually went native. He spent most of his time with his Barclay's Island friends, entertaining the women with fishing and shell-collecting expeditions on some of the islands and instructing the carpenter, Chadwick, to make "chests for those that have women." To further amuse them all, the captain "fired off four bomb lances to please the women," which Kirwin notes cost "Charley Gifford," the ship-owner, sixteen dollars. The lances, of course, were for killing whales, not pyrotechnics, but the next day Veeder fired off three more, "the women all raising the devil around deck in the afternoon and no work going on." When Captain Veeder was not entertaining on board, he spent time ashore, having ship's provisions sent to him:

> *Sent a boat in at 4 p.m. with the Capt.'s victuals and the women which we brought off the other day, 'four.' The ship came near going ashore while the officers were playing with the women and the mate half drunk. I was at the wheel and the mast head men came down.*
> (August 23, 1871)

The men on the mast heads, scanning the surface of the sea for whale spouts, were experienced enough to scramble down when the ship was in danger; if she struck a reef, the jolt would pitch them off their perches. The mate should have been giving sailing orders, but he was incapacitated and the captain was absent. Veeder stayed on shore at Barclay's for ten days, getting his meals from the ship and even extending an invitation to the crew to join him:

> *Capt. ashore sent off orders for each watch to go ashore half a day on Barclay's Is. with a pound of tobacco but the white men forward refused to go saying they wanted no such liberty and because we wouldn't go they called all hands to break out paint oil and the mate left orders to keep us at work.* (August 27, 1871)

A reversal of roles is evident here—instead of the captain trying to keep his men from deserting and running after native women, he was the real renegade, while Kirwin and the other "white" men on board appear to have been offended by his suggestion that they join in what must have seemed like true debauchery. The men of other races and nationalities that Kirwin

Scene of Polynesian women dancing in a grove of trees, engraved on a whale tooth by George Hiliott, mid-nineteenth century.

Gift of Robert Waggaman, 1977.141.1

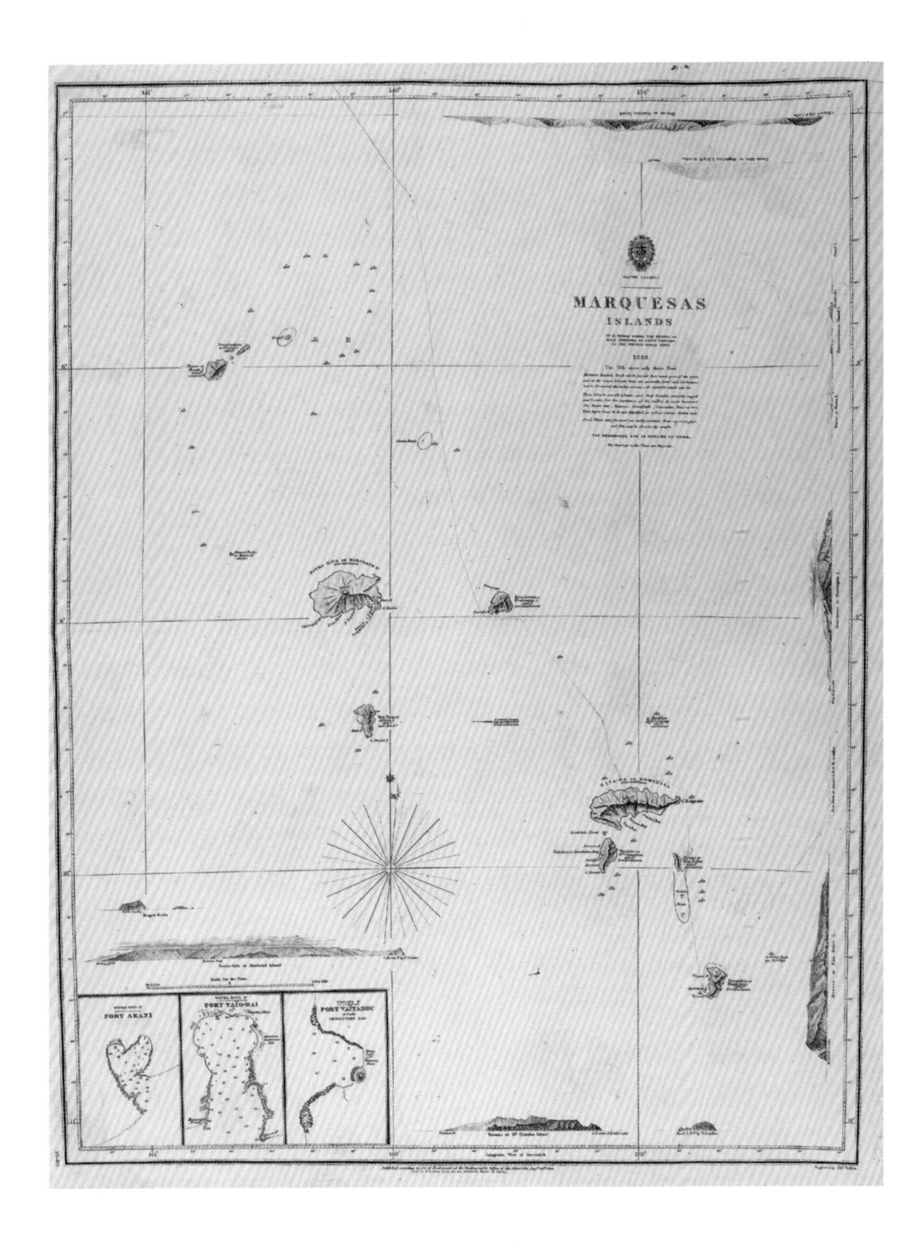

Marquesas Islands, **by M. Tessan under the orders of M. Le Capitiane du Petit Thouars of the French Royal Navy, 1838.**

Ms. 1000.4.1.18

eventually names in the journal—Joe Susa, Antone Brava, Joe Kanaka, Joe Spanish, Manuel, and Tarea—may have obeyed the captain's order, but Kirwin's coterie stayed on board. He retreated to his bunk to read *Percival Keene* by Frederick Marryat, a sea tale about a hero of lowly birth who has numerous stirring adventures and discovers that he is actually the son of a famous captain.

With Veeder back on deck August 31, the *William Gifford* headed to the Marquesas, arriving at Magdalena Island, or Fatu Hiva, the southernmost island of the group, on September 9. Kirwin and his compatriots were occupied making slings for pumpkins and baskets for oranges in anticipation of fresh fruit, while the carpenter fashioned wooden chests from old bread boxes to trade with the islanders. When they arrived, the stowaway Frenchman mentioned early on in Kirwin's narrative "swam from the boat ashore this morning and would not come back, is living ashore with the Chief." Kirwin doesn't mention the captain's woman during their ten-day sail, but when they leave Magdalena to sail to Nuku Hiva, he notes that she had been ashore with Veeder, her presence unremarkable as she took on the role of captain's wife. She must have marveled at rainy, mountainous, verdant Fatu Hiva, profuse with fruit and dripping with streams and waterfalls, a shocking contrast to the low-lying coral atolls of the Tuamotus.

By mid-September, when the *William Gifford* was still lying at Taiohae, Nuku Hiva, the crew had had enough of the paltry provisions allotted them, and "two of us," writes Kirwin, asked the captain for something to eat "and got a good cursing and was sent forward by the Capt. He has been selling salmon at a dollar a piece since we have been in here." The next day there was more solidarity in asking for more bread, for which they received a harsher reprimand from Captain Veeder:

> *In the morning painted the starboard side of the ship and at noon had pumpkins, taters & meat for dinner. Asked for bread and would not turn to until we got it and 11 of us were put in irons in consequence. One Brava Portuguese gave in and went to work while the rest of us stuck it out. Six hours*

> *and the Capt. gave us a good supper on the quarter decks asking us if we would turn to if we got like that all the time and we told him all we asked was enough to eat and he let us go.*
> (September 13, 1871)

The young men must have felt like they were in a workhouse. They certainly noticed the difference between their fare and what was served aft, not to mention the free-flowing alcohol and freewheeling women that were an almost daily diversion for the captain and mates.

From their small experiment with rebellion they learned the importance of sticking together. It's never clear if our journal keeper was the instigator and leader, but he never refers to anyone else in that role, so he is the primary suspect. Intelligent, educated, and self-righteous, he chose to watch and wait and to record the mounting evidence of the captain's increasingly inappropriate behavior and harsh treatment of the crew. All was not unpleasant, though. Kirwin managed to have a "jolly time" on shore, and, while the captain was on land, all hands went in swimming "that could swim." Considering the nature of their business, it's startling to realize there were those aboard who couldn't swim. Kirwin was one of the daredevils, however, jumping off the topsail yards into the ocean, even though they had caught a large shark from the stern the same morning.

While the *William Gifford* was in the Marquesas, and Captain Veeder and his mistress were enjoying themselves at the expense of everyone else, Susan Veeder was taking care of her girls on Nantucket. She records that George A. arrived from New York in the *Onward*; she and Susie went to church; and a lot of strangers were in town for the annual Agricultural Fair. Susie, who was twenty-three, was invited to the festivities by a young man from New Bedford, Mr. Swain, who took her to the ball, too, then sailed home. Susan must have remembered the ball she and Charles attended in Oahu in 1852, their time together on an exotic island magical with music and dancing, but she failed to reminisce about that episode. Her journal overlaps with Kirwin's only a few months, revealing mundane occurrences in the small town: the weather turned cool and she lit a fire in the stove in the front chamber of her house on Orange Street; she and her girls had tea with Mrs. Bailey; she went to Susie Baker's funeral; George sailed for New York with his wife, Sarah, while their children—Charles and Mary Frances—stayed with her. The last entry in Susan's diary is dated Saturday, September 30, 1871: "All well, nothing of any note," the entry made so often in her journal at sea. On the same day, thousands of miles away in the South Pacific, her husband was ashore with his mistress at Typee Bay, Nuku Hiva, when our disgruntled young journal keeper recorded, "Capt. is still ashore drunk for the last four days and no signs of his ever coming off."

* * *

Cruising off Nuku Hiva, the crew managed to snag a humpback whale that had been spotted from shore by their inebriated captain. It's a wonder any whales were taken at all:

> *The mate went ashore with a boat and come off at 6 p.m. dead drunk in the stern sheets of the boat bringing three boxes of wine with him for his own use. Capt. ashore just got over a week's drunk wants to sell the humpback oil and give us the money. No signs of the Capt. coming off.*
> (October 4, 1871)

While Veeder was ashore with his mistress, the officers brought women back to the ship and were "so much taken up with their women that they can't attend to their business." To make matters worse, if the crew were caught looking at the women they lost their watch below or their free time—and sleeping time—in the forecastle. Finally, on October 9, the captain came back to the *William Gifford* after twelve days absence and sailed the ship back to Barclay's Island. "He's so much taken up with his mistress that he could not listen to a man ashore who was trying to tell him where he seen whales a day or two ago."

After three nights in his mistress's village on the atoll, the captain returned to the ship, but with spyglass in hand, watching for as long as he could stand it, then back to Barclay's. When he returned to the vessel again, his woman—and a few more for the officers—accompanied him: "we have five aboard now all told. 7 p.m. the mate so drunk he can't stand up and the Capt. took his gin from him. Women are dancing like the devil and we are running down the land as usual." A week later, the female contingent appear to be having a grand time:

> *Seen two sunfish and lowered a boat but could not get any "for the women." At 4 p.m. a dead calm had to sling a stage over the quarter for the women to go in swimming off of. At supper time two women aloft at the main with their men.* (October 28, 1871)

Cruising for whales for a month without success, the captain playing cards, making squirt guns for the women and offering them a bounty for spotting a whale, eating roast pork aft and sending a few coconuts forward for the crew—it made Kirwin miserable. The women were everywhere, swimming alongside the becalmed ship and climbing up the masts with their lovers. On November 16 he wrote, "Women aloft with their arms around the officer's necks. Capt.'s woman sick and I wished she would dye." This was not what he had signed on for, not the kind of rousing sea adventure he liked to read about. His fear was returning home broke or in debt—his lay, or portion of the profits, was a small one. If they continued to have bad luck raising whales, then he would have nothing to show for his four years at sea but the physical toll of too much sun and too little nourishment.

Kirwin may have contemplated telling the story of the voyage of the *William Gifford* to a wider audience. He referred to himself as "author," so written on the title page of his journal, and he certainly had copious notes for the last year of the voyage. Unlike the typical whalemen in the forecastle, he enjoyed reading and writing and was apparently educated.

But an exposé and condemnation of the lusty and irresponsible whaling captain and his officers in the South Seas might be too explosive a topic for any publisher to accept. Melville's *Typee* was considered titillating more than twenty-five years earlier because it was about an exotic place where the way of life was different from American notions of society and home, and it was labeled fiction, even though based on the author's experience, and the author was a lowly seaman, not a captain. It was one thing to write about a foreign culture known for cannibalism and sexual freedom, quite another to shock readers with details about the Bacchanalian excesses of an American whaling captain, details that might open inquiries about other voyages in the South Seas. And who would believe him? More than likely Kirwin closed his journal and moved on to his next career, glad to have land under his feet and better food on the table.

On November 28, he remarked that it was "over six months since we seen a sperm spout," but on December 11, smack in the middle of the Tuamotus in the vicinity of Makemo, Taenga, and Nihiru Islands, they raised a shoal of whales. Unfortunately, they had no luck harpooning them, "owing to some of the officer's foolishness we could not get fast." Sperm whales appeared again a week later, and, even with more mishaps, the men managed to kill four of them:

> *At 8 a.m. our 3rd mate raised s[perm] whales on the weather bow and lowered four boats, chased them on between the two Is. and each boat got one. Got them alongside at 3 o'clock and cut two in by sundown. Folger got stunned by a whale kicking the oar against him. Mr. Rogers gun exploded in the head of his boat the bomb passing through the boat.*
> (December 16, 1871)

In a more typical logbook or journal, an entry like that of December 16 would be a highlight, a description of a whale hunt with minor disasters that proved the danger of the industry. On the *William Gifford*, however, it was often more dangerous to be on the mother ship with an unpredictable

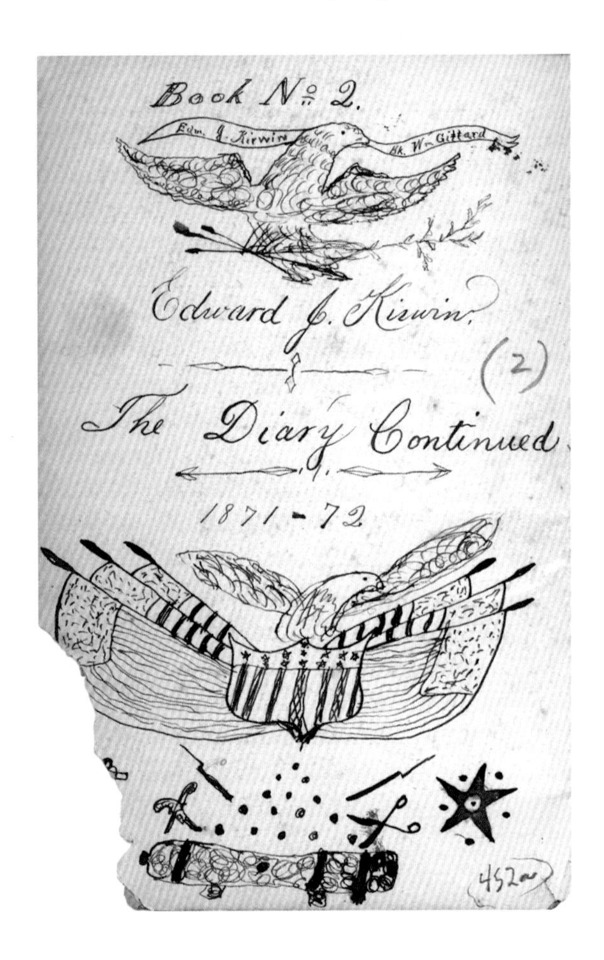

The second of four small booklets that record Edward J. Kirwin's observations on the voyage of the *William Gifford*, 1871–72.

Courtesy of the New Bedford Whaling Museum, KWM Log 452

captain and his distracted officers. While the crew was rendering the oil that would fill sixty-three barrels, Veeder made another exit: "Capt. went ashore this noon at Barclay's Is. with two days' provisions and his spy glass. I guess he is going to stand mast heads in the coconut trees."

Soon, the *William Gifford* was joined by another whaling bark, the *Oak* of Nantucket, the last whaler ever to depart from the island. How appropriate that our wayward captain should encounter this harbinger of the end of an era. Two years from home with eighty-four barrels of oil to show for it, the *Oak* was not having a profitable voyage. By the end of four years a captain would hope to have at least a thousand barrels, enough to cover the expenses of the ship and render a modest return for the owners with a little trickle-down for captain and officers. First mate James Russell had taken command of the *Oak* after Captain William B. Thompson left the vessel in November 1870, in Tahiti, for reasons we don't know. Captain Russell did not look at Captain Veeder and flee; on the contrary, he joined in the New Year's celebration on Barclay's Island. Perhaps Veeder's behavior was not particularly alarming to other whaling captains in those waters.

Christmas Day was uneventful. Veeder returned to his ship after a week on shore and the *Oak* joined in the inter-island transportation business, ferrying a group of local people to Ticoma Island. On December 26, preparations for a New Year's celebration began, with the cooper enlisted to make drums for the kanakas. Captain Veeder gathered up all the lanterns on board, along with the new drums and a roasted pig and back he went to the village on Barclay's. Meanwhile, Kirwin broke out a new blue shirt for the New Year, and "the evening's entertainment commenced with Cavanagh and Kirwin's combinational troup in the forecastle." Kirwin and his buddy, Ed Cavanagh, had entertained before, serenading Mr. Haughton's girls when they were lying off Tahiti, and they were at it again, a duo of Irish singers attempting to liven up the downtrodden crew.

The singing and dancing on shore were undoubtedly livelier, but Kirwin was not there to record the details. Both Captain Veeder and Captain Russell stayed overnight on Barclay's, returning to their respective commands the next day. The *Oak* was seen cruising in the same general area for another two weeks, but there were no whales to be found and Russell soon sailed away. The *William Gifford*, on the other hand, stuck close by Barclay's, while Chadwick the carpenter was kept busy making shutters for the captain's woman's house. In early January, they sailed the ship through a passage into the lagoon, providing the perfect setting for another party for the islanders:

> *Just before dinner there were a crowd of 20 kanakas or more consisting of the gov's and their wives of both is[lands] and several other kanakas come off to attend a feast which the Capt. got up in honor of them. He fired off a bomb lance and several blank charges, also his revolver several times to please them. They spread canvas across the quarter deck for a table and then put up two boat sail for a screen so that the vulgar gaze of the sailors would not disturb them as they sat there eating their fresh meat while we had to live on what fish we caught around the ship. Shortly after dinner some of the natives went ashore but two thirds of them stopped for supper which they eat in the cabin. There not being room enough for all the Capt. sent Mr. Tracy on deck to eat at the second table and let a ragged saffron-colored kanaka take his place as he was some relation to the old man's woman.*
> (January 7, 1872)

Whether mate Tracy was insulted or not, Kirwin certainly bristled at the slight to the officer, replaced at the captain's table by one of the islanders. He failed to appreciate the social hierarchy of the native population that Veeder treated with a degree of respect, careful not to offend the family of his sweetheart. His was not a casual liaison.

The crew dined on a "Baricota" caught in the lagoon. It made half of them so sick they were unable to work the next day, suffering the effects of what might have been ciguatera poisoning from toxins in smaller fish eaten by the barracuda. Symptoms include nausea, diarrhea, headache, and, in severe cases, neurological damage that can last for weeks. It must have been a mild case for the men of the *William Gifford*, as Kirwin does not mention the illness again. The local people knew the danger of eating certain reef fish from the lagoon, but no one warned the crew.

The lagoon was "smooth as a mill pond" according to Kirwin, and the flies so thick "we have to go around decks with our mouths shut tight." He was able to go on shore occasionally and to swim in the lagoon, breathtakingly beautiful with the underwater landscape of coral and a kaleidoscope of fish. Not one to ponder the natural beauty of the atoll, however, Kirwin was more interested in the plot of his unfolding story than the setting,

Detail of the Paumoto Group, from Susan Veeder's journal of the *Nauticon*.

Gift of the Friends of the Nantucket Historical Association, Ms. 220, Log 347

focused on the characters he saw as antagonists in the drama—the Old Man and his woman and the drunken first mate.

Leaving the lagoon proved to be more difficult than getting in. They planned to sail through the passage and into the open ocean on January 17 after twelve days inside, but the wind did not cooperate for another week. They gave it another go, with results that were very nearly disastrous:

> *We went ashore for the Pilot this morning and took a look at the passage, found everything favorable so we decided to sail. We run a line to the reef ahead of us and then took up our anchor and hauled up within a few fathoms of the reef when the hawser gave way and as we were fast drifting on a lee shore we made sail immediately and just got headway on in time to tack which we did just clearing the weather of one reef and keeping off for another. We had a strong current against us and by either the Capt. or Pilot's fault we struck a reef. ("The Capt.'s I suppose") We tumbled about there on the reef for a minute like an old tub when the tide swung us off clear. We whirled around there in the tide rip and everybody gallied, but at last we tried the pumps and found there was no damage that we knew of, but finally we got out and the Capt. & mate then had a growl . . . when the ship struck the women all hauled off their dresses and jumped for the rail all ready to swim ashore if it come to that. It was a miracle how we ever got clear.*
> (January 23, 1872)

CHAPTER SEVEN

Ship of Fools

For his services guiding the *William Gifford* out of Barclay's lagoon, the pilot—later identified as Mana Mana, the governor of the atoll—received five dollars and eight pounds of tobacco, a generous payment from a captain who was glad he had not lost his ship. The native passengers from Barclay's were deposited on Ticoma, and the *William Gifford* returned to sail under the lee of the favored island: "The Capt. is very uneasy about that woman of his, he took one masthead and watched the shore all the time." A few days of anxious spying from aloft were enough for Veeder, so back ashore he went in order to bring his woman on board, the better to keep an eye on her; she was joined by two other women and a few men. On February 1, Kirwin wrote, "Capt. got in the deck tub and had a wash with the women." The deck tub full of seawater was not intended for bathing but was a source of water for various shipboard chores. Veeder turned it into the equivalent of a modern-day hot tub, a social gathering place for the scantily clad, or naked, captain and his women friends who were accustomed to spending much of their time in the water. Not only did the captain bathe with his lover, but he also washed her clothes "while she is laying around decks too lazy to move." The unnamed mistress was not a submissive woman; in fact, she assumed a queenly role and may have been part of the Barclay's Island elite, related to Mana Mana, the governor. She asserted her position on the ship, accusing the crew of stealing from her, a ploy that did not make her popular with the sailors, who may not have been innocent of the transgression.

Fifty passengers from Barclay's boarded the *William Gifford* on February 4 for a trip to one of the windward islands a hundred miles distant, the ship so crowded it would have been difficult to lower the boats and chase whales even if they were spotted and impossible to butcher them and man the tryworks. But they saw no whales. For eight days it was roast pig for the captain and his friends and the skin and bones for the crew, until they ran out of pigs and watched their other stores dwindle. Kirwin noted on February 10, "Broke out water, flour and some molasses for the Kanakas as they came short of provisions and we were too. We had to give them ship's coconuts to eat as they had nothing." For a young man who was hungry, it was untenable to feed their passengers the ship's scant provender.

Finally, the band of islanders was delivered to Huahine Island, north of Tahiti in the Society Islands group. Kirwin and others rowed five boatloads of passengers ashore. "I got sunburned in the morning working for the Black Devils," Kirwin complained. The captain's woman did not exit with the multitudes, nor did the governor, his family, and four other women who stayed aboard to travel to Nuku Hiva, stopping first at a place Kirwin called Oahitahoo, a town on the island of St. Christina, or Tahuata, in the Marquesas. There, the mate found eight local women to bring on board, and some friendly competition began: "The Paumotu women are having a grand dance trying to beat the Marquesas women."

Although there is no mention of Captain Veeder's inebriation during the extended layover at Barclay's and the trip to Ticoma and Huahine—just feasting and fraternizing with the passengers—it may be due to the fact that he had not replenished his supply of spirits for several months, but apparently there was no shortage of liquor on Nuku Hiva, where the *William Gifford* arrived in late February:

> *Washington's birthday began with a mild breeze in the harbor. Commenced work before breakfast by breaking out what empty casks there were between decks with all the oil—8 casks. We filled the casks with salt water to give the ship a port list so we could put on some sheathing. There has been queer old*

> *works aboard today all hands aft drunk and nobody to oversee the work. We broke out beef. The Capt. just getting over a drunk sent ashore for a case of liquor, and the mate also is so drunk that he can hardly stand up.*
> (February 21, 1872)

The drinking bout that began on Nuku Hiva in late February did not truly end until the crew took matters into their own hands three months later, and it was not just the captain but most of the officers, too, who participated heartily. The crew began to desert at every opportunity; one of the men named Thurston stowed away on an unidentified cutter on February 25, the same day four other men from the ship—the steward, Chadwick, Antone, and Joe Kanaka—ended up in the local calaboose, or jail, for unspecified misbehavior. All the while, our journal keeper was busy on board sheathing the reef-scarred sides of the ship with copper and taking careful note of

Book number three of Edward J. Kirwin's four volume account of the voyage of the *William Gifford*.

Courtesy of the New Bedford Whaling Museum, KWM Log 452

all provisions brought on board—bread, beef, sugar, flour, potatoes, beans, onions, molasses, butter, cheese—plus supplies of tar, duck, and cordage. Some of the ship's whale oil—calculated by Kirwin at 2,001 gallons—was shipped aboard a schooner, bound for what market we are not told. Progress was being made for a continuation of the whaling voyage, even though the captain and mates appeared totally negligent. The captain went sightseeing with his Barclay's entourage, taking them on an excursion to Typee Bay while "all aft drunk and don't know what to do with themselves. Had a devil of a time in the evening trying to stop the mate from shooting Mr. Duane with an empty gun." The cook was drunk, too, and someone named Miller fell down an open hatch and almost killed himself. By March 9, after two and a half weeks in the harbor at Nuku Hiva, "the mate was seen ashore parading the beach with a woman's dress on, drunk as usual."

Kirwin and the young men from Nantucket found themselves in an increasingly bizarre reality, dependent on superiors who had leapt across every line of respectable behavior. They were in one of the most remote areas of the Pacific, surrounded by people only a generation or two removed from their cannibal past. Two days later Kirwin reported, "the natives from all the little sch[ooners] around have come aboard to get drunk and dance before the Old Man," who had progressed in his consumption of all available alcohol from liquor to absinthe. On March 15, Chadwick, the ship's carpenter who had made drums for the New Year's celebration on Barclay's Island and chests for the women's clothes, deserted the *William Gifford*, sailing on "Mr. Doom's cutter." It was obviously preferable to sail off with someone named Doom than to stay with Captain Veeder. Five days later, a seaman named Burdell was missing, suspected of being aboard a schooner that sailed in the night, and on Friday, March 22, three of the crew—Bill Wood, Samuel, and Tarea—stowed away on "Barstow cutter" and deserted as well.

Captain Veeder's ship was now seriously short-handed. He brought off the pilot and the local "brigadier"—the French officer in charge of the military station at Nuku Hiva—to assist him in looking for the latest deserters, but first they all got drunk, amused themselves with the women, played

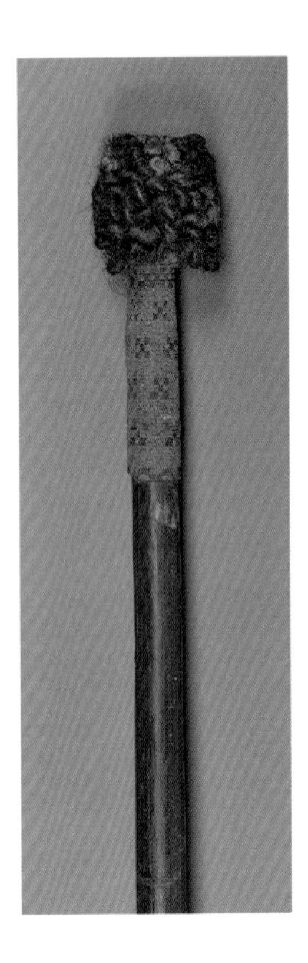

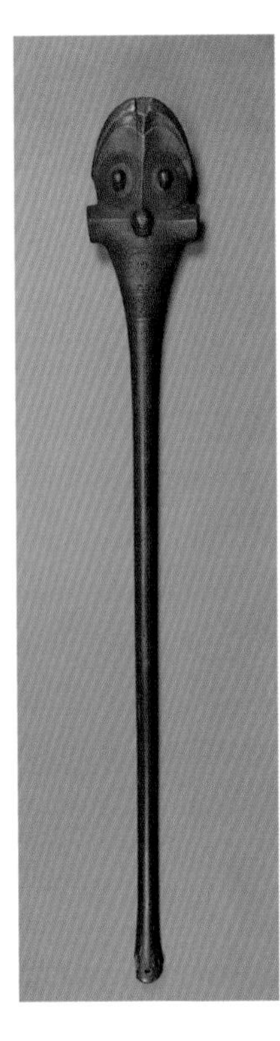

Left: **Ceremonial Marquesan staff composed of wood, human hair, and coconut fiber, circa 1830.**

Gift of Edward F. Sanderson, 1998.1101.273

Right: **An indicator of warrior status, this early-nineteenth century U'u club from the Marquesas Islands is both an artistic adornment and a utilitarian weapon.**

Gift of Edward F. Sanderson, 1998.1101.300

cards, and "the Pilot made himself at home and gave all the women a feast of some papoy and 3 cans of oysters." The Marquesan women remained on board as they sailed around the island in search of the cutter with the three latest deserters, who, as it turned out, had been apprehended and were in the local calaboose. Those unhappy men returned to the ship after the captain paid a bail of thirty-seven dollars. On March 30, five weeks after arriving at Nuku Hiva, the *William Gifford* turned and sailed back toward Barclay's Island. George Cash, one of the Nantucket boys who sailed with Veeder from New Bedford, was made boatsteerer just before they left the Marquesas, taking the place of one of the deserters. He would turn nineteen in two weeks, and if the year had been 1832 instead of 1872, he would have been well on his way to becoming a whaling captain—perhaps fourth mate on his next ship, then second mate, and, in eight or ten years, captain. But those days were over.

Captain Veeder stocked up on liquor in Nuku Hiva and was eager to keep the party going. When a boatload of islanders came off from Tahuata to trade, he added them to the shipboard mix:

> *A boat came off from Ohitahoo with only natives in it and the Capt. was so drunk he would not let them go ashore. He wanted them to stop overnight so as to see the Paumoutu kanakas dance which they commenced in good earnest at sundown. He gave them bread to eat and got up a jib for them to sleep on. P. S.: 11 a.m. my watch has just come below and the Capt. has been half crazy jumping around on the quarter deck trying to imitate the kanakas a dancing and feeding them liquor. He acts more like a lunatic than a Captain.*
> (April 2, 1872)

Other local boats approached the *William Gifford* to trade, but the captain would not send any of his boats on shore, for reasons Kirwin relates: "He told the Pilot that he could not trust a damned one of us and the next time we got our foot on soil would be in N. Bedford." While sailing along to Barclay's Island, Captain Veeder spent time washing his woman's clothes and watering the breadfruit, pineapple, and other plants she had collected in Nuku Hiva and transplanted in wooden bread boxes filled with soil. And he lost his bearings. Kirwin wrote on April 10, "I guess the Old Man don't know where he is as he has been trying to work out Longitude nearly all day and hasn't found out yet. He got Cash to help and learn him navigation." Veeder knew that the Nantucket boy, son of a whaling captain and schooled in the maritime arts and sciences in his native town, would be able to assist. Cash must have shown a great deal of ability, and, perhaps most important, he was sober. When they sighted Ticoma on April 13, the captain's woman took charge. "The Capt. and fourth mate have been washing their women's clothes. Capt.'s woman in a hurry to get back to her island told the Capt. to set the light sails which he did of course." No matter what Susan eventually discovered about her besotted husband's last voyage, she would not have imagined him allowing a young Polynesian woman to tell him how to sail his ship. Assisting with laundry was different; that she *could* imagine.

Arriving back at Barclay's on April 15 was cause for celebration, both for the native people going ashore and for Kirwin, who noted that there were eight of the islanders who had been with the ship two months and ten days, in addition to the fifty others who were transported to Huahine, plus those who came and went from Nuku Hiva while the *William Gifford* was at anchor in Typee Bay, and now "it seems like a new ship . . . everything seems so quiet." The departure of the captain's woman and her fellow islanders had been a final episode of barely controlled pandemonium:

> *. . . passed the settlement at 7:30 (a very moon light evening) so close in that the kanakas on shore were conversing with those on board. The Capt. and all his friends in the boats blowing fish horns and firing the bomb gun off about 20 times in succession. A regular fourth of July all hands jumping around and singing trying to make all the noise they can . . . Layed off & on Barclay's Is. all day and lowered both quarter boats and loaded them to the gunwales with the kanakas, passengers, women and their freight such as pumpkins, potatoes, onions, a bag of flour, some sweet biscuit, chests, cats, etc. also a flower garden consisting of nine or ten bread boxes filled with banana, pineapple, pumpkin, breadfruit plants and half of the Marquesas Is. and the Devil knows what.*
> (April 15, 1872)

Charles Veeder was the hero of Barclay's Island, the benevolent old man who ferried the islanders around and helped them gather necessities and luxuries that their atoll did not provide. His woman gained status because of her association with him; she wore gold earrings that he bought for her in Nuku Hiva and calico dresses that she made on board the ship and stored in her own wooden chest. Her house had shutters, which meant it was significantly more substantial than the traditional open-sided native hut. Material wealth, access to the ship's food and drink, and her power over the lusty captain separated her from the other islanders, but we don't know if she was respected within her community or reviled. Polynesian society placed an emphasis on sharing wealth and living in harmony with one's surroundings, and she was exhibiting a fair amount of hubris. But whatever her faults, the captain couldn't live without her:

> *The Old Man could not stand it for he waited until the turn of the tide after dinner and then went ashore on Barclay's Is. and brought off four women with about 100 coconuts dry and green together. He also brought off the cat he carried ashore the other day. He paid five dollars ashore for a sauce pan for his woman. At supper time we caught a large porpoise and are saving the blubber for the natives as it's the custom with us. Capt. keeps two of the women with him.*
> (April 22, 1872)

Tuesday, April 23, 1872, Kirwin noted, "My birthday 21 years old." If he had been born a hundred years later he might be celebrating his twenty-first birthday in his fourth year at college, not his fourth year at sea, disillusioned with the life of a sailor. He got an education nonetheless. At Barclay's in late April, Kirwin noted that one of the mates, Mr. Duane, was seriously ill, so the local doctor—dubbed "Tar Bucket" by our journal keeper—was brought aboard to treat him; ten days later his condition had worsened. The captain, who had no plan to leave Barclay's, ordered the feeble Mr. Duane to go ashore and wait for the next available transportation to Tahiti, and that's the last we know of him, another of the ship's company disappearing in the South Seas. Captain Veeder continued his activities of fishing and card playing with the women while the *William Gifford* was "running up and down the land as usual."

After an excursion on nearby Ticoma, the first lady of the ship exhibited one of her many talents:

> *Commenced at daylight to mind the boat that got stove yesterday on the reef and got through at half past nine when the Capt. with his kanakas friends went ashore on Ticoma and stopped till suppertime. The boat came aboard at four o'clock bringing four hundred coconuts in payment for two axes that we left there about ten months ago, the boat then went right in again and brought off the Capt. and his Kanaka gang with an extra woman. The boat anchor was foul and the Capt.'s woman dove down and cleared it.*
> (April 26, 1872)

Like her fellow islanders, the captain's woman was completely at home in the water and was an experienced diver. Twice in January natives of Barclay's had demonstrated their deep-water expertise: one dove down to retrieve a lost anchor, and another, called the best diver on the island, was paid ten dollars to dive twice and tell them "which way to kedge the ship." Captain Veeder would have been at a loss without their help.

In May, while six women aboard were "dancing and drumming tin pans" and the captain was "tinkering on tin boxes and pots for his woman," the crew spied blackfish, or pilot whales, and went after them, "Cash striking his first one." Recently made a harpooneer, the Nantucket boy had proven himself and could now boast to the girls at home that he was worthy. An old Nantucket legend suggests that island girls would not pledge their hearts to a man until he had harpooned his first whale, proving that he had what it took to one day be a captain. But it was now 1872, and not more than a handful of Nantucket boys would even get the opportunity to attempt the feat, so qualifications for engagement were necessarily less onerous. Cash knew what it meant though, and he must have been proud.

Kirwin's third tiny, easily hidden blank book was full by May 10, so he started on his fourth and final book, the dénouement of the South Seas whaling voyage of the *William Gifford,* with an ominous but appropriate beginning:

Today has been pleasant with a strong breeze. Cruising around Barclay's Is. as usual (if you can call it) and the Capt. went ashore at 10 a.m. with two of the women and came off at one o'clock bringing the women back again with a small pig, a few coconuts and fish. We sold 16 lbs. of cut nails ashore at 10 cts. per pound. We sewed a little on the gaff top sail and tried out the blackfish blubber in the afternoon. At 7 p.m. one of the women in the forecastle fainted from fright. Seen a "Tou Pa Pou" devil.
(May 11, 1872)

A devil in the forecastle! And, the first and only indication that any of the native women were in that humble domain of the ordinary seamen, who had been continually reprimanded for even looking at the women and trying to converse with them. Either Kirwin selectively withheld information all along, or the situation was changing on board.

Fourth small journal kept by Edward J. Kirwin on the *William Gifford*, 1871–72.

Courtesy of the New Bedford Whaling Museum, KWM Log 452

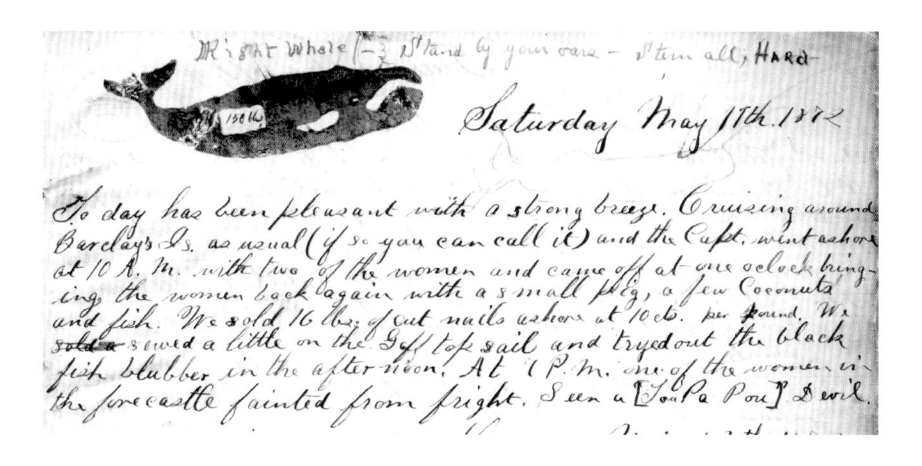
Right Whale [-] Stand by your oars - Stern all, Hard-

Saturday May 11th 1872

To day has been pleasant with a strong breeze. Cruising around Barclay's Is. as usual (if so you can call it) and the Capt. went ashore at 10 A. M. with two of the women and came off at one oclock bringing the women back again with a small pig, a few Coconuts and fish. We sold 16 lbs. of cut nails ashore at 10 cts. per pound. We ~~sold a~~ sewed a little on the Gaff top sail and tryed out the black fish blubber in the after noon. At 1 P. M. one of the women in the forecastle fainted from fright. Seen a [Toa Pa Pou] Devil.

Kirwin's journal entry for May 11, 1872.

Courtesy of the New Bedford Whaling Museum, KWM Log 452

A local schooner, *Favorite,* probably hailing from Tahiti, arrived at Barclay's Island; it appears to have been in the business of trading with the small islands in the area. Captain Veeder bought a case each of gin and brandy from her and began his final long drinking bout:

> *. . . has been drunk all day and ever since he got his rum . . . sent a boat into the reef and brought off seven passengers whom we are going to take down to Nehiru one of the leeward islands with a boat load of luggage consisting of coconuts, pigs, fish, chests, etc. Capt struck a porpoise this morning while the boats were down and sent it all ashore to his kanaka friends without giving us a mouthful. . . . The Capt. drunk all day wants to fight, half crazy, is going to [choke] a lot of us but is afraid, has been fooling with the women all day and is cross as two sticks.*
>
> (May 13, 1872)

Although the captain had been drunk numerous times on the voyage, Kirwin never divulged that it made him anything other than incompetent. The atmosphere was now charged, and our journal keeper was wary of him:

> *Hauled aback off Nehiru Is. after breakfast and the Capt. with three or four women and some Kanakas went ashore after a few coconuts and fish for the women to eat. Got off about noon and then run for the settlement where we landed our passengers and their luggage. We left eight ashore there and I don't know how many we have aboard as it is hard to keep run of them, they are going and coming so often. We have worked hard all day, chopping wood, breaking out and stowing it in the main hold and working ship as we were laying off and on nearly all the time. Capt. has been half tight all day. He would not let white men go ashore this morning. He got the women to wash off the break this afternoon and pick over potatoes, talking dirty vulgar to them all the time and yesterday giving them gin to drink. At 6 p. m. under double reefed top sails just luffed to the wind with coursers hauled up and Marutea Is. a little on our lee beam. So ends. Stand clear of Old Man as he is dangerous by his talk.* (May 16, 1872)

The next two days the captain was dead drunk on deck and "kept us moving the whole watch making and taking in sail and all sorts of unnecessary work. He has been cutting up all kinds of foolish capers with his woman. He got mad with her and beat her till she could hardly stand then took everything back from her that he had given her and wanted to drive her ashore on one of the islands." On May 18 Veeder went ashore at Marutea, the nearest atoll southwest of Nehiru, and found a drinking companion, a white man named Dan Snow "to have a good night's drunk." His belligerence continued:

> *We had a bad night of these last two nights as the Capt. kept coming on deck and making us work through his drunkenness. I had the middle watch out last night and when it was raining hard the Capt. come on deck and woke about all hands up beating his woman. She ran among the crew for protection but got none and "Dan Snow" had to separate them. She "dropped" right down on the wet decks. And then this morning just before breakfast the Capt. had a row with the Steward and put him in irons pointing his revolver*

> *at his head all the time saying it was loaded and threatening to shoot him and steward talking to him got three hard licks side the head, the third one knocking him senseless to the deck and cutting quite a gash in his cheek from which the blood flowed freely. He then put him ashore on Marutea Is. with the white man and when the boat went, Cash got in and stowed himself away ashore.*
> (May 19, 1872)

The rapid deterioration of the captain and the now violent bent of his drunkenness clearly scared young George Cash; he was willing to risk being apprehended for desertion and punished rather than stay on board with the irrational, gun-wielding captain in charge. Kirwin doesn't mention Cash again; he never returned to the *William Gifford*.

Meanwhile, the shipboard drama continued:

> *About two o'clock the boat got back from shore and it was my watch below, the boats crew were eating their dinner when the Capt.'s woman came running down there saying the Capt. had been beating her and was loading his revolvers which aroused our anger and shortly after, the Capt. came down himself and was just hauling her out of one of the berths when we grabbed him and made him fast with rope yarns then went aft and told the officers that the Capt. was down below bound and secured and we did not want to trouble them if they would only go on with their duty as before which they consented to seeing they could do nothing else.*
>
> *We told them that we wanted a boat sent in after the steward which was sent, but he would not come off saying the Capt. put him ashore and there he would stop. While we were lowering the boat the Capt. asked the cause of it and when I told him he almost cried, saying he did not want to see him again. We took him on deck and freed his legs but as he attempted to escape we took him below again and give him everything that is in our power to comfort him (except letting him go). I forgot to mention that he hit the steward with the barrel of his revolver as hard as he could. We looked for*

> *irons but could not get any large enough, so we made the best we could of our rope yarns. 7 p.m. it is hard telling whether he is crazy or drunk.* (May 19, 1872)

Mutiny! The crew decided that the fallout from mutiny would be less harmful than a drunken captain with loaded revolvers, so they did what they had to do in a bloodless coup. It is doubtful they took action to protect the captain's woman, since Kirwin, for one, wished her dead a long time ago. They were concerned for their own safety. The next line of Kirwin's journal is particularly interesting because he crossed it out. It is still legible, however, and it refers to an injury inflicted on the writer: "We took him on deck at his request but he attempted to escape by striking me in the face and skinning my cheek. We took him below again." Was it true, or in his retelling of the dramatic events did Kirwin get carried away and fabricate his involvement, giving himself the same injury as the steward? If he really wanted to omit the line he would have made his mark heavy enough to render it unreadable, but there it is, a comment upon a comment. He was certainly disturbed about what had just occurred, and he added more to the day's entry:

> *I forgot to state that last night when going below, as usual he left orders when to tack, which would certainly have put the ship ashore had we gone by his directions. For about half an hour after my watch got turned in all hands were called to save their lives as well as the ship and then we had hard work to get him to do right. He damned all his officers up and down too.* (May 19, 1872)

Captain Veeder gradually calmed a little as the crew kept him appeased with watered-down brandy, and he tried to bargain with the men:

> *He has been the whole time trying to buy us saying he will be perfectly satisfied if we will only put him on Barclay's Is. with one hundred barrels of oil. He says he will then give us "in writing" that he left the ship with his*

> *own free will. He also stated that if we took him to Tahiti he would lose all his voyage, "every cent" and it would be a disgrace to him having these women aboard, together with what we said about him. He said he would as soon be knocked in the head with a club hammer as go to Tahiti but all that, we refused, and told him we would go to Tahiti, if we could get there, and then whoever was in the wrong would get punished. He lays down below there talking and is the most vulgar mouth man I ever seen. He is singing out for his woman or brandy all the time and wants her to lay down side of him.*
> (May 20, 1872)

The captain, although drunk and possibly "crazy," was rational enough to know how his behavior would be perceived by the American consul in Tahiti, and he wanted to protect both his reputation and his money. Too late for that, though, as the *William Gifford* made its way to Papeete. It took a week to sail there, and with the lack of navigational skill among the officers it's a wonder they got there at all. In the interim the captain sobered up a bit with his watered-down ration of booze and a daily dose of laudanum, an opiate found in every ship's medicine chest; it would have helped to placate him. His abused mistress spent time with him in the forecastle, as the ever-interested Kirwin noted on May 25. "Just before 7 o'clock while reefing top sails the Capt. with his woman turned in the coopers berth about six or seven minutes for some purpose or other."

Two days later, they reached Papeete, Tahiti:

> *Pleasant with a light breeze. The pilot came aboard just after daylight and took the ship in about 11 o'clock in the lee'ard passage. She touched on the reef as she was coming in but done no damage. We hoisted our colors Union Jack down when we went in, which caused quite a sensation. The Consul came aboard to see what was the matter and then went down and released the Capt. but left the ship in charge of the chief officer Mr. Rodgers, and then commenced to investigate the matter. Not one of us is*

allowed to go ashore and no boats are allowed to come alongside. I think we are looked upon as a set of "Mutineers" but hope to be thought better of when the story is known.
(May 27, 1872)

It didn't take long for the consul to appraise the situation; in the meantime the captain had moved ashore:

The Capt. hired rooms up John Miller's house (a kanaka) he not being able to get them anywhere else they say. He sent aboard for some of his house hold articles, lamps, bed clothes, baskets and his woman's clothes, etc. Ed is writing off some of the last year's proceedings for the American Consul.
(May 29, 1872)

Kirwin's friend Ed Cavanagh was a better writer, as evidenced by the scrap of his journal that chronicles the post-mutiny passage of the *William Gifford* to San Francisco and beyond. He may have been selected as the most literate seaman aboard to report the activities of the captain and officers to the consul, so he must have had his own record of the past year to refer to. The American consul in Tahiti was Dorance Atwater, a survivor of two of the Confederacy's worst prisons in the Civil War and the man responsible for recording the Union dead at Andersonville Prison. For his service to his country, President Grant had appointed him consul to Tahiti just seven months earlier. Now, the problems on board the *William Gifford* would require quick action and diplomacy and test his ability to fulfill his new office. He went on board to investigate:

In the afternoon four Frenchmen with the A. consul and an interpreter came on board, called all hands aft and sent in for the Capt. to hear what he and the crew had to say about this woman's affair. Consul left orders to repair the rigging as he intends sailing Monday. We reckoned up today a summary account of the last years proceedings and it ran as follows.

> *Captain stopped ashore 49 days. We have had women on board 210 days and the boat has been ashore 158 times. So the reader may see that all that time has gone to H—— and no money in my pocket.*
> (May 30, 1872)

The next day the consul introduced the crew to Captain Sweet, the man he commissioned to take the ship to San Francisco, and "our old Capt. came on board and packed up his things and left." The last words of Captain Charles Veeder's whereabouts were written by Kirwin on June 1, 1872: "Capt. Veeder sent after his mats and shells and a pig."

On June 3, Consul Atwater sent the following dispatch to the secretary of state in Washington, D.C.:

> *Sir: I have the honor to report that I have removed Chas. A. Veeder as master of the whaling Bark Wm. Gifford of New Bedford and placed on board said vessel a new master with instructions to proceed to San Francisco and there await orders from the agents.*
>
> *I was actuated in this decision by substantiated charges of the officers and crew that the Captain, Veeder, had, through lewd women and intoxicating liquors rendered himself incapable of conducting the remainder of the voyage.*
>
> *That he had threatened to shoot and had struck some of the crew with a loaded revolver.*
>
> *That he had abandoned officers and men at different islands and by his brutal conduct caused others to desert the ship to her detriment.*
>
> *That he had kept native women for lewd purposes, on board ship from one to ten weeks at a time during the last twelve months thereby debauching and diseasing the officers and crew to the injury of the ship and her voyage.*
>
> *That he had often been in a state of intoxication and while in that state the vessel was twice nearly lost upon the reefs.*
>
> *That for months there was no one on board, save for the Captain, who understood sufficient navigation to navigate the vessel and that he had*

refused to ship officers understanding navigation thereby hazarding the lives of the officers and crew and the ship and her cargo.

That the voyage was being made contrary to shipping articles and against the interest of all parties interested in the vessel.

Believing that the foregoing a summary of the charges was sufficient cause for removal and appointment of a new master, I have this day dispatched the vessel to San Francisco with instructions as before stated.

I have sent advice upon the subject to the agents of the ship.

I may further state that I offered the late master Veeder a passage in the vessel to San Francisco, but that he declined it and I have good reason to believe that he is so far lost to self respect and decency that he will remain at one of these Islands with the native woman whom he had on board the vessel as his mistress.

Consul Atwater found the island women attractive, too, but he maintained propriety by marrying Moa, the sister of Queen Pomare of Tahiti, in 1875, and living the rest of his life there. It was not uncommon for Western men to fall in love with Polynesian women, and it's interesting to see that Veeder's behavior was viewed as lewd and scandalous, especially in light of the popular autobiographical novel written by Pierre Loti, *Tahiti: The Marriage of Loti,* first published in 1880. Loti, the Tahitian name given French naval officer Julien Marie Viaud, spent all of 1872 in Tahiti, *except* for the month of May, when his ship cruised to the Marquesas, so he was absent when the *William Gifford* sailed into Papeete on May 27. During Loti's time in Tahiti he fell in love with a fourteen-year-old girl and "married" her, but without legal ceremony or documentation, in what was called a "Tahitian marriage" by other writers, including Dora Hort, an English-born woman who spent a number of years in Tahiti in the 1850s and '60s and viewed the behavior of Polynesians and Europeans with the same critical eye and wit. It was a temporary arrangement, and Loti was well aware that he was destroying the innocent, beautiful child he plucked from the wilderness, brought to Papeete, and abandoned when his ship sailed. Loti spent his time with the native court, not the French authorities, and his view of Veeder's transgressions would perhaps have been less severe than that of Consul Atwater, but he does not reveal any knowledge of the incident.

Charles Veeder fell off the map in 1872. According to the ship's account book he was paid $500 in gold, but whether his mistress found him attractive when he no longer had a ship is a question with only one logical answer. He may have found passage back to Barclay's Island to live with the villagers he had befriended, and maybe they took care of the old man, sharing their fish and coconuts and continuing to dance and sing for his enjoyment until the great cyclone of 1878 blew them all away. Or maybe with his newly acquired capital he purchased a small schooner and continued to ferry islanders from one atoll to another until his alcohol-soaked navigational skills failed him, and he joined his sons—another Nantucketer "lost at sea."

CHAPTER EIGHT

The Lost Boys of the William Gifford

When Captain Veeder wandered off in Papeete with a purse full of gold and his mistress in tow, the men in the forecastle breathed a sigh of relief. Fearful for their lives, they had chosen the only course of action likely to remedy the situation, and it had been risky. The mates of the *William Gifford* could have resisted the demands of the desperate crew and insisted upon the release of the captain, but they didn't. That lack of action says something about the first mate, who should have stepped up, calmed the excited mutineers, and taken command of the ship. He may then have made the same decision as the crew, since the only appropriate next step was to deposit the captain with the nearest authorities. But there was a problem with the command of the ship starting at the top. Most of those who originally signed on were no longer on board, and with shifting roles and the addition of new officers in the midst of the shipboard mayhem, any semblance of order and authority was long gone. In 1868, a full crew of thirty-two men had set out for the Pacific: the captain, four mates, four boatsteerers, a cooper, cook, steward, carpenter, and nineteen sailors. They were all set to wreak havoc on any sperm whales encountered. Each of the four whaleboats headed by a mate and boatsteerer required four men to row, and with nineteen seamen there were three extra men. But ten of those mariners deserted in the course of the voyage as did one of the boatsteerers. Of the officers, only the fourth mate, Mariano Quenas, endured the entire three and a half years; by the end of the voyage, he was second mate. According to the account book kept by the owners of the *William Gifford*, the original first mate was Edward S. Davis, but he was paid for a "partial voyage" in 1870 when he left the ship and the second mate, Isaac P. Whidden, replaced him. When Whidden moved up to first mate, third mate Charles Weeden became second mate, and Quenas became third mate. The change in their lay in the account book—in Quenas's case from 1/55 to 1/40, and later to 1/32—reflects their change in position. Whidden must have been the mate who was sick at the beginning of Kirwin's account, replaced by Mr. Haughton in Tahiti in May 1871. Haughton's name does not show up in the *William Gifford* account book because he signed on in Tahiti and presumably stayed there when the ship returned in May 1872, reuniting with a family that was probably better off without such an intemperate and unfaithful man. Throughout Kirwin's account, the mate's drunkenness rivals the captain's, so he was not in any condition to take command of anything. By the spring of 1872, there were *no* competent mates on board, and Kirwin refers to Mr. Rogers, who signed on as boatsteerer in 1868 and was fourth mate in the fall of 1871, as "chief" mate. Only Veeder knew how to navigate the ship, and he needed help from George Cash, a frightened teenager on his first whaling voyage, to compute longitude.

That golden ticket for a whaling cruise with a renowned captain during the height of Nantucket's economic depression was too good to be true, literally, and it turned into a nightmare for the young men from Nantucket who were essentially imprisoned on a poorly run factory ship under the command of a drunken lunatic. It's a wonder they survived, but census records and other documents show that Thomas Winslow, George Cash, and Albert Folger lived to tell their tales of the South Pacific, as did their New Bedford crewmates, journal-keepers Edward J. Kirwin and Edward Cavanagh.

It was common for boys in their teens to go whaling in the nineteenth century, particularly boys from Nantucket and New Bedford, but that's not to say that it wasn't a harsh and sometimes deadly environment. All three of the Veeder sons emulated their father and became mariners, and two of them—Charles Edward and David—were lost at sea. The Nantucket boys born mid-century grew up with unemployment, abandoned houses, and sure signs of impending poverty surrounding them; regardless of the statistics of disaster and death at sea, the opportunity to go on a voyage and escape the local depression was appealing. To accompany one of the island's legendary captains made it even better—a captain who had sailed with his entire family would be the perfect caretaker and mentor for the local boys. Charles Veeder wore his successful voyages like badges of honor, and as one of the founders of that grand fraternity of whaling captains on Nantucket, the Pacific Club, he inspired the respect of the young men whose own prospects looked so desolate. The three untried Nantucket mariners who joined Veeder on the *William Gifford* were too young to have fought in the Civil War; this was their chance to see the world beyond their island home in the Atlantic and put some coins in their pockets. They probably had no dreams of getting rich or rising through the ranks to become captain in a dozen years or so, the common path of their fathers and grandfathers, but they would witness the watery world they had heard so much about, a world defined by ports, islands, atolls, reefs, and infinite stretches of empty ocean. And they would do battle with one of the largest creatures on earth.

Just a month after the *William Gifford* left New Bedford, *Lippincott's Magazine* published a travelogue about Nantucket, following an emerging trend in the national press to depict the island as a once-vibrant but now decrepit and charming locale populated by odd characters. "Nantucket now has a 'body-o'-death' appearance such as few New England towns possess. The houses stand around in faded gentility style—the inhabitants have a dreamy look, as though they live in the memories of the past." There was truth to the description, unfortunately. The wharves were no longer crowded with the dozens of ships whose masts once created a small forest in the harbor. While the ship-owners and whale-oil merchants who lived on Main Street still had fortunes to invest in the gasworks and railroads of the mainland, others who had no cash reserves left the island to find employment elsewhere or patched together a simple life of fishing and farming and odd jobs for those who could afford to hire laborers.

* * *

Consul Atwater arranged for the *William Gifford* to sail from Tahiti directly to San Francisco under the command of Captain Israel Sweet, whose wife joined him on the voyage, and on Monday, June 3, 1872, Kirwin recorded, "... we hove up our anchor and left Tahiti behind, all hands feeling bad as usual on leaving port." No rejoicing for the men who had come to expect harsh treatment, terrible food, and incompetent superiors, but the voyage turned out to be remarkably uneventful. With roast mutton and coconut pie on occasion and a plug of tobacco from the captain, life was good. On July 4, Kirwin wrote, "Work was suspended during the day and we got the best that the ship could afford, to eat and it was the pleasantest fourth that we have passed this voyage." On July 21, the ship anchored in San Francisco Bay at the foot of Howard Street. Captain Sweet went ashore immediately and sent a telegram to ship owner Charles Gifford, news of the turbulent voyage dotting and dashing over the wires to New Bedford and from there to Nantucket where it exploded like one of Veeder's bomb lances.

New Bedford's *Whalemen's Shipping List* broadcast the news on August 6, 1872: "Bark *William Gifford*, of this port, which arrived at San Francisco July 21st, was sent to that port from Tahiti, by United States Consul Atwater, under command of Capt. Israel Sweet. Consul Atwater writes from Tahiti, under date of June 1st, that the bark arrived there May 27th, the crew having possession of the vessel. The Consul investigated the cause and suspended the master, Capt. Veeder, from command, for gross misconduct and sent the vessel to San Francisco, as above."

Gross misconduct! All the old whaling captains on Nantucket read the *Shipping List*; it was their alumni news. They privately recollected some of their own questionable tactics and activities at sea and wondered just how far over the line Veeder had wandered. But the local paper, the *Inquirer and Mirror*, did not pick up the story, merely noting in the maritime news column of August 17 that the *William Gifford,* Captain Baker, had sailed from San Francisco for New Bedford.

The details Susan learned of her husband's last years in the South Pacific are not known, but her legal actions indicate that she got wind of the situation at least a day before the weekly *Whalemen's Shipping List* rolled off the press. Charles had given her a power of attorney in 1855, before his voyage on the *Ocean Rover*. It was a fairly common practice for a Nantucket mariner to endow his spouse with all the legal power she might need to live independently while he was at sea: the right to conduct business, buy and sell property, and secure a loan—in other words, to have the same rights as a man in an age when women were second-class citizens. Susan had not found it necessary to use her power of attorney before, but on August 5, 1872, she recorded the document in the Nantucket Registry of Deeds, along with a deed transferring all of the property owned by Charles to her brother, Edward.

Recently retired Nehemiah Baker, captain of the *William Gifford* on a previous voyage, was sent by the ship owners to California to bring the vessel home to New Bedford while attempting to snag a few whales along the way. The sailors of the tired and ill-kept whaleship were offered $35 a month to stay on board, or, as a couple of them later negotiated, $25 a month and 1/100 lay, but most of the crew had had enough of whaling and scurried like rats to get ashore, among them the two remaining Nantucket men, Tom Winslow and Albert C. Folger, who together "went in a schooner for $45 month." It was a chance to earn something, since Winslow's wage at the end of three and a half years was $40.94, or today's equivalent of about $800. He had signed on for a 1/200 lay, which meant that he actually made $236.94, but deductions ate up his meager pay. Every seaman on the *William Gifford*, from the mates on down, was charged twenty dollars for "expenses of ship," a sum reimbursed if they stuck with the ship. Those who wanted to take cash advances for their own use or to give to wives and mothers, paid an exorbitant interest of forty percent. Winslow took a seventy-five dollar advance and paid thirty dollars for it.

Added to that was another advance of ten dollars (no interest) and a bill from Captain Veeder's "slops" for $80.96. Slops was the name for anything purchased from the ship's store, like a new shirt, tobacco, or a knife. So from his grand total of $256.94, $216.50 was subtracted. And Winslow was one of the lucky ones. Of the nineteen sailors who began the voyage at either the 1/170 or 1/200 lay, thirteen were in the hole financially when the ship arrived in San Francisco, although ten of them had already, perhaps wisely, jumped ship.

The oldest of the Nantucket young men to sign on for a whaling voyage with Captain Veeder, Thomas C. Winslow, the "Tom" of Kirwin's account, was one of twelve children of Shubael and Ann Winslow. He had six older sisters, two older brothers, two younger brothers (one of whom died young), and a younger sister. If his father had been a mariner instead of a butcher, the family would have been much smaller. The Winslows of Nantucket were descendants of two brothers who married local women and settled on the island in the late eighteenth century: Joseph, a mariner, and Benjamin, a blacksmith. Benjamin's three sons were land-bound tradesmen as well, but grandson Tom joined the ranks of his seafaring cousins as a whaleman who rounded Cape Horn. One of his sisters would do the same. Phebe Winslow was married to Richard C. Gibbs Jr., who brought her along on a voyage on the *Talcahuano* in 1868, the same year Tom sailed on the *William Gifford*. Gibbs was second mate, so it was somewhat unusual for him to have his wife and toddler on board, but Phebe may have joined the excursion to keep the captain's wife company. The *Talcahuano* was commanded by George H. Cash, father of Tom's shipmate, George, whose mother Emeline was on board, too, with George's twelve-year-old brother Stillman. Captain Cash may have thought George would have a better introduction to whaling on a ship not so crowded with family; he could make his own way, under the kindly tutelage of Cash's friend Veeder.

A close community on shore became even closer at sea—the young whaling boys Tom and George on the *William Gifford* and the rest of George's family on the *Talcahuano* with Tom's sister and nephew. An even closer connection between Tom's family and the Veeders was his sister Sarah's marriage to George Veeder in 1860, making Tom uncle to Captain Veeder's grandchildren. Sarah was the second-oldest Winslow girl, fourteen years Tom's senior, married to the only surviving Veeder son. Captain Veeder should have showed Tom some special consideration since their families were united, but he treated the boy with the same sometimes cruel disregard he showed the rest of the crew.

Tom Winslow appears in Kirwin's journal three times, on two occasions because of unpleasant encounters with the captain, which were Kirwin's favorite episodes to record. On December 3, 1871, Tom and one of the boatsteerers went ashore on Nehiru Island and brought off three "fowl," which they cleaned and prepared for cooking, but the captain claimed them, ate them, and did not reimburse the men who had purchased or caught or traded for them. With good food in the forecastle a rarity, it was a low blow, worthy of note in the journal and greatly resented by Tom. Two months later, when the captain asked to borrow his deck of cards, Tom was not inclined to share. Veeder then confiscated the deck and threw it overboard, the kings and queens doomed to a watery grave and Tom wondering what his fate would be in the hands of such a spiteful and uncharitable man. Kirwin's last mention of Tom is on February 22, 1872, when he noted that Tom received a letter. From whom we don't know, but any communication from friends and family was a small miracle, envied by those who read and reread, carefully hoarded, and probably memorized their own letters from home. Tom may have learned that his father was not well; in San Francisco he got another letter: "Tom has received news of his father's death and is greatly affected thereby. Poor fellow! How he is to be pitied."

With no pressing need to return to Nantucket, Tom happily left the *William Gifford* and signed on for a passage up the coast from San Francisco on a schooner bound to the Pacific Northwest for lumber. He and Albert Folger went together, earning higher wages than either young man had ever imagined. Tom shows up in Bridgewater, Massachusetts, in 1873; his sister, Louisa, had married and moved to nearby South Abington a few years earlier, setting the precedent for the rest of the family to relocate to that booming center of the boot and shoe industry. The Abington area must have looked especially promising in comparison to Nantucket, where there was nothing happening and no employment for a young man fresh off a failed whaling voyage. During the Civil War, Abington had a contract with the government to supply Union troops with boots—roughly half of the army's boots were made there—and the industry was still vibrant after the war. Tom was a shoemaker the rest of his working life. In 1876, he married Florence A. Reed in South Abington, and they had two sons, Charles and George. If Charles was not such a common name—Tom's little brother who died at the age of two was named Charles, as was a notoriously eccentric uncle—one would wonder at his choice of name for his firstborn.

Neither of Tom's sons had children, and stories of their father's adventures on the *William Gifford* faded from family memory long ago. A descendant of one of Tom's siblings wrote of their seafaring relative, "Florence married Thomas Winslow, who sailed on a whaling ship out of Nantucket. If so, and it indeed seems that Thomas' family of birth was from Nantucket, apparently Thomas soon put that adventurous life aside for work more amenable to family life, because the federal censuses of 1880 and 1900 both show him to be employed in the shoe factories of the Abington Whitman area at that time."

* * *

Tom's shipmate, Albert C. Folger, receives even less notice than Tom in Kirwin's account of the last year of the *William Gifford*. Only once does Kirwin mention him, December 16, 1871, when, in the midst of a whale hunt, "Folger got stunned by a whale kicking the oar against him." In the roiling sea amid the three other boats and the frightened sperm whales, wham! powerful flukes knocked Folger's oar into his chest, or maybe his head, and he was momentarily out cold. Luckily, he didn't fall overboard, or crack his skull.

The oldest of the six sons of Albert C. Folger and Mary Ann Key, young Albert lost his father, a carpenter, when he was nine. As the first son in the family, he had responsibilities, the foremost being to get out of the house and earn his own living as soon as he was old enough. His widowed mother had a large brood to care for, none of them girls to assist in the domestic sphere; she remarried in 1869 and died a year later. While Albert was at sea, his siblings all moved in with their grandparents, Theophilas and Eunice Key, on New Street in Nantucket, a stone's throw from the Veeder house at 91 Orange. When the *William Gifford* accounts were settled, Folger was in the hole. The account book records, "loss in this man $47.16." He had taken an advance of $100 in 1868, money that probably went to his mother, and for that he paid the outrageous interest of $40. His slop bill was high because his family was too poor to outfit him properly before the voyage, and his 1/200 lay did not net him enough to cover his expenses.

After the arrival of the *William Gifford* in San Francisco in 1872, Albert and Tom made up for lost revenue working together on the unidentified lumber schooner. From 1873 to 1879, Folger's whereabouts are unknown, but an article about his career published in the *Inquirer and Mirror* in 1937 is both confusing and tantalizing:

> *Captain Folger went whaling to the Pacific with Captain George Veeder, in the ship Mount Vernon. The vessel was sold in Honolulu, and Capt. Veeder went into the trading business among the islands, buying a trim little schooner for the business. Folger went with him for a number of cruises and then drifted over to Yokohama, where he finally went sealing, commanding several schooners until he came into possession of the* Penelope.

Substitute Charles Veeder for George Veeder and *William Gifford* for *Mount Vernon*, a whaleship that sank in the Okhotsk Sea in 1856, and maybe we have a clue about not only Folger but Captain Veeder himself. It is nice to imagine Veeder in a trim little schooner, but there was no logical reason for Folger to return to Tahiti and work with the man he knew as drunk and dangerous. The report is so full of inaccuracies it can't be trusted on any level, but one thing is certain: Folger became a respected sealing captain and was known as a teetotaler, a lesson probably learned from the cautionary voyage of the *William Gifford*.

The next we know of Folger he was on an otter-hunting cruise in the North Pacific on the schooner *Alexander* of San Francisco in 1879, sailing to Japan, the Kamchatka Coast, the Bering Sea, and Victoria, on Vancouver Island, where the crew cured the pelts before taking them home to San Francisco. Folger must have liked Victoria; he returned there in 1880 and sailed out of the port for several years before making Yokohama, Japan, his headquarters.

According to the *Inquirer and Mirror,* Folger was to the sealing fleet what Captain Charles Grant (1814–1906) was to the whaling fleet, a high accolade indeed, since Grant was one of the giants of the local industry, a man who spent fifty-six years at sea and brought home more sperm oil than any other whaling master anywhere, *ever*. Folger did the same with sealskins and sea-otter pelts, but in much less time. In his schooner *Penelope* he discovered a seal rookery on Kyoku in the Kuril group, a chain of islands extending from the northernmost Japanese island, Hokkaido, to the tip of Russia's Kamchatka Peninsula. He brought back 4,070 sealskins and 55 sea-otter skins in less than five months of brutal massacre. He made a tidy sum, returning eventually to Victoria and becoming a Canadian citizen.

The impoverished young man who left Nantucket in 1868 returned to the island for the first time in 1894 to visit his younger brother, Arthur, a fisherman, and the only one of the Folger brothers still resident in their hometown. The summer scene on the island would have been shocking to the man who left when it was at its economic nadir. Nantucket had put on a new costume for its role as a resort; now there were throngs of well-dressed visitors around town, a train ran to 'Sconset, there were bathing houses and fishing-boat charters, hotels and ice cream parlors, all signs of renewed prosperity. Albert did not arrive until October, however, when the crowds were gone and the town had settled back into its offseason doldrums, but his wife, Florence, had spent the summer on the island with their infant daughter and regaled him with stories of a fashionable crowd at the baseball games, the annual Agricultural Fair, beach picnics, and squantums, a local term for clambakes at the shore.

Folger died in Victoria in 1929, preceded by Florence in 1923. Their daughter, Anna Rosa De Lima Folger, born in 1893, entered the United States in 1916 and exited from Seattle on her way back to Canada two years later; there her trail goes cold.

* * *

GEORGE A. CASH, the third and youngest Nantucket seaman aboard the *William Gifford*, did not witness the island's transformation to a summer playground for strangers. His experiences with Captain Veeder must have

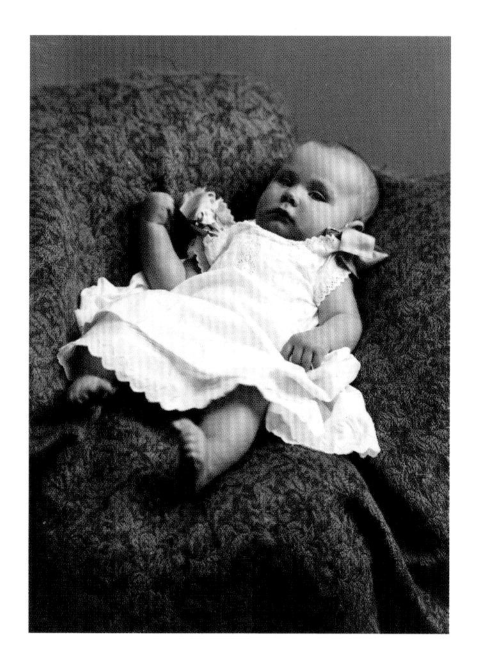

Rosa de Lima Folger (b. November 6, 1893), photographed in May 1894 when her mother, Florence—the wife of former *William Gifford* sailor Albert Folger—visited Nantucket.

GPN323

turned him against the sea; once he made his way to California, he went on shore and stayed there. When the ship's accounts were settled in 1873, his uncle—Captain William Cash, husband of Susan's friend, Azubah—signed for his wages, which amounted to $95.57. Young George had such a big paycheck because he had not purchased a single item from the slop chest. His parents supplied him with all the necessities for the voyage, since, unlike the parents of Tom Winslow and Albert Folger, they knew exactly what would be required and could afford it. Captain Cash's statement in the *William Gifford* account book is interesting:

> *Rec'd New Bedford 4 mo 15th 1873 from Chas. H. Gifford ninety-five and 57/100 dollars in full settlement for the voyage of George A. Cash and all demands against the owners which I agree to bear harmless by my settlement of his voyage and receiving the money he being a minor and having a discharge from his father. William Cash.*

Apparently George's father agreed not to hold Gifford liable for the lost voyage so grossly mishandled by his friend and neighbor Charles Veeder, whose violent actions scared young Cash to death—which is exactly what the young man risked when he stowed away in the whaleboat that took the badly beaten steward to Marutea, one of the lowest of the low-lying islands of the Tuamotus, in May 1872, just weeks before the crew mutinied. Kirwin wrote merely that "Cash got in and stowed himself away ashore." The story of Cash's escape, his life on Marutea, and how he eventually made his way to California is probably a good one, but like so many whaling tales, it is unrecorded and forgotten. And maybe even unconfided. Ashamed of his desertion or embarrassed by his association with the notorious voyage, Cash may have remained silent about that formative episode in his life. When his son donated a tapestry to the Nantucket Historical Association in 1969, he related that his grandfather, George H. Cash, was a whaleman and his grandmother, Emeline, decided to create the elaborate embroidery while her husband was away from home on his long whaling voyages. The large tapestry—approximately four and a half feet by five and a half feet—attests to the time Emeline had on her hands. It was given as a wedding present to George A. Cash who, according to his son, "had gone out west" and made his home in Washington Corners, California. In his interview with the local press, George's son made no mention of his father's whaling voyage

Emeline Cash (1823–1890), mother of George A. Cash of the *William Gifford*, went on a whaling voyage with her husband, Captain George H. Cash, and son, Stillman, in the Chilean ship *Talcahuano* in 1868.

GPN3822

Tapestry completed by Emeline Cash in 1862 and given as a wedding present to George A. and Ida B. Cash on June 30, 1880.

Gift of George N. Cash, 1969.27.1

with Captain Veeder. Census records and California city directories reveal that George worked as a butcher in San Francisco in 1875. By 1880, he was working as a laborer on the farm of George and Fannie Walters in Oakland. Their nineteen-year-old-daughter, Ida, became his wife that year, and George's mother sent him the meticulously worked tapestry. Twenty years later, George was a deputy assessor in Alameda County, where he lived in Washington Township on San Francisco Bay, in what is now Fremont, California. Although his education ended when he went to sea at fifteen, George appears to have been one of the most capable of the novice mariners on the *William Gifford*. He was promoted to boatsteerer, and he knew how to navigate a ship, which required mathematical knowledge he had learned in Nantucket. That education enabled him to leave butchery and get a desk job. George A. Cash died in 1907; his son, George N., died in 1970, a year after the visit to his father's birthplace. Neither George N. nor his sister, Fannie Cash Cramer, had children.

The Nantucket boys of the *William Gifford* sailed away in 1868 and did not return home. Although they all had extensive families on the island, there were no opportunities for them there, and the wider world beckoned. They had grown up in a community of cousins with family roots that reached back generations, but they dispersed and fathered small families in new communities where their past was not common knowledge to their neighbors. Neither Winslow nor Cash had grandchildren, and Folger's progeny is unconfirmed. During their four years at sea they grew from boys to men, learned to sail a ship, kill a whale, endure oppression, and take a stand against it. They reveled in the beauty of a Tahitian sunset and long remembered what it felt like to swim in a turquoise lagoon where native women seemed more fish than human. And they had their share of nightmares, too.

* * *

EDWARD J. KIRWIN, New Bedford seaman and journal-keeper, stuck with the *William Gifford* all the way home. He began the fourth and last section of his journal with the following lines:

> *Arrived in Tahiti May 27 with the Capt. in the forecastle and left there June 3rd 1872 for San Francisco, Cal. Crossed the Equator eight days out with a strong breeze.*
> (May 10, 1872)

Several weeks later, he briefly editorialized, proud perhaps of the recent notoriety of the ship:

> *Bark William Gifford (Sweet) Capt. bound for San Francisco under double reefed topsails with a crew of mutineers on board.*
> (June 16, 1872)

On July 21, 1872, Kirwin was introduced to a vibrant city that had been built on gold just twenty-three years earlier, when thousands of "forty-niners" arrived to stake their claims in the hills and streams of the Sierras. San Francisco was the hub, where the ships arrived, the men convened, and expeditions into the gold fields began. With a population of about 150,000 in 1870, it was then the tenth-most-populous city in the United States. New Bedford at the same time had a population of 21,000, and Nantucket held on to a mere 4,100. Boston and New York were larger than San Francisco, but chances are the young seamen of the *William Gifford* had never been to either city. With free time while the ship was in the harbor awaiting her third captain, Kirwin and his buddy, Ed Cavanagh, did some sightseeing in the big city. The young men who loved to sing went to the Metropolitan Theater and the New American Theatre, and they rode in the horse cars to "Woodward's Garden," a fabulous botanical garden that

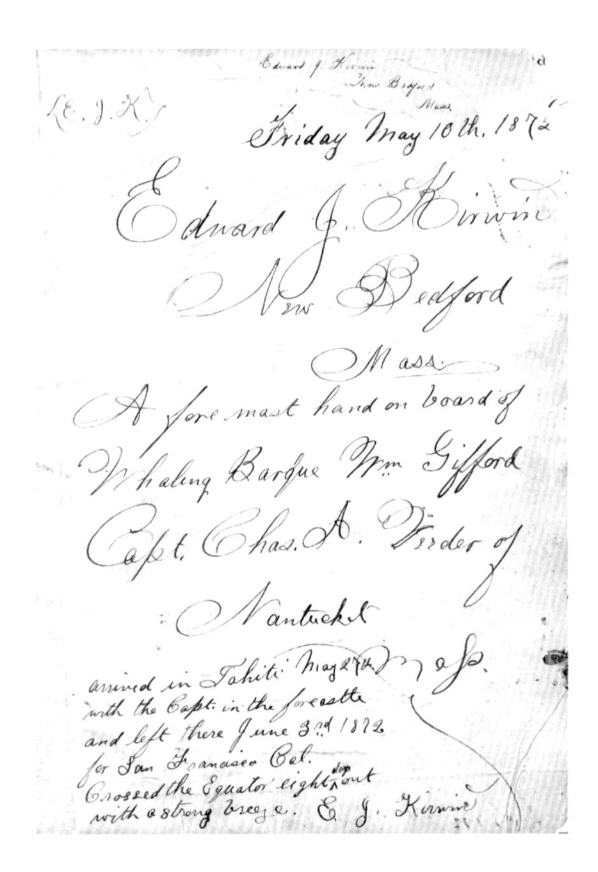
(E. J. K.)
Friday May 10th, 1872
Edward J. Kirwin
New Bedford
Mass.
A fore mast hand on board of
Whaling Barque Wm Gifford
Capt. Chas. A. Veeder of
Nantucket
arrived in Tahiti May 27th
with the Capt. in the forecastle
and left there June 3rd 1872
for San Francisco Cal.
Crossed the Equator eight day out
with a strong breeze. E. J. Kirwin

Page from Edward J. Kirwin's journal of the *William Gifford*, May 10, 1872.

Courtesy of the New Bedford Whaling Museum, KWM Log 452

included an amusement park and zoo. If Kirwin didn't regale his children with stories about Tahiti and Nuku Hiva, he probably felt comfortable describing the wonders of the manmade attractions in San Francisco. A thirty-dollar advance on their upcoming whaling voyage funded a good time in the city for the young men, although a large portion of the money was spent outfitting themselves for the homeward voyage; the lessons of the overpriced slop chest had been learned.

The third captain of the *William Gifford*, Nehemiah Baker, arrived on July 25. He discharged the entire crew and then rehired those who wanted to stick with the ship and try some more whaling. No one did, except for Kirwin and Cavanagh, the cook, and Mr. Rogers, who managed to get arrested for selling some of the ship's salt pork and was relieved of his commitment to the ship, going to jail instead. Ed Cavanagh tells us why he and his friend continued their journey in the whaleship: "Ed received a letter from his father who urged him strongly to stick to the ship and I guess we will although much against our inclination." After what was probably a regretful farewell to the charms of San Francisco on August 10, they sailed south, crossing the "line" on September 6. No sperm whales sported in the waters off the coast of South America; perhaps the albatross they caught off Massafuero, in the Juan Fernandez Islands, brought bad luck. Although Kirwin makes a few unflattering remarks about Captain Baker in his journal, calling him "rather savage," he finds no fault with the captain's management of the ship or the allotment of food for the crew, even mentioning a "bully dinner" on October 6, the day after they slaughtered a pig and a sheep from their onboard pen, but he may have regretted bargaining for twenty-five dollars a month and a 1/100 lay instead of a flat thirty-five dollars a month, since whales were scarce. In fact, Kirwin records only one whale killed on the return voyage, and a right whale at that.

On November 10, Kirwin wrote,: "Three months since leaving San Francisco and I would give my wages back to get there now." The dreadful passage around Cape Horn was imminent, but three days later, surprised that the return to the Atlantic could be so pleasant, Kirwin remarked, "Has been splendid weather for Cape Horn with a lite breeze from the northwest."

They made their way to Port Stanley in the Falkland Islands, where Captain Baker attempted to sail the ship into the harbor without a pilot, and, as Kirwin delightedly pointed out, "Old Baker was white as a sheet for once" as it proved to be a more difficult maneuver than he supposed. A pilot was engaged after some harrowing tacking, and Kirwin wrote, "I feel about worn out for we came about every five minutes." The bad weather found them as they lay at anchor in Port Stanley: "Has been a regular Cape Horn day. Commenced last night blowing strong from the South and called all hands at 10 o'clock to let go the other anchor. It was raining, hailing, snowing and I don't know what." The *William Gifford* rested in port for more than two weeks, the weather shifting from foul to pleasant to "very disagreeable." Kirwin and Cavanagh and the other crewmen re-housed some of the oil, taking it out of leaky casks and stowing it newly coopered in the hold. They painted the ship's rails, repaired sails, replaced glass in the after-cabin skylight, and loaded a ton of coal on board. They had time ashore, too, duck hunting, and on one occasion enjoying a bottle of wine with the captain, who did not overindulge. On December 2, 1872, they set sail, and the next day Kirwin wrote his last journal entry:

> *Splendid weather with a light breeze from the south but toward evening hauled around to the north. Crew engaged in knotting rope yarns and making spun yarn. Old Baker keeps us going from daylight till dark. Ed is going to stand mastheads with the boatsteerers. Lat 49.37 South.* (December 3, 1872)

Edward J. Kirwin, mariner mutineer, had run out of paper.

* * *

A LITTLE OVER TWO MONTHS LATER, the *William Gifford* sailed into her home port, New Bedford, Massachusetts, where there were ships in the harbor and industry on land—textile mills and glass factories were thriving, and there were opportunities for a young man who was adaptable, intelligent, and literate, with a sharp eye and a ready opinion. Kirwin's father, James, was a cooper, and his mother, Bridget, managed the family home on South Sixth Street where his five sisters and two brothers lived and that's where he returned. Throughout the 1870s, Kirwin is listed as a mariner in the New Bedford city directories, but by 1881 he had found the occupation that he would follow the rest of his life—glass maker. He worked at the Mt. Washington Glass Company, which produced a wide variety of items of cut and blown glass, including decorated lampshades and vases, as well as elaborate art glass. By 1890, the company employed three hundred men, all of them skilled craftsmen. Kirwin, who had spent four years on a "factory" ship, was now a factory worker again, creating a product he could be proud of: Peachblow, Burmese, Sicilian, and Royal Flemish glass, cut-glass chandeliers, and exquisite items such as a tea service sent to Queen Victoria, who was so impressed she ordered additional pieces from the company. His occupation is described in various records as a glass maker, glass cutter, and glass polisher.

In 1893, when he was forty-two years old, Kirwin married Catherine Cleary, a teacher, and they had two children, Mary A., born in 1895, and Edward Jr., born in 1897. Unlike his Nantucket shipmates, Kirwin stayed in his hometown as did his siblings. Sarah, Anna, Mary, Walter, and Henry shared the family home on South Sixth Street for decades, while Kirwin and his family lived nearby, first on Rockland, then on Court Street. None of his siblings married except for older sister Kate, but she had no children. The only progeny of the Kirwin family in New Bedford were Edward's two children. Edward J. Kirwin, glassworker, died in New Bedford September 26, 1924, age 73.

Ed Cavanagh, the constant companion of Kirwin who was last heard of "standing mastheads" on the *William Gifford* in Kirwin's final journal entry, signed in the ship's account book for his wages in 1873. What a different voyage it would have been for Kirwin if the "Ed" of his account had not been along to support his assessment of the conditions on board and to stand with him as they rebelled. Ed was frugal in his expenditures in the slop chest, too, and after four and a half years netted $307, today's equivalent of close to $6,000. Never mind that he had endangered his health with years of poor food and too much sun, the strictures of his Catholic upbringing had been sorely tested and shockingly flaunted, and he, like all the crew, had suffered at the hands of incompetent authority. He and Kirwin had seen how life was lived in the Pacific Islands, but they had no wish to spend the rest of their days there. New Bedford was home, and it looked good. Ed Cavanagh, remembered by his family as a story-teller with a beautiful singing voice, recounted tales of his voyage in the *William Gifford*—the trip around Cape Horn in howling wind, the old captain laughing gleefully when he pulled the wrong tooth from one of the sailors, the captain he called a sadist and a drunkard.

The trio of Nantucketers and their two New Bedford companions were eager boys when they left home in 1868 and lean, hardened men when they walked off the *William Gifford* to find their way in the world. Back in the domestic sphere of home and family, with solid ground under their feet, a coconut cake at Christmas may have reminded them of days when they ate watery stew and coconuts while Captain Veeder dined on roast pig and canoodled with his concubine. Or they may have remembered how much better a coconut tasted when you were nearly starving. Or they heard the rustle of palm fronds in the wind, felt the salt sting their skin, and remembered the laughing native girls dancing on the deck.

CHAPTER NINE

Eighty Years, Ten Months, Eight Days

Captain Veeder's bones lie somewhere in the South Pacific, on a sea floor littered with harpoons or in an unmarked grave on an atoll. Vital records kept by the town of Nantucket record that he died in the Society Islands in 1878, but there is no supporting documentation, no mention in the local newspaper, no trace of how the news reached Nantucket, although the likely story is that a whaling captain from New Bedford heard the news somewhere in the South Pacific when he stopped at Tahiti, or Huahine, or Nuku Hiva. The crazy old whaling captain who lived like a castaway had died, or wrecked his trading schooner on Lazareef, or was missing after the great cyclone hit Raroia in February 1878. A report of that calamity appeared in the May 1 edition of *The Friend*, a publication of the American Seamen's Friend Society, in a letter from Tahiti that described the heavy toll of destruction in the low islands of the Paumoto Group, particularly on Anaa, Raroia, and Kaukura: ten white men were drowned, 117 native islanders swept away, and 112,000 coconut trees destroyed. Veeder's mistress was from Raroia, or Barclay's Island as he knew it. He had befriended the governor and most of the inhabitants of her small village on his many visits there, so it may have been a last home for the old captain who was blown out to sea with the coconut trees and the piglets during the great cyclone.

Whether Susan expected the captain to come to his senses and come home, or not, she was no longer concerned that he would take control of his Nantucket assets; in 1876, her brother, Edward Austin, transferred all the Veeder property back to her: the Orange Street homestead, land around the corner on Warren Street, and other small parcels.

* * *

NANTUCKET WAS SLOWLY EMERGING from its economic lethargy in the 1870s, when it became known as an out-of-the-way summer destination for adventurous travelers and work-weary city dwellers in search of fresh air and good health. It was the dawning of the vacation era in America, and Nantucket, if not yet on the A-list, was one of dozens of beach communities developing into tourist destinations all along America's coasts and shores. The first local guidebook was published in 1871, *Historical Notes of the Island of*

Detail from *Bird's Eye View of the Town of Nantucket, State of Massachusetts, Looking Southwest*, J. J. Stoner, 1881.

Courtesy of the Prints and Photographs Division, Library of Congress

Nantucket, and Tourist's Guide, a promotional text featuring a heavy dose of local history. It was written by Richard A. Cook, a man "of more than ordinary intelligence" who worked as a clerk at the Ocean House, a three-story brick hotel situated in downtown Nantucket at the corner of Broad and Centre streets. Built as a residence by Jared Coffin in 1840, the grand house was sold to the Nantucket Steamboat Company in 1847, a year after the Great Fire and several years after Coffin and his family had relocated to Brighton, Massachusetts. The Steamboat Company turned the grand house into a hotel, enticing customers to take the steamer to the island and stay for a while in elegant comfort. By the time Cook wrote his guide, the Ocean House was in private hands and had expanded with a two-story wing that included a large dining room, where fish and chowder were specialties. Ulysses S. Grant visited Nantucket in 1874 and dined there, and more than two decades earlier, Herman Melville and his father-in-law, Judge Lemuel Shaw, traveled to Nantucket and almost certainly lodged there, as there were few other downtown accommodations at the time.

A hotel called the Atlantic House had been built in 1848 on Main Street in Siasconset, the village at the east end of the island, providing rooms for visitors who found themselves stranded seven miles from town or were charmed into lingering. Those two establishments were all that were necessary on the island until the 1870s, when the trickle of visitors began to turn into a steady stream. In the last quarter of the nineteenth century, hotels sprang up all over the island, from town to Surfside on the south shore, Wauwinet at the east end of the Great Harbor, and Siasconset perched on the far eastern bluff. Many Nantucketers earned a little extra income by renting rooms to visitors in the summertime. Susan Veeder did so, advertising for boarders in July 1875. She had a large enough house, and, although niece Susie would soon be married to a carpenter from Acushnet, Massachusetts, a town just a few miles north of New Bedford, Marianna was fifteen, old enough to help her mother as hostess and chambermaid. When the subject of Captain Veeder was raised, mother and daughter may have glanced at his portrait before asserting to their guests that he was lost at sea, like two of his sons.

Left: **Susan Austin Veeder (1816–1897), 1879.** *GPN768*
Right: **George A. Veeder (1834–1897), 1881.** *GPN1267*

Oldest son George, however, was present and well-known in town. He had had a long career on the ocean, both in the Pacific and in the waters around his home island. Although born too late in the era of Nantucket whaling to become a captain in that industry, he spent a number of years chasing the same mammals he was introduced to on the *Nauticon,* where he learned the finer points of whaling from his father. He was fourth mate on the *Young Hector* out of New Bedford from 1853 to 1857, and second mate on the brig *Eunice H. Adams* of Nantucket from 1867 to 1868, arriving home from a short voyage in the Atlantic a month after his father sailed on the *William Gifford*. George may not have known that the aging captain was planning to go back to sea, and he was not able to say a final goodbye to the man who had taught him everything he knew about the sperm whale. George sailed again on the *Eunice H. Adams* on an Atlantic whaling voyage in March 1869, the last year of Nantucket's participation in the business, then hung up his whaling hat in June 1870 when the voyage was over and the ship was sold to New Bedford.

Back on Nantucket with his wife and two children, out of long habit George kept an eye on the sea. In February of 1871, when the harbor was choked with ice and the winds were howling, the schooner *Mary Anna* of Hampden, Maine, struck a shoal and wrecked just a couple miles north of the town. With the temperature at four degrees, she quickly became encased in ice, imperiling the freezing crew. Nantucketers were accustomed to shipwrecks on the shoals around the island, and, regardless of treacherous conditions, when a vessel in distress was sighted local men would gather together and devise a plan of rescue. First, the steamship *Island Home* labored from Steamboat Wharf through the slushy water, attempting to reach the vessel but became stuck in the ice. When that attempt failed, George and seven other men set out in two dories at 10 p.m. on February 3, when the wind died and the ice had solidified enough for them to drag their boats part of the way on the ice, at some places throwing down long boards to bridge cracks and at others rowing where there was open water. Two and a half grueling hours later, they reached the wreck and rescued all five men aboard. The local newspaper reported, "No one who is not conversant with scenes of this kind, can appreciate the labor and sufferings of the rescuing party, to say nothing of the risk of life, or the torturing anxiety of their families and friends on shore during the five hours that they were absent." The heroism of these men was recognized by the captain of the *Mary Anna*, whose thank-you note to the Nantucketers was published in the next weekly issue of the *Inquirer and Mirror* along with a thank-you from the rescuers to their community for monetary donations: "We feel grateful for such prompt recognition, while we boast of no honor (nor did we look for any pay) for an act of duty by no means uncommon to humanity." A month later, another thank-you appeared in the newspaper, from the rescuers to Rowland H. Macy, a Nantucket son and founder of the New York department store that bears his name, for "his timely donation of money, so welcome to men in our circumstances and so entirely unlooked for." Rescuing men at sea would become George Veeder's mission in life, one in stark contrast to that of his father, who was contemporaneously threatening the survival of the men in his care. When the Surfside Lifesaving Station was built on the south shore of Nantucket in 1874, George joined as a crew member under the leadership of retired whaling captain Joseph Winslow, who had gammed with Susan and Charles and young George in the *Nauticon* in 1853 off the east coast of South America and subsequently taken his own wife and children to sea. Most of the shipwrecks that occurred around Nantucket were in what is now known as the "off-season"—fall, winter, and spring. That's when the lifesaving crew lived at the south shore station and patrolled the beaches day and night for eight months, risking their lives on a regular basis when they launched their surfboats into the stormy, frigid Atlantic in valiant attempts to save others. In the summer, the waters around the island were less treacherous, and George was able to spend time in the "pleasure yacht" business, taking parties of visitors on fishing trips and offshore cruises in his catboat *Favorite*. He was apparently a favorite himself; his yachting customers frequently gave him gifts—an American flag, a gold watch—and in a letter to the editor of the *Inquirer and Mirror*, one pleased customer referred to Veeder as "that Prince of Good Fellows." The local press was attentive to his fishing prowess and solicitous of his minor injuries, noting when he cut his finger or suffered frostbite on his chin or fell overboard from his boat. In fact, news notes about George appear in the newspaper more than three dozen times in the 1870s alone, in the decade of his father's disappearance from the public record.

* * *

THE NEW SUMMER TOURIST ECONOMY helped sustain the populace through the rest of the year, when everyone reverted to survival mode. In his 1875 *Handbook of Nantucket*, Isaac Folger, editor of the twice-weekly *Island Review*, wrote, "Nantucket is far from death. Having furnished light for the world she is now commencing to furnish health for the weary summer sojourner who lingers on her shore." Folger touted fresh breezes and squantums, and he advocated outings to Surfside, where a new cottage community was being laid out, and on to Siasconset, the village that would erupt as a celebrated resort and actors' colony by the end of the century. Nantucket was no longer a hopping-off place for voyages to the South Seas; it was a destination.

The local lens began to focus on long overlooked attributes of the island, and history was dished up along with clean air, fresh fish, cool nights, and surf bathing. Books touting the charms of Nantucket began to appear, too, many written by journalists and travel writers. One of the earliest is actually a romantic novel, Edward Bellamy's *Six to One; A Nantucket Idyl*, published in 1878, of particular interest because the startling demographic statistic of the title—six young women to every eligible man—was personified by six Nantucket girls, including one named Mary Veeder. Bellamy was referring to Susan's daughter, Marianna, eighteen years old in 1878, the same age as another character in his book, Lizzie Folger. A photographic portrait taken in July 1879 shows nineteen-year-old Marianna wearing a black-lace shawl; she was described in a letter written by Susan E. Brock in 1878 as "pretty little Marianna Veeder," and she was noticed by Bellamy, who described her in his book as a "placid blond." Although Bellamy's story is a lightweight romance, it acknowledges Nantucket's struggle with reinvention. One of the girls remarks, "I do hope the island will never become popular as a pleasure resort," to which Edgerton, the thinly veiled autobiographical character, replies, "The people over there on the mainland get so hungry for beauty in their nine months of toil and moil that they are on the look-out for every tid-bit of sea or landscape to devour in the vacation season, and they do devour it literally, spoiling and making an end of its charm by crowding to enjoy it, to say nothing of incidentally demoralizing the inhabitants by turning them into a crowd of lackeys and swindlers." This anti-tourism comment is nestled in a tale that glorifies the charms of Nantucket and promotes the very thing the protagonist disdains. His depictions of a squantum on Coatue, an outing to 'Sconset, and evening walks through the quiet town or along the foggy shore were all scenes to entice visitors, whether intentional or not.

* * *

Susan Veeder and her friends, many of them wives of retired mariners, witnessed the development of a different sort of town from the one they grew up in. In the summer the island swelled with strangers who were delighted to walk the quaint old streets and stare with curiosity at the genteel women in their grey houses, but not everyone liked being on display. One of the girls in Bellamy's story vehemently expressed the

Frontispiece of Edward Bellamy's *Six to One; A Nantucket Idyl*, 1878.

opinion, "We don't like to be regarded as curiosities, or have strangers come just to play for fun at the sort of life we live in sober earnest the year round. People don't like to have what is practical to them patronized as amusement by others."

But like it or not, Nantucket was on its way to becoming a summer playground. George Veeder managed to bridge the terrifying economic chasm between whaling and tourism by using his expertise on the water both to save men in peril and to entertain men and women of leisure who just wanted to go for a sail and catch some bluefish. Not everyone was as flexible or as skilled, especially younger men who needed opportunity and employment. None of the Nantucket boys on the *William Gifford* returned to the island, and neither of the Veeder girls—Marianna nor her niece, Mary Frances—married local men. Slim pickings on Nantucket.

Although Charles Veeder was long absent from the public record, the Veeder family was still newsworthy in the 1880s, their activities and accomplishments often in the weekly press. George's teenage daughter, Mary Frances, known as "Mamie," was something of a performer, noticed

Mary Frances Veeder (1864–1946), 1881.

GPN1274

for her talent in dramatic readings and debates. In 1881, she argued in an amateur debate that there was more happiness than misery in the world. In a photographic portrait of her taken that year she is stylishly attired in a wide-brimmed felt hat with a large white feather atop, and a white lace scarf around her neck. She looks confident and optimistic. Her grandmother Susan, sitting in the audience listening to her debate the topic, may have had arguments on the side of misery.

George Veeder became the second keeper of the Surfside Lifesaving Station in the summer of 1881. The first Coffin Family Reunion was held on Nantucket that year, a celebration of descendants of the most prolific progenitor among the early settlers of Nantucket that brought lots of transplanted sons and daughters back to the island and helped invigorate an interest in local history and landmarks. The reunion also spurred an ambitious real estate development plan for a cottage community at Surfside that never materialized. Excursions, speeches, dinners, and a

Surfside Lifesaving Station. Photograph by Josiah Freeman, circa 1881.

PH90-15-1

Grand Ball were held, and Marianna Veeder attended, wearing a gown of "garnet satin" embellished with "brocaded Spanish lace."

Marianna Veeder last saw her father when she was eight years old. He had been ashore on Nantucket her whole life up to that point, and then he disappeared. Did the solid reputation of her mother, her beloved older brother George, and her Uncle Edward Austin buoy her up? Was she tainted by her father's misdeeds, or was she embraced by her community? Marianna married Charles Hammond Vinal of New Bedford on February 12, 1885, at her mother's home on Orange Street in a ceremony led by the Reverend Louise S. Baker of the North, or First Congregational, Church on Centre Street. She was his second wife. A small group of family and friends gathered in the parlor where the coal stove warmed the wedding party. George and his wife, Sarah, would have been there, along with Mary Frances, who was twenty-one. Charles Edward had married Harriet Folger in October 1884, and the couple may have already moved to Minnesota, where their first child was born in late 1885. Susan's brother, Edward, and his wife, Phebe, had both died several years earlier, but longtime friend Azubah Cash, now a sixty-five-year-old widow, may have joined Susan in the celebration. The groom was the

Marianna Veeder (1860–1935), 1879.

GPN1268

son of a New Bedford whaling captain who had died in 1868, the same year Marianna waved goodbye to her father from the wharf in that city.

Although he started his career as a grocer, Charles Vinal later became registrar of the New Bedford Gas and Edison Light Company, working in the industry that made whale oil obsolete as the source of illumination. He and Marianna had two children, Elwin and Elise (or Elsie). Susan Veeder remained in her house on Orange Street in Nantucket, but she and Marianna visited often, and George's family came and went. Marianna's children grew up in New Bedford, and they, too, dispersed farther across the continent, shedding their New England maritime heritage like an old monkey jacket. When Elwin and his future wife, Grace Tripp, left Massachusetts to move to the Pacific Northwest, the true story of his Nantucket grandfather's last voyage was left behind. Elwin made his own mark on the other coast, helping to establish the town of Bend, Oregon, and then moving to Seattle, Washington, where some of his descendants still live. Who among his children knew that great-uncle David—lost at sea—had played on the deck of the *Nauticon* catching speckled haglets near Cape Horn, or that their great-grandmother had been carried up the hills on Pitcairn to see the descendants of mutineers just a month after her daughter died, the one whose stone they may have once visited in the old cemetery, tracing the outline of the tiare flower with their chubby fingers and wondering where, exactly, Tahiti was.

Susan Veeder's life spanned most of the nineteenth century. Born when Nantucket whalemen were poised to hit the high seas again after the War of 1812, just as they had after the Revolution, she lived to see the last whaleship leave the harbor. The catastrophic causes of the end of prosperity on the island—the Great Fire of 1846, the mass exodus of local men to California during the Gold Rush years, and that grim reaper of young men, the Civil War—all happened on her watch. And although these events were her very real concern, a large part of her life must have been spent thinking about the Pacific Ocean, remembering where she had sailed and contemplating the fate of her husband and sons. Susan died on

June 16, 1897, at Marianna's home in New Bedford. She had lived on land and sea for eighty years, ten months, and eight days. George, the beloved Nantucket son whose exemplary service to the maritime community preserved the family name, died two months later.

Susan, George, and his wife, Sarah, lie in the Newtown Cemetery in Nantucket, under matching headstones next to the small white marble marker of the final resting place of thirteen-month-old Mary Frances Veeder in her well-traveled lead casket. Susan's parents, George and Susan Austin, are in the same burying ground, as is Susan's sister, Eliza Foster, and a young child of hers, Edward Austin Foster, who died September 7, 1847, age 11 months. It's a small family representation. Descendants of Susan and Charles Veeder inherited portraits of the seafaring couple, along with Susan's journal of her voyage in the *Nauticon*, all of which were acquired by the Nantucket Historical Association in the 1990s. The ivory toy wagon that the captain made for his one-year-old daughter on the *Nauticon*, a relic of family harmony at sea, bounced from private to public to private hands the way beautiful artifacts sometimes do. Other pieces of the Veeder puzzle will surely appear as their story becomes better known, so the story may change, and memory and imagination and fact will be laid out on the table in a new scene, with a palm tree in the corner, a ship, a grey town, and a thousand leagues of blue.

Epilogue

TRAVELING TO A WEDDING in Seattle, I felt a little like the ancient mariner, carrying my tale with me: "She stoppeth one of three." I had begun a correspondence with Cindy, great-great-granddaughter of Susan and Charles Veeder, a couple of years earlier and now was invited to join her family for dinner on Mercer Island. Their house sits on part of the acreage that her grandfather Elwin Vinal had purchased in 1908, before the I-90 floating bridge was built, when it was necessary to sail over, or take the ferry to the island in the middle of Lake Washington. I found my way down the driveway to a cedar house surrounded by flower gardens, with a patch of green lawn like a welcome mat out front and a table under huge fir trees—dwarfing anything that ever grew on Nantucket. A young eagle screamed above the treetops. The view across Lake Washington was incredibly serene, the city barely visible, the lake calm. I felt transported back through the generations to 1850 when Cindy took my hand, as if I were meeting some part of Susan Veeder, finally.

Cindy had invited her brother Nile and cousin Steve, and there were husbands and wives and daughters and a very new granddaughter there, too. Everyone was remarking on the spectacularly clear evening and catching up on family news. I had no idea what to expect from this group—perhaps the pleasure of learning more about Susan would balance the dismay when I gingerly removed Charles Veeder's dusty skeleton from the closet. Cindy admitted that they didn't know a lot about their Veeder ancestors, less than they did about the Vinals of New Bedford, particularly Captain William Hathaway Vinal, who died in 1868, the year Captain Veeder left on his last voyage. Captain Vinal had heroic status in the family: he quelled a mutiny single-handedly and survived an episode in the jaws of a sperm whale. One of Cindy's relatives has his cellaret liquor cabinet, the musket he used to prevent mutiny, and his log of his whaling voyages.

In their small collection of family history, along with a Bible that includes a page crammed with birth and death dates in delicate script, are two typewritten pages titled "Excerpts from a letter written to your father, from your grandfather E. L. Vinal, upon Jan 5 1944." Elwin Vinal wrote the original letter to his son, Richard, to assist him in choosing a family name for a child soon to be born:

"It is not amiss to remember that you are a Vinal and that, unless you wish to deviate entirely from family names, it is well to consider names for your children that are connected with that side of the family, especially for the boys. You can always remember that you have come from good stock, on both sides, the traditional old New England stock which, with its descendants has been much of the back bone of the country."

In his letter, Elwin elaborates on the Vinal family—William and his wife, Lavinia, and their son Charles, who married Marianna Veeder. "Of course you know your grandmother's name was Marianna (née Veeder) . . . you were the apple of her eye." Elwin then relates the story of the last voyage of Captain Veeder: "When she [Marianna] was in her teens, he decided to make one more voyage for her benefit. He put nearly all of his resources, with some Boston associates, into a ship and cargo and sailed for the south seas. He never returned. His ship was wrecked in a storm. It broke the old man's heart and he died in Tahiti where he is supposed to be buried today."

Whoa. . . . Was this the story told to twelve-year-old Marianna in 1872, when Susan learned of her husband's betrayal? To console her daughter, did she assure her that her father was thinking of her welfare only, that he didn't abandon her for reasons she may have heard whispered around town. Absolutely not, she was told. He only hoped to make a tidy profit and fund her future, but, alas, he wrecked his ship. Tired and heartbroken by misfortune, he died in Tahiti, where he is buried. Either that was the story Marianna accepted and chose to tell her children or it was Elwin who revised the tale for the next generations.

Elwin also writes about the three sons of Charles and Susan and gets them a little mixed up, stating that David was washed overboard in a storm wearing boots and oilskins and didn't have a chance; that actually happened in 1858 to Charles Edward, on the ship *Midnight* out of Boston. If he got the two lost brothers confused, what he relates about Charles Edward would refer to David: "After having been away a long time, he wrote from Liverpool that the ship was, at last, sailing for home. The ship sailed but was never heard from again; one of those mysterious disappearances that were not uncommon for ships in those days." Who knows if David Veeder was ever in Liverpool, which was not a common destination for a whaler in the mid-nineteenth century. His gentle erasure from the family story may be another polite fabrication that masks some other tale. About George, the "prince of good fellows" and only surviving son, Elwin merely states that he left the sea at about middle age and lived on Nantucket where he raised a family, and died "from the effect of a sunstroke several years before from which he never fully recovered."

One of the highlights of Elwin's short chronicle of the family is his summation of the life of Susan Veeder, who visited Marianna frequently in the last decade of her life, her trips to New Bedford noted in the local newspaper. Her grandson, eleven years old when she died, remembered her well, but the stories she told him, or his memory of them, were slightly warped by 1944, when he recorded them.

"She was a dear old lady. She travelled around the world 4 times with her husband on his ship—which was some travelling in those days. I have the original of a letter (dated 1852) written her from Pitcairn Island, referring to their visit there 2 years before, and signed by Abinah [Albina] Young, one of the daughters of Thursday Christian."

Well . . . Susan went on one voyage with Charles, not four, although it lasted four years and she did see a lot of the world. Charles traversed several oceans, too, but in none of his voyages did he circumnavigate the globe, so there is some hyperbole in the family mythology. And no one knows where the Pitcairn letter is. This long game of "telephone," when stories morph from generation to generation as the whispers are misheard, or intentional edits are made just to confuse the person at the end of the line, is a common one. Without Susan's journal as catalyst, much of this story would not have unfolded.

I've yet to find a single word written by Charles Veeder, but there are traces of the handsome captain in the gene pool here, and from Susan a trait that draws the women to the water; they are a family of voyagers. Cindy tells me that her mother, Lee, had a sailboat named the *Windy Lee* when she was a teenager growing up on Lake Washington, a boat her father Elwin (called Skipper) built or bought for her; the stories don't all agree. When Lee married at eighteen, she chose for her husband a man who had built a twenty-six-foot Norwegian pilot boat, and their kids—Cindy and her five brothers—grew up sailing. Lee kept a journal of their time on the water.

Following family tradition or genetic predisposition, Cindy and her husband acquired a sixty-five-foot tugboat soon after their marriage and in the summers cruised the west coast of Canada with their four children. One of Cindy's brothers runs a sailing charter; a cousin builds boats. She and other siblings honeymooned on Tahiti, unaware that their great-great grandparents had spent six weeks and lost a child there in 1850, or that Captain Veeder was deposited there in 1872 with his mats, his shells, and a pig.

How much we have of our ancestors in us and what it does to us is a mystery. Cindy tells me she traveled to Hawaii recently and went on a whale watch, to see the creature that shaped Susan's life. When a whale breached near the ship, astounding her with its size and power, spraying her with drops of the same Pacific water the *Nauticon* sailed over, she threw up her hands in a moment of joy and shouted her great-great-grandmother's name.

* * *

SUSAN VEEDER was just one of a community of women whose husbands, fathers, brothers, and sons chose to make a living at sea, continuing the tradition of Nantucket mariners who been sailing from the island since the early eighteenth century in search of whales or engaging in commerce along the Atlantic seaboard, in Europe, South America, and China. Maritime wives understood their role in the community, precarious as it was, while they awaited the proceeds of their husbands' endeavors and the return of the men in their families. They managed households, cared for children, and supported each other as friends and as kindred. Susan Veeder was willing to leave the small world she knew and enter the realm of men at sea, gaining a perspective that few of her peers enjoyed, and setting an example for other women to follow.

Charles Veeder was the epitome of the Nantucket whaling captain—multi-talented, reliable, and resourceful, but, in the end, he betrayed everything that had made him successful, the ties to family and home not strong enough to combat the attractions of a warm climate, a young woman, and a simple life among people he genuinely enjoyed, although his choice was clouded by alcohol and possible derangement. The twisted, extraordinary journeys of this family are a footnote to Nantucket whaling history, a cautionary tale, and a reminder that there are always human stories behind enterprise and industry and the scramble for wealth. As enigmatic as they are, Susan and Charles are full of spirit, driven by curiosity and desire to break with tradition and find a new way forward.

Acknowledgements

Many people offered commentary and support for this book as it took shape during the last eight years, and I sincerely thank them all. My interest in the details of Susan Veeder's life began in 1995, when, in my role as librarian of the Nantucket Historical Association, I sat in my windowless office in the old Peter Foulger Museum on a Saturday afternoon and by telephone placed the winning bid on Susan's *Nauticon* journal, which was being auctioned by Eldred's auction gallery. Fifteen years later, while researching the lives of women who went on whaling voyages for the book *Sometimes Think of Me: Notable Nantucket Women through the Centuries*—a celebration of Nantucket women that accompanied an exhibition of the stunning embroidered narratives of Susan Boardman—I became more intrigued by Susan Veeder and curious about her errant husband. Pulling together the story of their lives on Nantucket and at sea led me to some wonderful people and places.

To Michael Harrison, the NHA's Obed Macy Director of Research and Collections, my sincere thanks and appreciation for his role as editor of this book. His wide-ranging intellect, deep knowledge of maritime history, and close attention to detail have tightened the screws on a leaky vessel and made it more seaworthy. My thanks to former NHA chief curator Ben Simons, former executive director Bill Tramposch, and long-time photo archives specialist Ralph Henke for their support of this project. My gratitude extends particularly to the late research associate and NHA research fellow Libby Oldham, a friend and critic who championed this book from the get-go. To James Russell, Gosnell Executive Director of the NHA, kudos for establishing a publications program at the NHA that supports the scholarship that is the basis for interpreting local history, and to Amelia Holmes, associate director of the Research Library, for her behind-the-scenes efforts to digitize the NHA's collections and improve online access. Thanks to Sarah Ballard, NHA volunteer who transcribed the *Nauticon* journal, and to NHA interpreters Karen McNab and Peggy Godwin for encouraging me to write this book. My thanks also to the generous staff at the New Bedford Whaling Museum Research Library—former librarian Laura Pereira, library director Mark Procknik, and volunteer Jan Keeler, who shared her books about French Polynesia with me.

In a true test of friendship, the following people took the time to read and comment extensively on this book, and I am so grateful to them: Nat Philbrick, Jonny Rizzo, Ben Shattuck, and Morgan Van Vorst. Other attentive readers include Susan Boardman, Christine Harding, Joanne Marcoux, Debra McManis, Joyce Van Vorst, and Barbara White. Thanks to my dear friend John Meffert for sharing the Veeder story with passengers as they cruised to Tahiti on the *Paul Gauguin*. Wish I had been there!

I could not have written this book without the peace and quiet (and fortifying meals) provided by the Vermont Studio Center during two writing retreats there.

My thanks to the crew of the *Aranui III*, who did an exemplary job of sharing information about the remote islands of the Tuamotus and Marquesas, and to anthropologist Sidsel Millerstrom, onboard lecturer, for her insights into Polynesian culture.

Special thanks to Cindy Peterson of Mercer Island, Washington, great-great-granddaughter of Charles and Susan Veeder. Cindy invited me to dinner with her extended family, including other great-great grandchildren of the Veeders, Nile Clarke and Steve Hiltner. I was also fortunate to spend a day with Dolly Vinal, a descendant from the same generation, when she visited Nantucket on a tour of locations related to her whaling heritage. She kindly donated to the NHA an umbrella that once belonged to Charles Veeder. Thanks also to William T. Vinal for sharing his ship portrait, and John Clarke for his interest in this project.

Genealogical research led me to Linda Johnson and Pamela Rossbach, descendants of seaman Edward Cavenagh. Linda had in her possession a journal of the tail end of the voyage of the *William Gifford*, which she kindly lent to me before donating it to the New Bedford Whaling Museum. Pamela Rossbach, also descended from Cavenagh, relayed stories of Captain Veeder's conduct that had been passed down in the family.

My gratitude to Joan Sanderson of the Victoria Genealogical Society for pulling together every scrap of information about Nantucket whaler and sealer Albert C. Folger.

Thank you, Eileen Powers, for another beautiful book.

Finally, thanks to my family, whose love and support is everything.

Betsy Tyler
2019

NOTES

Abbreviations:

AOWV	*American Offshore Whaling Voyages 1667 to 1927* (online database) by Judith N. Lund, Elizabeth A. Josephson, Randall R. Reeves and Tim Smith (New Bedford: Old Dartmouth Historical Society, 2010)
BGR	Eliza Starbuck Barney Genealogical Record (online database)
HN	*Historic Nantucket*
I&M	*Inquirer and Mirror*
NBWMRL	New Bedford Whaling Museum Research Library
NHARL	Nantucket Historical Association Research Library
Starbuck	Starbuck, Alexander. *History of the American Whale Fishery* (1879)

Prologue

The *Aranui 3* was replaced by the *Aranui 5* in 2015 (four is an unlucky number in Tahiti). Although the earlier ships *Aranui 1, 2,* and *3* were, as far as capacity goes, primarily cargo ships, the newer ship shifts the emphasis to more passengers and more of a cruise experience, since that has become the most cost-effective way to run the ship. See Paul Theroux's *Happy Isles of Oceania* for a description of a cruise on the *Aranui 2*.

Naval officer Charles Wilkes led the United States Exploring Expedition 1838–42 and wrote *Narrative of the United States Exploring Expedition* published in five volumes in 1844. Nathaniel Philbrick brings the voyage to life in *Sea of Glory: America's Voyage of Discovery, The U.S. Exploring Expedition 1838–42* (New York: Viking, 2003).

For details of the *Essex* tragedy, see Philbrick's *In the Heart of the Sea* (New York: Viking, 2000). Resources for the study of *Moby-Dick* are widely available.

Chapter One: Islands Seen by the Ship *Nauticon*

Susan Veeder's journal "Islands Seen by the Ship *Nauticon*" September 13, 1848–March 24, 1853 is in NHARL Ms. 220, log 347. Most of the quotes from her journal retain her original spelling; punctuation and capitalization have been modernized for clarity. Although Susan was the earliest whaling wife sailing from Nantucket, captains from other ports had been known to bring their wives along on whaling voyages. Three decades before Veeder sailed with her husband on the *Nauticon* in 1848, Nantucket-born Mary Hayden Russell joined her husband, Laban, on the *Hydra*, out of Plymouth, England, and sailed with him again, in 1823, on the *Emily*, out of London. Mary wrote a long sea-letter to her daughter on Nantucket, a mini-journal of sorts that explains her presence on board as her wifely duty; see NHARL Ms. 83, folder 1.

See *AOWV* for a complete list of Veeder's voyages as master of whaling vessels. Although he was to take the *Joseph Starbuck* on a whaling voyage in 1842, the ship was wrecked in a storm on her trip from Nantucket to Edgartown, under the care of an experienced pilot. There is no evidence Veeder was on the ship at the time. See Obed Macy's account, NHARL Ms. 96, journal 6, November 28, 1842 (p. 93) and *I&M*, December 3, 1842. Veeder is listed as first mate on the *Christopher Mitchell* 1834–37 in an article in the *I&M*, October 22, 1910, and he sailed on the ship *Charles* out of New Bedford, 1830–33, as noted in the American Crew List database at Whalinghistory.org. Details of all ships spoken by the *Nauticon* can also be found in *AOWV* and Starbuck.

George and Matthew Starbuck and their younger brother, William, lived in the iconic Main Street houses known as the Three Bricks, identical houses built for them by their father, Joseph Starbuck, a wealthy whale-oil merchant and ship owner. Poems written by Elizabeth Starbuck are in NHARL Ms. 43, Poets and Poetry/Songs and Music Collection, and she is no. 28 of Grace Brown Gardner's "Fifty Famous Nantucketers"; see NHARL Ms. 57, scrapbook extra 3, 19. Elizabeth's parlor at 97 Main Street was the setting for the inaugural meeting of the Nantucket Historical Association in 1894. Catherine Starbuck, Matthew's wife, was known for her gardening expertise; she was the founder of the Botanical Society of Nantucket in 1878. Melanie Ried conducted extensive research about women's whaling journals for her doctoral dissertation, *"The Captain's Best Mate": Gender, Genre, and Representation in Women's Whaling Journals 1823 to 1915* (Honolulu: University of Hawaii, 2013). In correspondence about illustrated women's journals in October 2012, she wrote, "Susan Veeder is the only woman journal keeper I came across who did watercolors, or any elaborate images. Harriet Swain (NHA) has a few small ships and/or ship ensigns drawn in the margins when ships were spoken, and some of these are water colored; however, I believe her husband, Obed, drew these in her journal. His journal on his previous voyage includes these small images as well. Jerusha Hawes has a partial journal aboard the ship "Emma C. Jones", 1858–59, New Bedford Public Library, which contains some simple landscape drawings in ink. Betsy Ann Tower's formal log aboard the "Moctezuma," 1847–50, New Bedford Whaling Museum, has a few small landscape drawings in ink. Both of these women simply outlined the landscape, and neither of these come anywhere close to the lovely artwork completed by Susan Veeder."

Portraits of Susan and Charles Veeder were acquired by the NHA in 1994 and 1999 respectively. The provenance of both can be traced back to the Barbara Johnson whaling collection auctioned by Sotheby's on several occasions in the 1980s and '90s. Susan's previously undated portrait can fairly certainly be ascribed to the time Captain Veeder was in Hong Kong. The log of the *Ocean Rover* (NHARL Ms. 220, log 178), kept by an unknown crew member, states that the ship "came to anchor at Hong Kong" on February 2, 1858; it remained in the harbor until March 15. I have suggested that Susan's portrait was framed and hung in the captain's cabin; the painting might also have been rolled and wrapped for transportation.

William Wilkes Morris advertised a Mariner's School in the *Nantucket Inquirer* in the period 1821 to 1836. See also NHARL Ms. 250, folder 1 for Morris's journal.

First mate Mr. Archer was most likely James Archer (1810–1869), the only Archer in the BGR who would have been of suitable age; at 38, he was a contemporary of Captain Veeder. In 1853, James Archer was captain of the bark *Afton* of New Bedford, sailing from that port five months after the *Nauticon* returned to Nantucket.

Although the Crosby name was a well-established one on Nantucket in the nineteenth century, Consul William Crosby (1809–1872) does not appear to have close Nantucket connections. According to an obituary notice of Crosby in *The Record: Containing Reports of Evangelical Efforts in Chile* (Valparaiso, 1873), vol. 3, p. 18, he was born in New York but grew up in Columbus, Ohio. Crosby served as U.S. consul in Chile from 1846 to 1860. He married Lucinda Anter in 1841 and the couple had two children born in Ohio—Narcisa and William—and three born in Talcahuano—Alfred, Porcia, and Andrew, the latter two born after Susan's visit in early 1849. Captain Stetson, according to the *Nantucket Journal* April 2, 1849, was at Talcahuano "recovering in health." *AOWV* lists him as George M. Stetson, captain of the New Bedford ship *Trident*, 1846–50; he was replaced by Marcus W. Taber, who was captain on two subsequent voyages of the ship. Stetson did not return to the sea as a whaling captain.

Joan Druett's *She Was a Sister Sailor: Mary Brewster's Whaling Journals 1845–1851* (Mystic: Mystic Seaport Museum Inc., 1992) is a richly annotated woman's journal from the same period as Susan Veeder's voyage. The most comprehensive book about women who joined their husbands on whaling voyages is Druett's *Petticoat Whalers: Whaling Wives at Sea, 1820– 1920* (Auckland: Collins Publishers, 1991). She quotes from a variety of journals that describe women's shipboard accommodations. The recently restored *Charles W. Morgan*, a New Bedford whaleship now belonging to Mystic Seaport in Mystic, Connecticut, is the only surviving American whaleship. It is the same length as the *Nauticon* and was built just seven years prior, making it an appropriate model for the Veeders' home at sea.

John Munkley was born in Norway in 1811. Captain of the *Emerald* on three voyages (1843–47, 1847–51, and 1851–56), he died of "apoplexy" on the voyage home in 1856. He and Caroline had a son named Henraie (1855 Massachusetts State Census) born in Chile in 1849 and a daughter Carolena born in 1851. Whether Caroline accompanied her husband on the voyage of 1851–56 is not known.

Third mate James F. Roberts records the taking of a sperm whale on Tuesday, January 23, 1849, in his journal (Nicholson Whaling Collection, Providence Public Library, copy in NHARL Ms. 220, log 403).

Nantucket whaleman Peleg Folger kept some of the earliest American whaling journals; originals are at the Nantucket Atheneum (logs 1 and 6) and the NHARL (Ms. 220, log 318). An educated, droll young man, he recorded the high and low points of his chosen occupation, from the much-anticipated meals of haglet pie and mutton, with an occasional drink of rum flip or hot chocolate, to the brutal incidents of the chase and capture. See Thomas Philbrick's *Remarkable Observations: The Whaling Journal of Peleg Folger* (Nantucket: Mill Hill Press, 2006).

Chapter Two: Paradise Lost

Asa Hoxie and Mary Swift Kelley married in 1835. He was captain of the *Pacific* 1844–48, and again 1848–52, the latter voyage when Susan Veeder met them in Talcahuano. William A. West was captain of the *Globe* sailing out of Mystic, Connecticut, 1845–49. According to Starbuck the ship was condemned at Valparaiso in 1849.

The record of the decimation of Galapagos tortoises by whalemen is revealed in dozens of logbooks and other accounts of the whaling industry; by some estimates more than 200,000 were captured and eaten in the period 1830–70. See Mary K. Bercaw Edwards, "Of Melville, Tortoises, and the Galapagos," *HN* Fall 2014, and Charles Townsend, "The Galapagos Tortoises in Their Relation to the Whaling Industry: A Study of Old Logbooks," *Zoologica*, vol 4, no 3, 1925.

Nowhere in her journal does Susan Veeder list the names of the crew of the *Nauticon*, nor are the records of the ship available in any public repository, but third mate James Roberts listed in the back of his journal the names of those who spotted whales. The incorrigible Barney Jones had the most sightings (5), followed by Mr. Simpson (4), Charles Swain (3), the cooper (2), and the rest of the men one each: Thomas Barnard, Mr. Ellis, Captain Veeder, the cook, H. Dennis, Jack, Harry, and Roberts himself. The men referred to as "Mr." would have been mates. James Archer was first mate, Mr. Simpson was second mate, James Roberts was third mate, and Mr. Ellis was fourth.

Although the ivory toy wagon is attributed to Charles Veeder, and may well have been crafted by him for his daughter, it is also possible that first mate James Archer made the wagon. A similar small ivory wheelbarrow purportedly made on the *Nauticon* in 1851 was also auctioned by Northeast Auctions in 2008. An example of Archer's extraordinary scrimshaw work—a three-drawer dressing case and mirror decorated with ebony and ivory inlay—is in the collection of the

NHA (1906.71.1); it was constructed on the ship *Afton* 1853–57 by Archer, then captain of that ship.

Although written directions from Christopher Mitchell & Co. admonished Captain Veeder to maintain strict order and forbade liquor on board for anything other than medicinal purposes when he was in charge of that company's ship, *Christopher Mitchell* (1838–41), there were no cautions against trysts with island women (NHARL Ms. 132, book 2). No instructions from the Starbuck brothers to Veeder for conduct aboard their vessel survive. Druett discusses prostitution on board whaleships, with and without wives present, in *Petticoat Whalers*, pp. 178–80.

Edward T. Perkins, *Na Motu; or, Reef Rovings in the South Seas* (New York: Pudney & Russell, 1854), describes Papeete around the time the Veeders were there, as does Ida Pfeiffer in *A Lady's Travels Round the World: Travels from Vienna to Brazil, Chili, Otaheite, China, the East Indies, Persia, and Asia Minor*, translated by William Hazlitt (London: G. Routledge & Co., 1852). Pfeiffer began her first voyage around the world in 1846. See also *The Old Broom Road Tahiti: 100 Years of Adventure Writings from Tahiti, 1829–1929*, edited by Fran Dieudonne and Ann Kuhns (Encinitas, Calif.: Neptune House Publishers, 2004).

The "Dr. Johnson" who prescribed the lethal powder for Mary Frances Veeder was Dr. Johnstone, described by Perkins as having a house with a shady verandah facing the harbor (*Old Broom Road*, p. 29). The American consul at the time was Horace Hawes.

Chapter Three: The Billows Rolled as They Rolled Before

Thomas Barnard may have been Thomas H. Barnard (1831–1869), who worked as a captain in the coastal trade in the 1850s and '60s, volunteered for the U.S. Navy in 1862, and was promoted to quartermaster. In 1869, he and his brother, Charles W., were lost with the rest of the crew of the schooner *George H. Rogers* on a cod-fishing voyage to the Grand Banks. (*Nantucket Weekly Mirror*, August 30, 1862, p. 2; *I&M* July 24, 1869, p.2)

Cornelius Rust is harder to identify. The 1860 U.S. Federal Census records one Cornelius Rust, 36, in Baltimore, Maryland, of German birth, married to another

German, Christina, also 36, with two children, John (7) and Levi (5). This Cornelius would have been twenty-four years old in 1848.

A log of the *Navigator*, George Palmer, master, is in NHARL Ms. 220, log 162. In his file on Pitcairn (NHARL Ms. 335, folder 1042), historian Edouard Stackpole lists visits to the island in the period 1808–30; see NHARL Ms. 335, folder 963 for his reference to Mrs. Palmer at Pitcairn. A logbook kept by the first mate of the *Potomac* (1849–53) under Captain Charles Grant is in NHARL Ms. 220, log 204.

The 1880 U.S. Federal Census for Asa Hoxie's family lists a daughter, Phebe, born in 1852 in the Pacific Ocean and a son, Rufus, born in 1858. Either the date of Phebe's birth is recorded incorrectly, or the child born in 1850 did not survive.

Starbuck presents a different statistic of the *Lafayette*'s oil cargo, stating that the *Nauticon* saved 600 barrels of sperm oil and 200 of whale oil from the ship; there is no mention of the participation of Captain Benjamin T. Sisson of the *Callao*. See "Disasters" column, *Sailors' Magazine and Naval Journal* (American Seamen's Friend Society), vol. 23, no 4, December 1850.

The story of the wreck of the *Essex* was told by survivor Owen Chase in his *Narrative of the Most Extraordinary and Distressing Shipwreck of the Whale-Ship Essex* (New York: W. B. Gilley, 1821) and by Nathaniel Philbrick, *In the Heart of the Sea* (Penguin, 2001). The sinking of the *Ann Alexander* was described in "A Ship Sunk by a Whale," *Littell's Living Age*, vol. 31 (November 29, 1851), 415–16, and in Edouard Stackpole's "Ann Alexander's Scrimshaw Set Tells the Story of a Ship Sunk by a Whale," *Historic Nantucket*, July 1980.

Cocos Island is now a protected national park belonging to Costa Rica and a UNESCO World Heritage Site. For its appeal as a premier dive site, see "Journey Beneath Jurassic Park—Cocos Island" by Michael Salvarezza and Christopher P. Weaver in *Advanced Diver Magazine* (Issue 6, [2000]); more details about the natural history of the island are in the authors' report at http://www.ecophotoexplorers.com/coco_island.asp. An earlier description of the island is in *The Arcturus Adventure: An Account of the New York Zoological Society's First Oceanographic Expedition* by William Beebe and Ruth Rose (New York: G. P. Putnam's Sons, 1926).

The captains and ladies in Lima in November 1850—MacDonald and Hooper—were likely from merchant ships and do not appear in sources for American whaling voyages. Charlotte Coffin Wyer's journal kept on board the *Young Hero* is in fact a long letter to her sister Eliza Ann Chadwick; see NHARL Ms. 220, log 268.

"Maritime oil fields" is a poetic description, not a literal one; the designation was not used in the whaling industry in the 1850s.

Whaling captains and crews were more familiar with the Galapágos Islands than anyone else in the early- to mid-nineteenth century. Herman Melville wrote about the islands in *The Encantadas* or "Enchanted Isles" published in 1854; the essays were included in his *Piazza Tales* (New York: Dix & Edwards, 1856). For specifics on the whaler's mailbox see the "Galapagos Islands, a History of their Exploration," by Joseph Richard Slevin, Occasional Papers no. 25 of the California Academy of Sciences, issued December 22, 1959. Slevin describes Post Office Bay on Charles Island, in use as early as the 1790s, pp. 108–09.

From the U.S. Federal Census of 1870 and "Biographical Sketches of Bourne, Massachusetts," *History of Barnstable County, Massachusetts 1620–1890*, edited by Simeon L. Delo (1890), we learn that master mariner Nathaniel Burgess of Bourne—and later New Bedford—and his wife, Ann, had four children: Margaret (Maggie) and Robert W., born in 1846 and 1847, respectively, in Peru (both on a previous voyage of the *Robert Edward*); Helen, born in early 1849 in Chile, and two younger children, Edward and Lucy born after they returned to Massachusetts. Another son named Edward, born in the Marshall Islands in 1852, did not survive. Helen must have been the sick babe referred to in Susan's entry of February 17, 1851. Azubah Cash, in NHARL Ms., 220, log 312, February 8, 1851, mentions that she could give Ann Burgess news about her daughter, Maggie—who had not traveled with her parents—because Azubah had seen the girl more recently than Ann had. Mrs. Russell was most likely Abby Russell, traveling with her husband, Elihu Russell, aboard the *Peri* of New Bedford.

For more on baleen see "Useful Products of the Whale," *Penny Magazine of the Society for the Diffusion of Useful Knowledge*, nos. 516 and 517, April 18 and 25, 1840.

James Roberts's journal of the *Nauticon* is in the Nicholson Whaling Collection, Providence Public Library; a copy is in NHARL Ms. 220, log 403. Little is known about him. His mother, Statira S. Marstow, came to Nantucket from Maine and was married briefly to a man named Roberts, but whether in Maine or Nantucket is not clear. She wed her second husband, Nathan Drake, sometime around 1834, and they had three children born on the island. The BGR lists James Roberts's middle initial as H., but his signature in Log 403 and a death notice in the *I&M* Dec. 29, 1851, confirm that his name was James F. Roberts.

In *Leviathan: The History of Whaling in America*, Eric Jay Dolan describes bowhead hunting in the Arctic in chapter 19, "Ice Crush," describing in particular the disaster of 1871, when an entire fleet of thirty-three whaleships was lost in the ice. The *Mary Mitchell* was formerly a Nantucket whaleship, sailing from that port on seven voyages between 1827 and 1847, when she was sold to California.

Chapter Four: That Old Road Home

Charles B. Swain II of the Nantucket ship *Enterprise* (1850–54) and his second wife, Eunice, were in Maui in October 1851. Whether Eunice sailed with her husband or met him in Maui is not known. The identities of Captains Joy and Gwen are undetermined.

Azubah Cash's journal of her voyage in the *Columbia* is in NHARL Ms. 220, log 312. She does not write in her journal in the period August 3, 1851–March 6, 1852 (William Murray Cash was born August 20, 1851), but in a brief description of that period recorded four months later, she relates that she and the captain paid the Veeders a visit: ". . . we went on board of the Ship Nauticon (which was the 29th [October, 1851]) and spent the day with Capt. and Mrs. Veeder and had a pleasant visit."

Rowe's Olympic Circus arrived in Honolulu (Oahu) in December 1850, according to *The Polynesian*, Saturday January 4, 1851. Apparently, it became a somewhat permanent fixture as it is mentioned in the Honolulu newspaper throughout 1851. Laura Fish Judd, *Honolulu: Sketches of Life, Social Political, and Religious, in the Hawaiian Islands from 1828 to 1861* (New York: A.D.F. Randolph & Co., 1880), p. 236, lists the amusements of Honolulu at mid-century, after several decades of missionary labors had tamed the town. Francis Allyn Olmsted, *Incidents of a Whaling Voyage to Which Are Added Observations on the Scenery, Manner, and Customs, and Missionary Stations of the Sandwich and Society islands* (New York:

D. Appleton and Co., 1841) describes Honolulu in 1840, where "the laws for the restraint of licentiousness are very strict" (p. 194); he discusses haglets (p. 323).

Several of Susan C. Sprague Winslow's letters written at sea on the *Constitution* to her sister-in-law Mary Ann Morrow Winslow on Nantucket are in NHARL Ms. 160.

Chapter Five: Nantucket in Decline

In the 1840s, Nantucketers had attempted an ingenious solution to the problem of a shallow harbor entrance, a double-pontoon device called the "camels" that lifted ships high enough to float over the sandbar. Although marginally successful, the camels were no longer in use when the *Nauticon* returned in 1853.

Melville's famous whaling tale, originally titled *The Whale,* was first published in three volumes by Richard Bentley in London in October 1851. New York publishers Harper and Brothers brought out a one-volume edition the next month, titled *Moby-Dick; or, The Whale.* See Susan Beegel's "Herman Melville: Nantucket's First Tourist?" *HN* Fall 1991, for details about Melville's visit to Nantucket.

Nantucket's contributions to the mining and entrepreneurial activities in California in the mid-nineteenth century are many; the ships, men, and sometimes women who left Nantucket for California in the early years of the Gold Rush are recorded in the miniature booklet (measuring 2 x 3 in.) *A List of Persons from Nantucket Now in California, Or On Their Way Thither Including the Names of the Vessels in Which They Sailed, The Time of Sailing and Of Their Arrival There; Also Persons Returned, &c.* (Nantucket: Jethro Brock, 1850). Edward A. Austin is listed as the captain of the *Montano.* Austin had two very successful voyages as captain of Nantucket whaleships: *Young Eagle*, 1840–43, bringing home 2,544 barrels of sperm oil, and *Henry Clay*, 1844–47, with 2,847 barrels. His voyage to California was a plum, a paid trip with his wife as passenger and a chance to witness the gold mania that was turning San Francisco into a city. He may have planned to retire after that, but in 1853 he was sent to New Zealand to bring home the ship *Edward.* Details are scant, but according to the *Whalemen's Shipping List*, May 31, 1853, p. 98, "Ship *Edward*, Mosher, of Nantucket, is reported to have put into Auckland, New Zealand, in the latter part of January last, where the captain had disposed of all or a part of his cargo. The ship was abandoned by her crew. At last accounts, the *Edward* had 20 bbls sperm 1200 d[itt]o whale oil." On October 4, 1853, the same publication reported "Capt. [Oliver C.] G[ardiner Jr.] reports ship *Edward*, Mosher, of Nantucket was in Auckland, having abandoned her whaling voyage on account of the difficulty of obtaining a crew, and is now engaged in the lumber trade." Starbuck reports that the ship arrived in Nantucket July 27, 1854, brought back by E. E. [*sic*] Austin.

Peter P. Veeder is a real mystery, not appearing on genealogical sites that detail the Veeder family in America, particularly the descendants of Simon Volkertse Veeder who settled in New Amsterdam in 1652. There is a record of one Peter P. Veeder serving in the New York militia in Monroe Country during the War of 1812, but whether he is the same Peter who married Rachel Allen of Nantucket in 1808 is not known. The first real estate transaction of Peter P. Veeder on Nantucket was in 1818; all his transactions recorded in the Nantucket Registry of Deeds are as follows:

> Book 25, p. 252: Tristram Bunker to PPV, house in Newtown, 1818.
> Book 32, p. 213: PPV to Reuben Meader, house in Newton, $100, August 2, 1832.
> Book 33, p. 112: Rochester, January 14, 1835, At sight pay to order of Mr. Robert Swain 611.71 and charge to account. To Messrs. Elihu Swain and Reuben Meader. Peter P. Veeder.
> Book 33, p. 438: Rochester, May 1, 1834, At sight for value received please pay to the order of Charles A. Veader [*sic*] $1500 and charge the same to account of your ob't servant Peter P. Veader [*sic*]. Messrs. Elihu Swain, Reuben Meader.

Obed Macy's reference to Peter P. Veeder is in NHARL Ms. 96, journal 5. Nantucket Supreme Judicial Court records for 1832 include no information on the Veeder case, which appears to have been dropped once he absconded. In the account book for the *Loper*, NHARL Ms. 335, folder 1000, all crew sign for their lay except Veeder, who earned $2,045.95. On September 1, 1832, he was paid in oil, 2,407 gallons at $0.85 per gallon.

John Cotton, master of the *Loper*, was later the master of the New Bedford ship *Victory* on a voyage that left that port in 1835. Eight years later, his wife, Mary Cotton, petitioned the Supreme Judicial Court of Massachusetts for divorce, on grounds that her husband abandoned her in 1835 and that since 1840 he had been consorting with lewd women in Tahiti. John Cotton did not return to Nantucket; local genealogies state that he died at sea. See William Aeberli's articles "Captain Peter P. Veeder: The Nantucket Settler" May 10 and May 17, 1973, in *The Greece Post* (Pittsfield, New York). Copies are in the NHARL "Blue" file.

Peter P. Veeder's farmhouse in North Greece is still standing.

Charles H. Robinson advertised in the Nantucket *Inquirer* in 1853, "The subscriber will keep constantly on hand a good assortment of first quality Italian and Marble Grave stones and Monuments, finished in first rate style, and cheaper than can be got elsewhere." Robinson, who more than likely carved the tiare flower on Mary Frances's gravestone, later became the preeminent architect/builder of Victorian houses on Nantucket.

The poem "Nantucket Girls Song" is found in the back of Eliza Brock's journal of the *Lexington*, NHARL Ms. 220, log 136. Brock stayed at the Russell Hotel in the Bay of Islands, New Zealand, in February 1855. There she met Mrs. Ford, who gave her the poem and may have written it. See the author's *Sometimes Think of Me: Notable Nantucket Women through the Centuries* (Nantucket: NHA, 2010) for biographies of Eliza Brock, Betsey Morey, Susan Veeder, and other Nantucket whaling wives.

Advertisements in the Nantucket *Inquirer* in the early 1850s reveal the range of goods and services available on the island. See the March 30, 1853, edition of the newspaper for the luxury items listed.

Statistics of the *Young Hector* are in Starbuck. Joseph Marshall's letters written on board the *Sea Queen* to his brother-in-law William H. Crosby in Nantucket are in NHARL Ms. 283, folder 8.

Veeder's property in Shimmo was purchased from Moses H. Swift (Deed Book 42, pp. 15–16, November 5, 1841); Charles N. Cottle (Deed Book 42, pp. 346–47, June 6, 1842); Frederick Arthur (Deed Book 48, pp. 13–14, August 23, 1848), and Joseph W. Folger (Deed Book 48, p. 26, September 8, 1848). The advertisement of cows for sale ran in the Nantucket *Inquirer* January 19–March 19, 1855. Records of the Nantucket Agricultural Society are in NHARL Ms. 171.

Other master mariners mentioned in relation to the Veeders—William Cash, Israel Morey, Joseph Marshall, Joseph Winslow and Peter Brock—were not on the Nantucket *Inquirer's* September 6, 1853 list of men who owed more than $50 in taxes. Susan's brother, Edward Austin, does appear, with a personal estate of $12,500.

Susan's power of attorney dated June 30, 1855, was recorded August 5, 1872, Deed Book 62, pp. 25–27.

Edmund Pomeroy Collier's *Cohasset's Deep Sea Captains* (Cohasset Historical Society, 1909, reprint 1984) includes a brief biographical sketch of John Warren Bates (1815–1895), captain of the *Flying Eagle* on a voyage to San Francisco in 1856, when young Charles Edward Veeder first went to sea. Bates engaged in the West Indies trade for many years and made voyages "to San Francisco and around the world" in the *Flying Eagle*. A Chinese painting of the *Flying Eagle* is on p. 42 of Collier's book and a photograph of Bates on p. 43.

Doubling Cape Horn was written by Susan Emma Brock in 1926 and published by the *Inquirer and Mirror*; a 1941 edition was published by the NHA. Brock was the first curator of the NHA. The *Inquirer* editorial, January 21, 1860, is a eulogy for William H. Swain, 19, son of Joseph S. Swain, who fell from the main royal yard of ship *Golden Eagle* on November 7, 1858, in latitude 41 south , longitude 83 west, five days before arriving at Talcahuano, Chile, on his passage to San Francisco. Edgar Kelley was lost at sea July 30, 1858, six months before Charles E. Veeder.

There is no mention of David Veeder's demise in the *Inquirer*.

The Pacific Club was founded in 1860 by whaling captains Samuel Wyer, George Palmer, Obed Swain, William S. Chadwick, Charles A. Veeder, James Wyer, and Samuel Swain. See the *I&M*, September 29, 1917, for "The Real Story of the Pacific Club of Nantucket and the Historic William Rotch Building."

Nantucket was "discovered" by magazine writers in the 1860s. Strother's article in *Harper's New Monthly Magazine* in November 1860 was followed by a travelogue in *The Atlantic Monthly* in March 1866, titled simply "Nantucket." *Lippincott's Magazine* followed suit with "Nantucket" in September 1868.

For more about Nantucket 's participation in the Civil War, see NHARL Ms. 93, Grand Army of the Republic Collection; Ms. 94, Civil War Collection; as well as numerous collections of family papers with Civil War correspondence. *The Civil War: The Nantucket Experience, Including the Memoirs of Josiah Fitch Murphey* by Richard F. Miller and Robert F. Mooney (Nantucket: Wesco Publishing, 1994) focuses on Nantucketers in the 20th Massachusetts Volunteer Infantry.

Although there is no Nantucket record of Rachel Veeder in the local newspaper or any other source, she was most definitely a member of the Veeder household for a few years. See *Genealogical Memoirs of the Burns, Kirk and Newcomb Families* by Arthur R. Newcomb (1957) in the collection of the Greece Historical Society.

Chapter Six: Song of the Siren

Susan Emma Brock, who sailed on the *Midnight* with her parents and wrote obliquely about Charles E. Veeder's tragic death in *Doubling Cape Horn,* wrote to her friend Benjamin Sharp, December 3, 1882, about her boredom on Nantucket. Conditions were probably similar in the 1860s; see NHARL Ms. 270, Sharp Family Papers, folder 4.5. Susan Veeder's home journal is in NHARL Ms. 482. Edward J. Kirwin's journal of the voyage of the *William Gifford* is in NBWMRL, KWM log 452. According to the 1870 U.S. Federal Census, Edward J. Kirwin (17, at sea) was the oldest son of James (45, cooper) and Bridget (39) of New Bedford, Massachusetts. He had an older sister, Kate (23), and six younger siblings: Sarah E. (15), Anna M. (14), Mary J. (12), Susan J. (7), Walter J. (5), and Henry H. (4).

Raroia was the landing place for the *Kon-Tiki* in 1947, when, after a one-hundred-and-one-day journey from Callao, Peru—4,300 miles due east—the raft of Scandinavian adventurers and scientists led by Thor Heyerdahl wrecked on one of the uninhabited motus of Raroia. Heyerdahl was attempting to prove that Polynesia could have been settled in prehistoric times by people from South America using rafts similar to his forty-five-foot-long one made of balsa wood. The *Kon-Tiki*'s landing brought some attention to Raroia in the mid-twentieth century when Swedish anthropologist Bengt Danielsson, one of the *Kon-Tiki* crew, traveled back to the atoll with his wife a couple of years after the scientific expedition and settled down to write his doctoral thesis about life and work there. They stayed three years and Danielsson's books—besides his published dissertation he also wrote a more popular title, *Raroia, Happy Island of the South Seas*—present a picture of life on the atoll seventy-five years after Captain Veeder was last there, when it was feasible that some residents may have heard their parents or grandparents talk about the old whaling captain who became so involved in village life. But if they talked to Daniellson about Veeder or any other interlopers, he chose not to record the information.

Details of the *William Gifford* cruise come from Kirwin's log (KWM log 452): August 12, 1871, carpenter's job making chests; August 16 and 17, firing off bomb lances; August 22, sending victuals ashore; Sept 19, swimming; October 6, losing a watch if you look at the women; October 13, captain ignoring news of whales; October 19, women dancing like the devil; December 18, captain standing mast heads in the coconut trees; December 29, Cavanagh and Kirwin singing; January 11, 1872, lagoon smooth as a mill pond.

For great narratives and descriptions of the Marquesas, see Herman Melville's *Typee: A a Peep at Polynesian Life* (London: Wiley & Putnam; John Murray, 1846) about his captivity by the inhabitants of Typee Bay in Nuka Hiva, Marquesas Islands, after he escaped from the harsh conditions of the whaleship *Achusnet* in 1842; and Thor Heyerdahl's *Fatu Hiva: Back to Nature* (London: Allen & Unwin, 1974) an account of a near-disastrous year (1937–38) spent attempting to live in an unspoiled paradise on Fatu Hiva, the southernmost and most isolated of the Marquesan islands with his wife, Liv.

The *Whalemen's Shipping List,* January 24, 1871, p. 2, reported, "A letter from Capt. James Russell, dated at Tahiti, November 18th, states that he had taken command of bark *Oak,* of Nantucket, (displacing Capt. Thompson,) and would sail next day to cruise off Sunday Island.... Capt. Thompson would return home." James M. Russell (1823–1897) and William B. Thompson (1820–1886) were both veteran whaling masters working out of Nantucket and New Bedford.

Chapter Seven: Ship of Fools

Kirwin's log: January 28, 1872, Capt. took one masthead; February 7, washing his women's clothes; February 12, black devils; February 19, grand dance of Paumotuan and Marquesan women; March 3, mate attempts to shoot Mr. Duane with an unloaded gun; March 9, mate in a woman's dress on Nuku Hiva; March 11, natives drinking and dancing on board; March 26, papoy and oysters for the women; April 3, no shore time for the crew until New Bedford; May 9, Cash harpooned a blackfish.

Historically, victors in battles among Marquesan factions are believed to have dealt with their captured enemies by practicing a ritualistic cannibalism. In *Fatu Hiva*, Thor Heyerdahl recounts meeting and living with an elderly Marquesan who had practiced cannibalism in his youth.

Papoy, or popoi, was the Marquesan version of the Hawaiian dish poi, made of fermented tarot.

The fourth book of Kirwin's four-part journal has a long-winded subtitle added later, after the events that led to the captain's removal, "Edward J. Kirwin, New Bedford, Mass. A foremast hand on board whaling barque Wm. Gifford, Capt. Chas. A. Veeder, Nantucket" and the subtitle: "arrived Tahiti May 27th with the Capt. in the forecastle and left there June 3rd, 1872 for San Francisco, Cal. Crossed the Equator eight days out with a strong breeze, E. J. Kirwin." Opposite the title page is a listing of "Latitude and Longitude of Places," fifteen in all, from Honolulu to Cape Horn.

Veeder may have suffered from elephantiasis, a swelling of the legs caused by parasitic infection; it was a common affliction among South Pacific islanders. Cirrhosis of the liver is another possible cause of the swelling that made his legs too big for the irons, or shackles, on board the *William Gifford.*

American consul Dorance Atwater, a Union soldier during the Civil War, was imprisoned at Belle Isle, Virginia, and Andersonville, Georgia, where he kept a list of all the Union prisoners who died, with detailed information found nowhere else.

Chapter Eight: The Lost Boys of the *William Gifford*

An account book kept for the owners of the *William Gifford* is in NBWMRL, Ms. 58, series A, of the William Gifford Business Records. It lists all those who signed up for the voyage, their role and lay (percentage of profits), their expenses (cash advances, purchases from the slop chest), and how long they served.

"Nantucket," *Lippincott's Magazine*, September 1868, p. 284. Even though the island appeared almost dead, it was "becoming more and more famed as a place of fashionable resort" according to the anonymous writer.

Israel Sweet was a merchant captain, not involved in whaling. He is listed as captain of the *Eliza* of Tahiti in 1868, on a voyage from Ovalau, FIji to Sydney, New South Wales, in *State Records Authority of New South Wales: Shipping Master's Office; Passengers Arriving 1855–1922*, NRS13278 [X119120], reel 421, but is not listed in *AOWV*.

Susan Veeder's Power of Attorney is recorded in Nantucket Registry of Deeds, Book 62, pp. 25–27.

See the BGR, on the NHA website, for vital statistics of all Nantucket families mentioned, as well as decennial U.S. Federal Census Records, available online. For more details about individual members of the Winslow family, see *Winslow Memorial: Family Records of the Winslows and Their Descendants in America, with the English Ancestry As Far As Is Known*, by David-Parsons Holton and Frances-K. Holton (New York: F.-K. Holton, 1877–88).

The *Whalemen's Shipping* List, November 24, 1868, p. 2, reports, "Chilian bark Talcahuano, (late British bark Swansea,) Capt. George H. Cash, of Nantucket, sailed from this port [New Bedford] November 20th, 1868, for Talcahuano and whaling in the Pacific Ocean William P. Gallagher, first mate; Richard C. Gibbs Jr., second mate; Oliver C. Coffin, third mate; Albert P. Fisher, boatsteerer; Charles H. Barnard, Alexander M. Eldridge, Obed A. Morris, and Sylvester B. Raymond, seamen; Mrs. Cash and son, the captain's family; and Mrs. Gibbs and son, the second mate's family."

It was Ed Cavenagh, Kirwin's friend, who wrote in his journal about Tom's sad news on July 26, 1872. The journal, a daily record of the voyage from June 3 to September 10, 1872, has recently been donated to NBWMRL by Cavenagh's descendants. When he received payment for the voyage, Ed Cavenagh signed his name "E. Cavenagh, Jr." in the account book of the *William Gifford*. His father spelled the family surname Cavanaugh, and Ed later changed his spelling of the surname to Kavenagh, the name used by his descendants.

The boot and shoe industry was established in Abington, Massachusetts, in the 1840s; a number of factories are described by Benjamin Hobart in *History of the Town of Abington, Plymouth County, Massachusetts, from its First Settlement*

(Boston: T. H. Carter and Son, 1866). Several of Tom's siblings and his widowed mother relocated there, too, in the 1870s, according to U.S. Federal Census records.

The short bio of Tom Winslow was posted on Ancestry.com, noting the source, "Chester Lynn, author of a 1968 typescript Reed family history and who was a first cousin once-removed of Thomas Winslow's wife."

Albert Folger was the most difficult of the "lost boys" to track down, primarily because he moved to Canada and was therefore absent from U.S. Federal Census records. Joan Sanderson of the Victoria Genealogical Society's "Queries Team" helped track down sources of information about Albert C. Folger, including death records for Folger (1929) and his wife, Florence (1923), and the birth record of their daughter, Annie Rosie (1893), a.k.a. Anna Rosa de Lima Driscoll Folger on baptismal records, as well as the following sources: Frank Kelley, "Captain Dick Folger," *Daily Colonist* (Victoria, B.C.), March 16, 1952 (all facts in the article, including a Nantucket birth, indicate that the subject is Albert C. Folger); Archie Wills, "Sealing Brought Riches to Victoria . . . But It Had Sad Ending," *The Islander* (Victoria, B. C.), April 4, 1982 (refers to "Gus" Folger); and Peter Murray, *The Vagabond Fleet: A Chronicle of the North Pacific Sealing Schooner Trade* (Victoria, B.C.: Sono Nis Press, 1988).

The *I&M* reports Mrs. Albert C. Folger's visit to the island, April 21, 1894, and her husband's arrival October 13, 1894. His obituary was printed in the issue of January 11, 1930, noting that in his boyhood days Captain Folger was known as "Butt Folger." The 1937 article about Folger appeared in the issue of October 23.

George A. Cash married Ida Walters; their children were George N. Cash (1902–1970), married to Bertha Peggy Cash (d. 1968) and Fannie Cash (1882–1960), married to Vincent Cramer. The Cramers lived with Ida in Washington, California, at the time of the 1940 U.S. Federal Census. George A. Cash's obituary notice is in the *I&M*, October 12, 1907, where he is noted as being the only brother of Stillman Cash, proprietor of Cash's Fish Market in 'Sconset. The tapestry worked by Emeline Cash in 1862 is in the collection of the NHA (1969. 27. 1); an article titled "Old Tapestry Returns Home to Nantucket" is in the *I&M*, September 18, 1869.

Both Kirwin and Cavanagh describe their time in San Francisco in their journals. Cavenagh's comment about Kirwin's parental advice is noted July 24, 1872. He mentions the crime of Mr. Rogers on July 31; Kirwin mentions it, too, although he says that Rogers sold salt beef, not salt pork. Cavenagh's journal ends one month after leaving San Francisco, when he filled up the last page of the little booklet that was probably one of many he kept of the voyage. An elderly descendant of his recalls seeing a more extensive journal, with illustrations in the margins, but no one in the family now knows where it is. Kirwin records on October 4, 1872, that Baker is "rather savage"; November 18, Baker white as a sheet; November 23, Cape Horn day; November 24 (top of page), drawing of a right whale, 100 barrels; November 30, wine with the captain.

Annual New Bedford city directories list Kirwin's residence and occupation. See George C. Avila's *The Pairpoint Glass Story* (New Bedford: author, 1968) for a history of the Mt. Washington glass works and Kenneth M. Wilson's *Mt. Washington and Pairpoint Glass: Encompassing the History of the Mt. Washington Glass Works and Its Successors, the Pairpoint Companies: Volume One* (London: Antique Collectors Club, 2005). Kirwin's death record is in vol. 25, p. 79 of *Deaths Registered in the City of New Bedford*. Edward J. Kirwin (Junior) died in New Bedford, August 17, 1982 according to the New Bedford *Standard Times*, August 18, 1982, p. 28. Edward Cavenagh (also spelled Cavanaugh, Cavanagh, and Kavenagh) was born July 10, 1850, married Sarah Elizabeth Edgerton in 1880, and had four children. According to Linda Johnson, "The story about my grandmother's 'Papa' shipping off on a whaler as a teenager is well known in our family, as well as the story about the mutiny against Capt. Veeder." Another descendant, Pamela Rossbach of Sag Harbor, recounted family stories of Veeder's cowardice and cruelty.

Chapter Nine: Eighty Years, Ten Months, Eight Days

James L. Green briefly describes the cyclone in Raroia in his "Letter from Tahiti," *The Friend* (a publication of the American Seamen's Friend Society), Honolulu, May 1, 1878.

Clay Lancaster's *Holiday Island: The Pageant of Nantucket's Hostelries and Summer Life from its Beginning to the Mid-twentieth Century* (Nantucket: NHA, 1993) chronicles the yearly growth of hotels, inns, boarding houses, restaurants, and other businesses serving the tourist industry.

The *Whalemen's Shipping List* provides evidence of George Veeder's career in whaling: *Young Hector*, November 1, 1853; *Eunice H. Adams*, May 7, 1867; March 31, 1869. The rescue of the crew of the *Mary Anna* is reported in the *I&M* February 11, 1871, p. 2; February 18, p. 2; and March 4, p. 2; special thanks to R. H. Macy is from March 18, 1871, p. 3. Accolades for George Veeder as a yachting captain are in the *I&M* September 5, 1874, p. 2; August 14, 1875, p. 2; July 12, 1879, "Prince of Good Fellows," p. 2; October. 7, 1882, p. 2. See Edouard Stackpole's *Life Saving Nantucket* (Nantucket: Life Saving Museum, 1972) for a complete history of the subject.

Edward Bellamy is known best as the author of *Looking Backward: 2000–1887* (New York: Houghton Mifflin, 1888), a view of a future utopian United States that gave rise to the short-lived Nationalist Party. His visit to Nantucket in the summer of 1877 is not mentioned in the local press, but the publication of *Six to One* the next summer is noted in the *Island Review*, July 24, 1878, p. 1. The quote about lackeys and swindlers is on p. 40; "patronized as amusement," p. 39.

Mary Frances Veeder in the press: declamation prize *I&M*, March. 20, 1880, p. 2, and *Nantucket Journal*, March. 25, 1880, p. 2; debate, *I&M*, February 19, 1881, p. 2. Susan Brock's description of Marianna Veeder is in NHARL Ms. 270, Sharp Family Papers, folder 4.5. Charles E. Veeder in rowing regatta, *I&M* July 5, 1879, p. 2; arranging "Hop" *I&M*, July 15, 1880, p. 2.

The Vinal family was well known in New Bedford. A biography of Charles Hammond Vinal is included in Zephaniah W. Pease's *History of New Bedford* (New York: Lewis Historical Publishing Co., 1918), vol. 3. Elwin Vinal married Grace Tripp, daughter of educator and librarian George H. Tripp of New Bedford in 1908. They had three daughters and one son. Elise, sometimes spelled Elsie in public records, married Herman "Harry" H. Baker, and they had two daughters.

INDEX

Page numbers followed by *fig* indicate illustrations or their captions.